Praise for

The Color of Food

What a book! Dive into the stories and photographs Natasha Bowens shares in these pages and you come up for air with a profound apprecation for the diversity of people planting the seeds and harvesting the foods to keep alive cultural traditions and nourish communities around the country. Anyone who eats should read this book: You will come to the table with new appreciation for the intersections between race and food that so often go unsaid and undocumented. Kudos to Bowens for creating this powerful and important book.

—Anna Lappé, author, *Diet for a Hot Planet* and *Hope's Edge*

Natasha Bowens, through her compelling stories and powerful images of a rainbow of farmers, reminds us that the industrialization of our food system and the oppression of our people — two sides of the same coin — will, if not confronted, sow the seeds of our own destruction.

—Mark Winne, author,
Closing the Food Gap: Resetting the Table in the Land of Plenty

The Color of Food captures the heart and souls of farmers of color... farmers that are frequently forgotten as the stories of agriculture in our country are told. Through the lens of a camera we step into the cultural history of our foods and the beautiful and proud people that grow them.

—Cynthia Hayes, Executive Director,
Southeastern African American Farmers Organic Network

True to her ancestral ties, Natasha brings forth the hope of a new generation of young people of color fixed on recapturing the energy, history and tradition of farming. The power of storytelling is etched in each farmer's tale of courage and resiliency as they look at farming, not as oppressive, but as a vibrant celebration of who they are. *The Color of Food* makes the ancestors rise up in triumph!

—Karen Washington, farmer, activist, and cofounder,
Black Urban Growers

It is impossible to understand food in America without digging
deeply into "race," class and culture. People's perceptions are their realities,
and *The Color of Food* contributes to changing our reality by changing our
perception of the hands, hearts and faces in the food movement.

—Malik Yakini, executive director,
Detroit Black Community Food Security Network

Natasha Bowens brings us two critical reminders:
the potential and pitfalls of "a movement" in any singular form;
and the importance of vision and determination in doing truly groundbreaking
research. *The Color of Food* represents the best kind of research—inspired and
independent, a project of deep listening and unbounded sharing. Our task
is to cultivate the questions she scatters, in a rich and colorful light.

—Philip Ackerman-Leist, author, *Rebuilding the Foodshed* and director,
Masters in Sustainable Food Systems, Green Mountain College

The food movement has woken the world to joy of food,
but the beauty of the people who grow it is too often hidden. That's why
The Color of Food is so gorgeous. This is a book that celebrates the food movement
leaders to whom I've been honored to be able to turn for wisdom. To read Natasha
Bowen's journey through North America is to draw from the rich, exquisite
and too often hidden work of people of color in reinventing the modern
food system. From First Nation to immigration, there isn't a topic on which
Bowen's curiosity doesn't latch, nor her camera capture. It's a must-share book
for anyone who holds hope in their hearts about the future of food.

—Raj Patel, author, *Stuffed and Starved*

THE COLOR OF FOOD

Natasha Bowens

STORIES OF RACE, RESILIENCE AND FARMING

new society
PUBLISHERS

Cover design by Diane McIntosh.
Photography © Natasha Bowens

Printed in Canada. Third printing July 2021.

New Society Publishers acknowledges the financial support of the Government of Canada through the Canada Book Fund (CBF) for our publishing activities.

Paperback ISBN 978-0-86571-789-3   EBook ISBN 978-1-55092-585-2

Inquiries regarding requests to reprint all or part of *The Color of Food* should be addressed to New Society Publishers at the address below. To order directly from the publishers, please call toll-free (North America) 1-800-567-6772, or order online at www.newsociety.com

Any other inquiries can be directed by mail to:
New Society Publishers
P.O. Box 189, Gabriola Island, BC V0R 1X0, Canada
(250) 247-9737

New Society Publishers' mission is to publish books that contribute in fundamental ways to building an ecologically sustainable and just society, and to do so with the least possible impact on the environment, in a manner that models this vision. We are committed to doing this not just through education, but through action. The interior pages of our bound books are printed on Forest Stewardship Council®-registered acid-free paper that is **100% post-consumer recycled** (100% old growth forest-free), processed chlorine-free, and printed with vegetable-based, low-VOC inks, with covers produced using FSC®-registered stock. New Society also works to reduce its carbon footprint, and purchases carbon offsets based on an annual audit to ensure a carbon neutral footprint. For further information, or to browse our full list of books and purchase securely, visit our website at: www.newsociety.com

LIBRARY AND ARCHIVES CANADA CATALOGUING IN PUBLICATION

Bowens, Natasha, author
        The color of food : stories of race, resilience and farming / Natasha Bowens.

Includes bibliographical references.
Issued in print and electronic formats.
ISBN 978-0-86571-789-3 (pbk.).—ISBN 978-1-55092-585-2 (ebook)

        1. Minority farmers—United States. I. Title.

HD8039.F32U55 2015   338.10973   C2015-900788-7
                                                       C2015-900789-5

Contents

Prologue: Sowing Seeds for the Road

> **"** In search of my mother's garden, I found my own. **"**
>
> — Alice Walker

THE LONG, LONE ROAD stretches out in front of me and Lucille's steering wheel feels sturdy under my grip. Dust from the farm road flies off of her windshield and the wind stirs all the beads and feathers hanging from her rearview. We glow together in the light of the setting sun, heading south to the next farm. Lucille sputters gently, and I pat her dashboard, "Easy girl, easy. We've still got a long way to go."

After four consecutive months driving across this country, I have driven almost 15,000 miles, traveled through 16 states, laid my head in 49 different places, interviewed 53 farmers and taken roughly 3,500 photographs. It's been quite a journey. And it's not over yet.

I never would have imagined that my desire to dig in the dirt would lead me

here, digging instead into the stories of farmers of color across America — Black, Latina, Native, and Asian farmers and food

activists. All I wanted to do when this all started three years ago was grow food, know exactly where my food was coming from, and live more in tune with the Earth. But as I began to feel rooted in my life as someone who worked the land, I quickly realized all the cultural and historic baggage that came with that. My father's ancestors worked in the fields as slaves; in fact, they were slaves owned by my *mother's* ancestors. I'm literally the product of ownership and oppression reuniting, as if to rewrite the story. So when I ended up in the fields myself, I felt deeply conflicted. It was as if all of my feelings about my family

history and this country's agricultural history were converging at once. It was as if my agrarian story was already written.

The chosen story for people of color in agriculture seems to play out on repeat, reducing our agrarian identity to slavery or farm labor and summing up our communities as deserts in need of water and food. But I know our story is so much richer than that. I can feel that richness when kneeling in the sunshine to sow seeds into the damp soil. I can sense it at the community garden when harvesting side by side with elders born on foreign soil. I can see it when volunteering on urban farms led

by Latina mothers changing the health of their communities. I know that if we don't change the story being told, we will continue to lose that connection to our food, culture and land. We will continue to be known as the underserved communities instead of the strong and resilient communities that we are. We will continue to scoff at the idea of tilling the land instead of embracing the beautiful tradition. If we don't tell our stories, we risk being pushed further into the shadows of the national dialogue on whole foods and sustainable living, a dialogue promoting the diets and practices our ancestors had well before the term "organic" came into vogue.

Living off of the land was the life of my ancestors, yet it's also a hip new trend for my generation. However, this trend doesn't seem to include people of color. Working in the fields is often tied to times of traumatic oppression for people of color, yet it provides me a sacred space to connect with nature and spirit. Most folks in my family wouldn't dream of becoming a farmer, yet the stories of those who are making it work aren't being told.

I felt the need to redefine our agrarian identity as people of color, in my own small way — possibly motivated by my own conflicted feelings. I saw that raising awareness of all the issues and inequities that intersect with race and food was imperative. Storytelling from other farmers of color seemed like the perfect answer.

So after just three years of transforming myself from a self-taught backyard gardener to a farm hand on small organic farms, I decided to put down the pitchfork and pick up a pen and a camera. It was as if I could not dig my hands into the soil any further until I dug into these stories. It was time to hit the road.

As a lifelong lover of photography and the written word, I decided this project would be more powerful, more rooted in a tradition of storytelling, as a photo documentary. With the help of my community, I was able to raise $10,000 in 60 days to set out on a five-month journey across the country to interview and photograph farmers and food activists of color. The result brings me out here on the open road.

In these pages you will find a past-due compilation of portraits, oral histories, storytelling and insights into the food movement and agrarian life in communities of color. As you travel with me from farm to farm, we are invited into farmers' personal lives where we'll learn of family histories, successes and struggles. We will explore food system obstacles, food culture and community building. We will see food and farm realities through the eyes of the marginalized.

This book first introduces you to more of my story and the path that led me to this project, then it takes you on the road and begins introducing you to the farmers — who you'll hear from in their own words. Through the stories and cultural legacies preserved in this book, my hope is that the picture of the American farmer can be seen in its true colors.

Part 1:
Brown Girl Farming

To tend the soil is to tend the soul.

— Anonymous

Before the Journey

THERE I WAS, barefoot in the mud wondering, "Why am I the only brown person here? This whole organic farming thing can't just be for hipsters. I mean, we all came from the land, so why does it seem like young White folks are the only ones going back to it? People of color farm too, right?"

I sure didn't grow up on a farm or anywhere near farmers. I was born in industrial Newark and raised in metropolitan South Florida, not exactly what you'd call farming towns. I didn't come from a farming family, but I know my ancestors did. Down in South Carolina, they knew what it meant to eat well and grow okra with their own chicken waste fertilizer. But they didn't call it "organic." Nor did the first stewards of this soil, before their land was taken. They showed the pilgrims how to grow food and what golden treasures hid beneath those husks. So where were they now?

I might have been in the wrong place out there looking for solidarity in the middle of West Virginia, but it hadn't been much different in the good food movement when I was living in Washington, D.C. Before I left the city for the farm, I worked for a non-profit as a political organizer and blogger on environmental issues and health care reform. It didn't take me long to see the elephant in the room, stomping on our environmental and health problems and making them worse. The elephant was the food and agricultural system. I became captivated by it. I immersed myself in the healthy food and farm movement and morphed into a crazed activist, overly excited to grow my own food.

I went to conferences, worked at farmers markets, volunteered at community gardens and eventually left my job to move out to an organic farm. Even though my grandmother would have slapped me for this kind of decision — you just don't leave a stable job in my family — I was passionate about making the move to agriculture. I was right there alongside other "back-to-the-land" hipsters, but I remember feeling out of place and a little irked, not only because I didn't own a bike or have a beard, but because I was often the only woman of color.

The farmers markets in D.C. were everywhere *but* in communities of color, as were the good grocery stores for that matter. The urban farms and community gardens sprouting up all over the place might have been in some Black and Latina neighborhoods, but they weren't necessarily run by the folks from the neighborhood or even accessible to them. Any exceptions to that, I would find out, were just not getting the same visibility.

It seemed to be the same deal with the national trend of young folks picking up the pitchfork and heading back to the land. I thought all the talk about farm-fresh food and backyard chickens was great, but wondered where all the faces of hipsters of color donning muck boots were. I wanted to know where to find the permaculture workshops led by the farmers of color we needed as our mentors. I wondered where all the books on Amazon were that held knowledge and wisdom *our* ancestors had passed down.

I knew it was all out there, but the lack of visibility was killing me. Sure, the visibility of agrarian life in general has been dwindling. America has been trying to

forget its agrarian identity since industrialization took everyone off the farm. But I could clearly see that life coming back — even if it was with the modern twist of growing on rooftops, in empty lots, or without Roundup. And people still loved that identity. Society still loved to romanticize and honor the American farmer. So I couldn't help but ask why faces like mine weren't showing up in those Super Bowl commercials or in the rest of the media's portrayal of agriculture.

I started thinking, "Are people of color being excluded from this food and farm movement? Are we simply not on the farm anymore? What's caused our departure from the farm? Or are we staying off the farm by choice?"

I still remember sitting in my office in D.C., two years before I decided to transform myself into a farmhand, telling my friend Paula that I wanted to quit our place of employment and move to a farm in the country. She'd looked at me as if I suddenly had two heads and then preceded to remind me that working out in the fields was supposed to be a thing of the past for our people. "You won't find me out in those fields," she huffed, "Too much like cotton picking for me." I remember rolling my eyes and opening my mouth to remind Paula that farming didn't equal slavery. But I hesitated.

As descendants of African slaves, we do have an ugly history with farming. I think of my own family history. Both sides of my family are coincidentally from the same tiny town outside of Greenville,

South Carolina — a state through which 80 percent of African slaves entered this country. A few years ago, I discovered that my mother's European American ancestors bought my father's African American ancestors to work their fields. The Colemans (my mother's family) literally owned the Bowens (my father's). As a product of the two families' reunion, it's hard not to think about that history. The thought kept me conflicted about my new love for farming. Was I returning to a trade my ancestors worked to free me of? Or was I bringing back a powerful connection to the land that my generation has lost?

I'm sure this thought exists for many families and communities of color in this country. For many, agriculture can represent deep pain because of the history of slavery, but also because of current land loss, forced migration and oppressive farm labor practices. But I remember thinking, "Could this be enough to keep us from picking up the plow again?" I think, for some people, possibly it is. But I'd like to think we recognize that our legacy with the land is so much more than that. As Dr. Monica White, author of *Sisters of the Soil*, states, "Our history is much richer than sharecropping, tenant farming, and slavery." We have legacies of innovative and cooperative agriculture, traditional food ways, family heritages and powerful stories rooted in the land. How could we not embrace farming as part of our culture and a sacred connection to celebrate?

However, I know that simply choosing to farm or to continue a family heritage on the land is unfortunately not enough. There is a long history of barriers for farmers of color resulting in a system today laden with inequities which make it hard to survive.[1] There are farmers of color fighting to keep the land they are losing at three times the rate of White farmers.[2]

We have also been losing our connection to the land, our food and our culture as each generation leaves the farm and rural towns for jobs in urban areas, and we become dependent on the industrialization of agriculture and corporatization of our food system. The system itself is also severely imbalanced in its distribution of healthy food options, resulting in inequitable access for many communities. And the results are diet-related illnesses such as diabetes and obesity plaguing these communities at disproportionate rates.[3]

Even with the recent effort toward equality from the "food justice" movement, there's still a perpetual problem.[4] We have policy makers and organization leaders spouting statistics about and introducing solutions for communities they have never lived in or fields they have never plowed. We have farmers markets opening in predominantly ethnic neighborhoods without farmers of color, bilingual staff or culturally relevant foods — which does not help increase food access in these neighborhoods labeled "food deserts."[5] Most of the decision makers and shareholders in food and ag do not represent the diverse communities most impacted by the broken systems, which makes it difficult to effect real change.

I knew there were farmers and food activists of color trying to shed light on the solutions, but felt that maybe they weren't being heard. I knew there were communities of color revitalizing farms and gardens to combat the health and access issues in their communities, but maybe they weren't being supported. Maybe their organizations weren't receiving the funding. Or their hard work was going unrecognized in articles about food revolutionaries and new sustainable farm projects. Or their names and faces weren't showing up in the food and farm aisles of the bookstore. But I knew they were out there fighting.

I knew because I had been searching for them. Feeling alone and frustrated out in West Virginia, I began searching for answers to all of my questions. I began searching for solidarity. I started searching for *our* stories of food, instead of continuing to feel like I was living in someone else's.

I decided to leave West Virginia, and found myself on an urban farm in the heart of Brooklyn.

It was a good move. I was living off of savings from my D.C. job and crashing on an old friend's couch while I worked odd jobs at juice bars and volunteered on urban farms. These farms were throughout Brooklyn and the Bronx, growing food in communities labeled as "food deserts," but residents were taking their food system into their own hands — residents like those of the South Bronx who started La Finca del Sur, an urban farm run by Black and Latina women in the neighborhood. Or those of Harlem and Brooklyn who

have come together as the Community Vision Council led by Asantewaa Harris, a woman who has been promoting community health and the support of local Black farmers for longer than I've been alive. I instantly fell into this amazing network of food activists and urban gardeners of color who taught me a lot about the history of the movement as well as their struggles and successes.

I attended countless workshops and conferences addressing issues for communities of color in the food movement, including a few outside of New York City. From Detroit to Chicago and Oakland to Milwaukee, I was discovering a movement of people of color working to revolutionize the food system and tell their own story of food.

It was a sigh of relief. It was beyond powerful.

At this point, I had started my blog Brown.Girl.Farming. and was also writing for a few online magazines about people of color in the food movement. I was inspired as more and more folks reached out to tell me about their work and where they were in the country. I began dreaming of a way to connect all of us together — to share our stories.

At the end of 2010, Black Urban Growers hosted New York City's very first Black Farmers and Urban Gardeners Conference. I was ecstatic. Black farmers came from as far as Mississippi and California to share knowledge, resources and stories. Gary Grant of the Black Farmers and Agriculturists Association

(BFAA) shared his experiences fighting for the discrimination lawsuit against the USDA on behalf of thousands of Black farmers. Black farmers from upstate New York shared their feelings of isolation and struggle as some of the only Black farmers in the state. There were retiring farmers meeting beginning farmers, rural farmers connecting with urban farmers, farmers who thought they were alone finding kindred souls. It felt to all of us like a giant sigh of joyful relief.

The room where we all gathered after a day of workshops and presentations (such as "A Place for Us: Black Farmers in the Organic Movement" and "Reclaiming and Reframing Black Farmer History in the U.S.") was so full that people were lining the back walls and trickling into the over-flow room. At a conference where most attendees were used to being the minority at other food movement gatherings, we were now overflowing the space. The energy in the room was thick as presenters like Will Allen from Growing Power and Karen Washington from La Familia Verde received standing ovations after making moving statements such as, "There is no reason why people of color should not be leading this movement. It's amazing how thinking ahead is really going back, back to our roots." The support and excitement for our young presenters like the youth from East New York Farms and Rooted in Community gave us all hope for the future. There was cheering, laughing, crying and head-nodding among elders and youth alike. We were bonded together, and the pride and determination in the room was palpable.

It was that feeling that I knew I wanted to capture and spread to other farmers of color — those that had been reaching out to me on my blog, those who couldn't be at that conference, those I hadn't even met yet. These stories were what I wanted to share with the larger movement. It was that pride and joy engulfing the room that I wanted to preserve and celebrate somehow.

I knew then that these stories were what I felt connected to when my hands were in the soil. That fierce and resilient agrarian identity was what I knew was buried there. And I wanted to unearth it. For myself, for all of us.

Part 2:
Rooted in Rights

 We cannot grow without our roots.

— Anonymous

As I DRIVE SOUTH from New York with my hands steady on Lucille's steering wheel — having spent the last year farming upstate, working hard to build this project and finally raising the funds to get on the road — I reflect on the fact that my original quest to grow food and connect with the land has left me feeling more landless than ever. Thus far, I have only worked other people's land and moved from place to place. I think of land ownership and the stories of sharecroppers and migrant farmers and the inequity of power over land and resources throughout history impacting farmers of color.

The land and its resources support us day in and day out, but most of the time we don't give much thought to who controls it all. We might forget that someone else has control of our water, our food. We might not think about who the land belongs to or who it belonged to before us. We might not think about whose feet walked the very soil our feet now touch

or what was gained and lost in its depths. Most importantly, we might forget that the land beneath our feet holds endless stories of struggle to claim it.

Of course, there was a time when there was no concept of land ownership. All of this land was once a commons. Our ancestors roamed it freely, hunting and gathering. Common Indigenous philosophy was that the land, the water, and the web of life on Earth were not things to be owned. There were tribal territories of course, but the concept of owning the land itself was nonexistent. However, as we know, Indigenous peoples who spanned the continent were abruptly and violently introduced to that concept with the era of European settlement. Suddenly the land and resources under their feet were no longer for them. Native peoples of this land were forced to watch as their homes were burned and the land they cherished was disrespected and destroyed. Many were evacuated from their homelands and given new land on which to survive. Boundaries were drawn. Borders and regulations were applied to what was once communal.

All of our states, counties, private land and neighboring countries were essentially created in this way: by force of power. What we know today as the Mexican border only exists because of the Mexican American War. Indigenous people of the region lost roughly half of their national territory. The rest of the Indigenous communities that lived here also lost the lands they called home. Out of the 2.3 billion acres of land that stretch from sea to sea in the U.S., Native Americans have been left with about two percent.[6]

Native communities were not the only ones affected by the land and power dynamic. Forced migration from homelands also took place overseas in Africa with the era of slavery. Africans captured on the land they called home were brought here to work this land for the wealth and benefit of others. Even after emancipation, many African Americans continued to work the land in order to survive and eventually acquire their own land — which today is being lost at a much higher rate than White landowners. According to the Black Land Project, Black landownership makes up less than one percent of all privately owned rural land in the United States. Many more Black Americans farm, but do not hold title to the land they till. Japanese American landowners also lost much of their land when deported to internment camps during World War II, and now they belong to the smallest percentage of farmer/landowners in the country.[7]

It is important to connect the dots of the history of land ownership in this country to the reality of land loss today. Every minute of every day we're losing more than an acre of farmland. Every state is affected. The American Farmland Trust says that in just 25 years over 23 million acres of farmland was lost to development.[8] And that doesn't count the urban community farm land loss due to development. In this country, it's called "development" or "industry"; in other parts of the world, it's called "land grabbing."

Governments, development corporations and ag corporations are buying up huge pieces of land in Africa, China and India to secure food production or extend development, causing farmers to go so far as burning themselves in their homes out of protest and desperation to keep their land in their family. Here in the U.S., big agriculture and development are key players in land loss, as are farm foreclosures. Small farmers struggling to compete in a growing corporate ag system and lacking federal support are losing their farms and their land to foreclosures. And farmers who have been, as the USDA calls them, "historically disadvantaged" are seeing higher foreclosure rates.

This land-grabbing dynamic is alive in policy as well, and it results in a twisted cycle. International trade policies like NAFTA are driving land loss for communities who don't hold the power.[9] These policies that govern our global food system allow crops produced in industrialized countries to be sold in developing countries at cheaper prices than local farmers can sell them for. This puts farmers out of business and forces them off their land, causing a migration to the very same industrialized countries that passed the trade policies. Seeking opportunity for survival on new land, these migrant workers end up in fields working for the very same agricultural corporations that put them out of business.[10]

This power dynamic has made it nearly impossible for communities of color to hold on to land. Yet they *are* still holding on. From discriminant federal laws and legal loopholes to racist politicians and money lending agents, barriers throughout history have made it very difficult for communities of color to even acquire land. Yet many *did*. However, much of the land sold or allotted to these communities has been some of the worst land in the most hostile environments — from the swamps and floodplains of the South to the harsh deserts and dry prairies of the Plains and the Southwest. Yet survival and resilience persist.

There is survival, despite efforts to control the very genes of the living things we depend on for our food. There is survival, although other resources, like water and minerals, are out of our control as well. "Industry" is causing groundwater depletion and pollution and the degradation of the environment. And communities of color are the targets once again.

Someone once told me that to understand is to dig deep, so we must always carry a strong shovel and an open ear. The following stories give us some understanding of the struggles and triumphs over land and resources in different communities throughout history and today.

Portrait 1:

Land Is Freedom

Mr. Daniel Whitaker at 93, Retired Hog Farmer and WWII Veteran, Tillery, North Carolina.

> Land is the only real wealth in this country and
> if we don't own any, we'll be out of the picture.
>
> — Ralph Paige, Federation of Southern Cooperatives

I DECIDE THERE IS NO BETTER PLACE to begin digging than in the Carolinas, where my family history begins and where history for African American agriculture runs deep.

I head to a place where land rights have historically been at the forefront of life for its large population of Black farmers and former sharecropping families. The Black Farmers and Agriculturists Association (BFAA) in Tillery, North Carolina, invited me down to talk with some of their farmers. And as I drove into town, the hot, flat road was flanked by cotton fields and dotted with historical markers that transported me back in time.

❧

"In my first life — I was just a small kid you know — my daddy was a sharecropper. As time would go on, I would often wonder about why we were living in such a broke down house. It got in my mind that it was just the traditional way for opposite folks [White folks] to get ahead in life: by working people. We would make 10 cents a day or 25 cents a day, and a lot of people don't believe that was good, but that's the way it was. Your parents would work all the year and the opposite people would come up and tell ya you didn't

earn any money this year. I was watching all those things. And I thought, 'I don't wanna get no family if I can't provide for them.' Those things rested hard on my mind. So I didn't ever try to live like my dad and uncles who were sharecroppers. I knew I wanted to try and do something for myself."

Mr. Whitaker, a sweet and gentle man whose sturdy voice radiates pride, sits with me in his living room in front of a case of sentimental keepsakes collected throughout his many lives. "I don't see too well and I don't hear too well," he says, "but you ask me anything you want and I'll answer in a proper manner."

I met Mr. Whitaker just the day before at a community meeting of the Concerned Citizens of Tillery, to which I was invited by Mr. Gary Grant, one of their founders and a leader in the BFAA. As I sat in the community room where elders gathered to discuss issues and good news in this small rural town of North Carolina, I was surrounded by some of the most vibrant elders I've ever had the privilege of being in the company of. I noticed Mr. Whitaker sitting calmly with his hand on his cane and wearing his dark prescription sunglasses. My neighbor at the table informed me that if I wanted to talk to the farmers of Tillery, he was my guy. A 93-year-old retired hog farmer, Mr. Whitaker, like many citizens of Tillery, came from a family of sharecroppers. However, unlike many elders from Tillery, he never did participate in what they called the "40 Acres and a Mule" project.

"They had divided the land for '40 Acres and a Mule,'" Mr. Whitaker explained, "but I bought my own land. I never did get into that '40 Acres' because I couldn't understand it. Sometimes they don't want you to understand it."

What many Tillery citizens refer to as "40 Acres and a Mule" was actually the second version of the program. After the Reconstruction era, the first "40 Acres and a Mule" policy promised freed slaves land to get started, but the policy was reversed and the promise was never fulfilled. Roosevelt's New Deal in the '30s and '40s made a second attempt with the creation of the Resettlement Administration, and 113 rural resettlement projects began to relocate struggling families into government-planned farming communities. Of those, there were 15 Black resettlement projects, and Tillery was one of the largest. Black families who had been sharecropping in the area came to Tillery for a fresh start.

I point to an old money belt in Mr. Whitaker's case and ask him its significance. "I got that during World War II," he answers proudly, "I wore it everywhere I went. I worked with my daddy until I was 22, and then I decided it was time to go. So I went on to the service. I joined the Army, and then Pearl Harbor was hit

and there I was. I fought overseas for three years.

"When I came back, I wanted to be a farmer who worked for himself. I grew up working for people with my daddy and I would watch everything 'cause I was hoping and praying one day I would be a landowner and I would know how to take care of the land and make crops. But I didn't want to sharecrop, that was for my dad. It wasn't for me. I could understand working for myself but I couldn't understand working for nobody else. Fighting a war was good and it was OK looking out for the United States, but fighting everyday working for somebody else, just to make it, I knew that wouldn't be too good."

Said best by Dr. Gail Myers, anthropologist of African American agriculture, "The sharecropping system after slavery became the plantation institution reincarnate." Black farmers were often cheated out of fair earnings by their landowners, and, as Mr. Whitaker remembered from his childhood, they also began going into debt due to the nature of the sharecropping system — like having to borrow seed and fertilizer from their landowners to get started.

Another member of the Tillery community, Mrs. Hazel Hendricks, spoke of her family's experience coming to Tillery from sharecropping. "We moved here at the end of 1937. We moved from Rocky Mount, where we were sharecroppers," she explained. "You know in sharecropping you get all your supply from the man in March, and we never did come out ahead; the man always got the money and we didn't. So we found out about '40 Acres and a Mule' and we came here."

However, government-allocated land wasn't exactly a bright new start. The ideologies of slavery and discrimination still remained and were deeply woven into our nation's systems. Black families coming to Tillery were allocated land to farm, but were required to pay off that land with their earnings. Moreover, they were given land on the floodplain of the Roanoke River, and every year, due to crop loss, they would fall behind trying to compete with surrounding White farmers who had dry land on higher ground.

"We bought fruit trees and set them out," recalled Mrs. Hendricks, "but then the flood came in '40. The river dam busted and came all the way here, and there wasn't nothin' but water. We had chickens. My brother wasn't a month old. The chickens got drowned, and the farmers had to replant everything. The land that came with the Resettlement was river land, and after the flood there wasn't too much left. Another year it was a hail storm that beat all the cotton back. We couldn't make the cotton that year, and so we were foreclosed on."

From a young age, Mr. Whitaker vowed to work for himself and provide for his family, and that's exactly what he did. Upon his return from World War II, with money he saved from the service, Mr. Whitaker bought his land.

"I bought two parcels of land up the road and got my daddy on it 'cause he had never been free," Mr. Whitaker smiles as he remembers. "I put him on one parcel and got my brother and put him on one. I stayed first with my dad on the land I bought him. For six years we worked together, and then I went to buy another farm. I was blessed to find another farm. It took me awhile to get started right and everything, but I did pretty good.

"I got some hogs and calculated their breeding and had them breed three times a year and sold them at a certain price and was able to make 30,000 dollars in four or five years. I made the money and paid off the land.

"I was a person who liked to grow hogs and so that's what I kept doin'. I sold them to the Rio Market in Rocky Mount and at the Glaston Stock Yard. I had an orchard too. It was good for about 25–30 years. I used to sell peaches, apples, pears and corn, some of everything."

I then point to a cowbell in the case behind Mr. Whitaker, "Oh that's Bessie's cowbell," he chuckles, "it increased my earnings. Getting started in life, I sold a lot of vegetables in the street, and I would ring the bell to bring people out of their homes. I would make 300 dollars a weekend sometimes. I've been a self-employed person in that manner. I had my 314 acres of land, and that's where I've been ever since '52."

"I did it all because I wanted to be free."

❧

Mr. Whitaker ran his farm as a land-owner for over 30 years. He passed away in 2014 leaving his remaining land to his five children and eight grandchildren.

Alma Maquitico, 35,
El Centro de Trabajadores
Agrícolas Fronterizos/
The Border Agricultural
Workers Center,
El Paso, Texas.

We all had land, but because of colonization —
a scheme focused on the exploitation of economic
opportunities — we have lost it.

— Alma Maquitico

A S THE ROAD STRETCHES OUT in front of me, I think about freedom and what it means. Freedom to exercise our rights, to keep our rights. I think about how quickly all that can be lost and the price we are willing to pay to get it back — the sacrifices and struggles we are willing to endure. It makes me think of the parallel stories of Latino farmers in this country currently experiencing what many Black farmers went through centuries ago: either working the fields for the benefit of the agricultural industry or struggling to gain access to land and a just system. I decide to head to the Mexican border in El Paso, Texas, to hear from migrant farmers.

❧

"I think there are a lot of similarities between Black farmers and migrant struggles," offers Alma, an incredibly warm volunteer for the Border Agricultural Workers Center in El Paso, Texas. "We each have histories of owning land and losing it to the powers that be." Alma and I sit together outside of the Center taking shade from the hot summer sun. I came to the Center on the border between Ciudad Juárez, Mexico, and El Paso to talk with the volunteers who run its projects and the

campesinos (farmworkers) who use its services. The Center started after the work of César Chavéz in 1975, who led labor and civil rights activism for farmworkers in the '60s and '70s. The Center offers a range of services for the more than 12,000 migrant farmworkers in the border region, including a clinic, cafeteria and a safe haven for workers to sleep.

As we sit and talk about land loss, we are frequently interrupted by a helicopter flying loud and low overhead. I look up to the sky and Alma says, "Oh, get used to it. It's the militarization of the border. We have drones, we have helicopters that are here constantly, every day. And we always just have to put up with it. One time, a drone fell into someone's backyard, can you imagine? This is some of our everyday. We're trying to build an alternative here in a very militarized community."

The Center is situated directly across the street from the international bridge between the U.S. and Mexico, making it an opportune recruitment area for agricultural employers looking for migrant workers, but also a highly patrolled area by border security.

"A lot of the farmworkers who come here to the Center were small producers in

Mexico," Alma continues on the topic of land loss. "They were producers who lost their land at one point in history. Some still have their land but are unable to produce anything due to the international control policies, especially NAFTA. These policies have devastated the Mexican farm and the Mexican peasant economy."

NAFTA, the North American Free Trade Agreement, was passed in 1994 to eliminate tariffs on agricultural trade. This essentially allowed the U.S. to export heavily subsidized crops like corn to Mexico tax free and below cost. This resulted in the loss of over 1.3 million farm jobs in Mexico.[11] Mexican farmers and landowners were not spared in this competitive environment and were forced to leave their own farms to look for work.

"So, you see, with the Black farmers in the South, it's the same history. We all had land, but because of colonization — a scheme focused on the exploitation of economic opportunities — we have lost it.

"Some of these migrant workers today come here to work for someone else and get paid very little. I help them with their IRS forms for income taxes, and I can see that some of them only make between $3,000 and $6,000 per year. Often, the IRS defines their work as subcontracting or consulting, so they then have to pay $1,200 in taxes. Additionally, many of the employers will collect workers taxes but never report them, so the workers think they are doing the right thing, but the IRS is never receiving their money. It's

extremely unfair and is blatant exploitation for cheap labor. It's like enslavement or sharecropping."

Emancipated Blacks began sharecropping or continued as slave labor in order to survive. And this fight to survive is what drives many Mexican workers across the border today.

One of the *campesinos* (to remain unnamed) from the Center joins our conversation and shares his story of migration, "I came here because of hunger. Producing in Mexico was impossible. I was unable to produce because the price for my crop dropped by 50 pesos a bushel. I can't survive on that. I was forced to rent out my land. I had to come here and work for the commercial ag industry."

And he was not alone. Some Mexican farmers most impacted by NAFTA were those raising pork or growing corn. According to Alejandro Ramírez, of the Confederation of Mexican Pork Producers, Mexico imported 30,000 tons of pork in 1995, the year after NAFTA took effect. By 2010 pork imports, almost all from the United States, had grown more than 25 percent. As a result, pork prices received by Mexican producers dropped 56 percent. Corn imports also rose from 2 million to 10.3 million tons from 1992 to 2008.

"We lost 4,000 pig farms," Ramírez estimates in a 2012 article in *The Nation* by David Bacon. "On Mexican farms, each 100 animals produce five jobs, so we lost 20,000 farm jobs directly from imports. Counting the five indirect jobs dependent on each direct job, we lost over 120,000 jobs in total. That produces migration to the U.S. or to Mexican cities."

This forced migration and land loss does not rest solely on NAFTA's shoulders. The Mexican government and large corporations are key players as well. The Mexican government has denied rights to their peasant landowners, favoring development and corporate growth instead.

"In my village, we lost our land because the government changed Article 27 of the Mexican constitution," Alma explains, "which guarantees our right to land. For example, we had land that was allocated to us during the Revolution, and we couldn't sell it; that was gonna be our land, and our kids' land no matter what. But the new president, Salinas, just changed the constitution and said our land could now be for sale. He gave corporations a free hand to buy up our land and push us out. So in my village, a cement corporation bought land and opened their factory; now a lot of my family no longer own their land and are peons working at the cement company. Either that or they come to the U.S. and work here."

Before the Mexican Revolution of 1910, most of the land in Mexico was owned by a single elite ruling class, which meant a small percentage of rich landowners owned most of the country's farmland. Indigenous wage workers and peasants were essentially debt slaves to the landowners. With so many people suppressed, revolts and revolutions were common in Mexico. To relieve the Mexican peasant's plight and stabilize the country, various leaders tried different types of agrarian

land reform. Some of that reform included restoring the traditional Aztec system of *ejidos,* a system of using communal land for agriculture. This meant that landless farmers sharecropping or leasing land from wealthy landlords could petition the government to create an *ejido* which they could have rights to use indefinitely as long as they kept the land in production. They could even pass those rights on to their children. Peasant farmers were thus protected and given land security, until 1991 when the new president eliminated this constitutional right in preparation for the opportunities NAFTA would bring.

"This greed is driving corruption," adds Ramon, a founding member of the Center who joins our conversation. "Distributors working for the state are taking advantage of small farmers. For example, the price of beans in Mexico is 25 pesos a bushel, but you try and produce the beans and sell to the distributor and they will only buy the beans from you for 8 pesos. It's very corrupt. We call them *coyotes.* We have no rights. Even our water rights are gone. Water is supposed to be communal in Mexico but that is not happening, they are controlling the water."

Mexico has a long and well-established tradition of water resources management which started in the 1930s. The *ejido* sector and rural communities were subject to direct federal control over water while private landowners enjoyed the benefits of federally subsidized irrigation and guaranteed market prices. Over time, large landowners got rich, while small farmers, by the 1970s, were suffering from the effects of water monopolies. Privatization of public water is on the rise around the world, and could become a reality here in the U.S. There is already over-exploitation of groundwater, causing scarcity here and worldwide. Governments, including our own, are scrambling to secure water, taking water rights away from Indigenous and peasant communities.[12]

All of this brings Mexican families across the border to find work and hope for a fresh start. But many are just being met with more exploitation here. Ramon explained how many workers come to the Center and express their fear to speak up or protest. Though they know they are being treated unfairly and paid very little, they can't afford not to get on the bus that day and work.

The Center is there to support workers as they struggle, but Texas is a right-to-work state, so it is hard to unionize. Alma is part of a younger volunteer team at the Center that thinks simply supporting the workers as they are exploited is essentially helping the ag companies get what they want. Her generation is trying to take the Center on an alternative mission toward sovereignty over their lives, their food and the land.

Alma and her colleagues are starting the program called El Instituto to train more leadership at the Center and bridge the generational gap between *campesinos* and volunteers. She also partners with La Mujer Obrera, a women-led social purpose business cooperative, on an initiative called SURCO in which migrant women,

Indigenous communities and ag workers are developing alternative food systems in the region. In joining the two programs, they have three strategies:

"One is to train ourselves in ecological practices, to remember and rescue a lot of the traditional knowledge from our community. Because, remember, a lot of us have forgotten how to plant and farm without pesticides because a lot of us have worked on farms that are in the industry using pesticides and chemical fertilizers. Another strategy is to access land and infrastructure to launch a much bigger project. It's not only about producing but creating unity in very adverse conditions. Look at the soil; our soil is very sandy, and it's also been polluted. We have the militarization of the border here, and people are very discouraged to organize because of fear. So we want to create a safe space for coming together. Third is to build trust. People have been working at this for many years, and they've been promised things that have never happened. So we need to build trust and bring back hope.

"What we're doing as younger people . . . it's a very daunting task. We want to take responsibility for advancing the rights of our own community. We want land because we are landless and we need to be able to produce our own food and distribute that food among our low-income communities who can't afford and don't have access to healthy fresh foods.

"We are surrounded by farms and harvest America's food, yet our communities are considered food deserts."

Portrait 3:

Lifeblood of the Land

Tyrone Thompson,
North Leupp Family Farm,
Navajo Nation, Leupp,
Arizona.

> Our future depends on that water, it's a vital resource.
> This water's been building up for thousands of years,
> and they'll deplete it in just generations.
>
> — Tyrone Thompson

A COMMUNITY LACKING FOOD is called a "food desert," but using the word "desert" suggests a desert is a place where food doesn't exist. And that is just not true — I know Alma and the *campesinos* would agree.

As I continue my drive through the Southwest, I find food and a fight to survive emerging from the scorched earth with a fierceness. The community I meet with is working hard to sustain agriculture in the desert and preserve their cultural traditions. Yet their rights to a vital element for survival are under threat.

⟨≋⟩

My toes wiggle in the cool water as I take in the scene around me. The dry sand that seems to stretch on forever through the desert stirs with the light breeze. The squat trees that dot the landscape look as if they are shrinking under the rays of the hot sun. The farm in front of me glows green with corn stalks and melon plants. One of the young farm interns hurtles over my head in the shape of a cannonball into the water tank where I am floating. We are cooling off after pulling weeds all day on the North Leupp Family Farm (NLFF) on the Navajo (Diné) Nation in northern Arizona.

I was invited to the reservation by NLFF, a non-profit community farm run by and for Navajo families. They work to re-engage the local community in time-honored farming practices and culinary traditions as well as preserve language and culture with youth groups who learn farming skills on the farm. I spent two days on the farm, talking with the farmers as I helped them pull weeds in the fields.

The Navajo reservation is the largest in the United States, covering over 25,000 square miles across Arizona, Utah and New Mexico. Navajo people, or Diné as they call themselves (meaning "the people" or "children of the holy people"), inhabit a land that is considered one of the most arid parts of the Great American Desert. The average rainfall in the lowest lands is three to five inches per year, while the higher lands receive 10 to 15 inches. For comparison, most other states in the U.S. get about 30–50 inches of rain each year.

The boundary of the Navajo Nation was defined after the war between the U.S. and the Navajo and their forced migration and four-year internment away from their homeland, also known as "The Long Walk."[13] When the Navajo were permitted to return to their land, the Navajo Treaty of 1868 — a first of many land treaties — was signed. However, historic Diné land, or Diné'tah, is traditionally defined by what they call the Four Sacred Mountains and covers a much larger area than the current reservation. Much of that land was taken for ranching because it is wetter and more verdant, so the Navajo were left with the driest one third of their traditional homeland.

Although this limited their hunting, gathering and grazing areas, Navajo people continued raising livestock, but they began relying more heavily on farming. However, dry land produces only limited forage, which is harder to sustain, so overgrazing and soil erosion quickly became a problem. In the 1930s, the federal government restricted the amount of livestock Navajo families could have by enforcing livestock permits. The government also reduced grazing areas with grazing districts which disrupted the Navajos' traditional system of shared grazing areas

North Leupp Family Farm.

among families. These restrictions are still in place today.

In addition to the limitations of dry land farming and restrictions on their subsistence and income from livestock, Navajo people have been enduring battles to keep their much-needed water. Since 1908, Navajo and Hopi Nations have had treaty-guaranteed priority water rights to the Little Colorado River. Yet fast-track backroom deals among the federal government and large energy corporations now threaten to take those rights away forever.[14]

"They're trying to steal our water," says Tyrone Thompson, who goes by "Farmer Ty" at NLFF. "Big water companies, the state of Arizona and Nevada, they're trying to take our water. Our people are gonna be hit with hard times pretty soon as droughts continue. And all the while, they're asking us to waive our rights to water. The settlement is *this thick,* and they're trying to just rush and push it through with a lot of legal terminology that people don't understand."

The North Leupp Family Farm is situated on nearly 100 acres that lie just north of the Little Colorado River on floodplains that have served generations of Diné families with fertile soil and water for farming. Today, the farm serves over 30 families as a community owned and operated farm with plots available to each family. Tyrone is one of the staff members keeping the farm running, coordinating youth workshops on the farm and providing all the plots with irrigation. This is the only irrigated farm in the southwestern part of the Navajo reservation. The farm pumps its water from an underground well fed by the Coconino Aquifer. That water is pumped through an antiquated system and fed into a holding tank (the same one we used for cooling off after a hot day's work) at the back of the farm. The cost of running the diesel pump depends on the cost of fuel. This puts a high price on the water. With fuel costs rising, climate change encroaching, and local water already under siege, Navajo farmers are becoming increasingly concerned for their future. (Note: As of 2013, NLFF has transitioned to a solar-powered water pumping system acquired through funding from the USDA.)

"Our water is already being pumped elsewhere," Tyrone continues. "They're getting Navajo water for free, and a lot of electricity created from it is being pumped off to Vegas and the like. The Navajo president is not fighting for us. He came to our local chapter house to talk to us about the water settlement, and he had 15 police guarding him, and there was apparently a sniper up on the water tower aimed down at us. We had old ladies and little girls getting patted down — It's crazy times. Our own president is scared of his people. It's because he's all for giving up our water rights even though all the people are against it. Even our leaders — our council delegates that are supposed to be speaking on our behalf — it's just that dollar bill they're after."

The Navajo Nation has long been fighting corruption from within its governing body as well as exploitation of its people from outside of the nation.[15] From uranium to water running underneath Navajo land, resources have been taken to be used elsewhere and profited from, while the health, environment and economy of the Navajo Nation have suffered. Over half of the Navajo Nation live in poverty, with a more than 50 percent unemployment rate. Over half of homes on the reservation lack indoor plumbing and rely on hauling water from nearby sources intended for livestock and prone to contamination. The water aquifers they rely on are also sensitive to fluctuations in precipitation during drought.[16]

"Our future depends on that water, it's a vital resource," Tyrone emphasizes. "This water's been building up for thousands of years, and they'll deplete it in just generations. They [the Peabody Coal Company] depleted 500 years of water in 20 years at Black Mesa."

Black Mesa is a sacred Navajo mountain on top of a large water aquifer that shares the same name. Black Mesa is also home to two coal mines operated by the Peabody Coal Company. Coal mined there is used to produce energy that is sent to surrounding cities like Las Vegas and Los Angeles — while 40 percent of Navajo homes remain without electricity. The process of mining coal requires large amounts of water for coal preparation, including washing the coal and suppressing dust caused by mining. This water is taken from groundwater aquifers and rarely returned (with the significant exception of the runoff and improper disposal of the uranium-polluted

water discharged from the mines after the coal is extracted). Black Mesa has become a famous site for environmental justice and water rights activism; young activists have been fighting there for land and water sovereignty.

(Note: In August 2014, a grass-roots conservation planning initiative was funded by the Navajo Nation. Twenty Navajo communities or chapters are involved in this effort. This one-year model community-based water and conservation project is intended to respond to worsening drought conditions and climate change by identifying, mapping and developing surface and ground water for the present and future. This will also quantify water in the Little Colorado River watershed, which can be used to leverage claims to Aboriginal water rights.)

Tyrone is wearing a t-shirt with a blue ribbon of water running across it with the word "Tó" printed in blue letters. "Tó or Tóh means the life blood of the people, water," he explains. "A lot of our stories start from the earth in this way. We live from the water and take the plants and animals as our medicine. Us five-fingered people, whether Native or not, we were provided here on this Earth with everything that we need, but the way things are now are really backwards, and it's hurting us holistically."

Another member of the farm, Stacey, joins us as we pull weeds in the field. We all sweat under our sun hats, and I tug on the stubborn roots of camelthorn, a common weed in the area that is full of sharp thorns.

Stacey masterfully works the weeds out of the cracked earth, and I can sense the energy he has invested in this land.

"Before the farm was here I used to herd sheep through this land," he shares, "and at that time the river would flood and we'd catch catfish and eat them out of the river. And this stretch of land here was dotted with cornfields. People would migrate and set up cornfields until the water would run out, and then you'd be dry farming. But corn used to grow like crazy here. I remember when I was little, I used to look up at the stalks so much taller than me. I remember the diet we used to have, none of it was processed food, it came from the corn fields, the livestock in the corral and some of the wild plants that we have here. Like wild carrots and yucca, and wild game like cottontail — one of my favorites. We had everything we needed right from this land.

"But things are changing. The climate is changing, which is why our water is more important than ever. I remember years ago it used to rain like crazy here. It would just pour and pour and pour. Not anymore."

The Navajo Nation has suffered extreme drought since 1996.[17] And in the summer of 2013, the Navajo president declared a drought emergency for the Nation, with precipitation falling 65 percent lower than normal. It seemed to me like everyone on the reservation was feeling the effects of drought.

The next day, after sleeping in my hot tent and experiencing one of the Navajo Nation's notorious sand storms that blow in across the desert every evening, I am blessed with the opportunity to speak with many of the families farming at NLFF. Hank, another founding member of the farm who extended the invitation to visit, organized a potluck to welcome me and provide a time to speak with everyone. We enjoy fry bread, a common (and delicious) Navajo staple made from blue corn meal, as well as kneel-down bread (or nitsidigo'í) that gets its name from the old process of kneeling down to grind the blue corn before it is stuffed in the husk and roasted. We all eat and talk and laugh, and I listen to the native Diné language being spoken by many of the elders.

Two of the elders happen to be the previous owners of the land before they donated 99 acres to NLFF. Jackie Thompson, 83 years old, and his wife, Carrie Thompson, 76 years old, had been farming the land since the 1980s.

The present farm at North Leupp dates back to the early 1980s, when it was organized into an economic development cooperative funded through the Seventh Generation Fund. The cooperative included several family farms across the southwestern and western portion of the reservation. The cooperative was disbanded in the early 1990s, and Jackie and Carrie Thompson became the sole operators. With Jackie's failing health, the farm sat idle for several years until the late Justin Willie took on the task of revitalizing the farm with Jackie's blessing. In 2005 Justin enlisted the partnership and funding of

Northern Arizona University's diabetes prevention program to re-start the farm.

Carrie's sister, Orsi Terry, translates for Jackie and Carrie as they tell me about the farm in the '80s and '90s.

"We grew alfalfa and we used to take it to sell for hay and feed to the people that wanted it," Jackie recalls, "and the money that came in went back to the farm. We irrigated from the same water source they use now, the same well. We grew up farming. Our parents grew corn, squash and watermelon. We have seen a lot of changes over the years, and they all have to do with water. They are taking the water and sending it to other communities. There is less water now than before."

Orsi and others at the potluck chime in with their experiences. "I farm here and there when I can find water," Orsi says. "I found out about North Leupp through my church. I like it because they have water right here. We used to farm when we were small, we used to have water then,

Jackie Thompson, 83 years old, and his wife, Carrie Thompson, 76 years old.

but there's no water anymore, no place to farm anymore."

"I've been farming about two years, I just started," says Daniel Many Goats, a 71-year-old member of the farm. "A long time ago, when I was younger, my father had a lot of land and planted corn, and I learned a bit from him. We had squash and watermelon, and we had lots of rain where I grew up. I grew up about 30 miles east of Tuba City. We didn't irrigate, we just waited for the rain. This farm here is great, the only problem is the water."

"I've been farming for 35 years," shares Jonathan Yazzie, the youth coordinator who brings teenagers to the farm and can trace his family farming history back ten generations. "I'm growing a variety of vegetables with my father, who's from Sand Springs. We're part Hopi, part Cherokee. We did dry land farming mainly, but some irrigation for vegetables. The irrigation systems came from Israel. We would pump water from the wash and run it through tanks and filters. We grow a lot of the same way that we were taught. Now we use a little modern technique, but it's too expensive, so we keep our traditional way and it is cheaper for us. We grow our native corn. We were taught to pray to our Creator, and we have prayers and songs right before we plant. We use corn pollen for prayers — prayers for rain."

The Hopi reservation, or Hopi, is located within the Navajo Nation on 2,500 square miles. I was actually able to meet with a Hopi farming organization while I was there, but since their agricultural practices and cultural traditions are so sacred, they asked me not to publish their interview. However it is well known that agriculture, and corn in particular, have always been a part of Hopi life. Their traditional ceremonies mark the different phases of the Hopi agricultural cycle, and corn plays a big part in ceremony and prayer.

Hopi people are also known for their dry-farming methods, which rely solely on natural precipitation. Since there is not much precipitation on the reservation, this method is based on keen observation and Hopi scientific procedures that include their own research and soil analysis. Their crop yields of strong and sturdy corn, squash, beans and melons give hope to a hot and drying planet.

Many say that Hopi farming is based on faith and what the ancestors say is "a heart full of prayer." Maybe a prayer for water is one we will all need to keep in our hearts in the future.

Portrait 4:
Home, Land

Gary and Kaye Kozuki,
Kozuki Farms,
Fresno, California.

> We have raised our kids here on this land. We have been here for over 50 years. We're proud of that.
>
> — Kaye Kozuki

THE NAVAJO TOWN of Leupp, Arizona, where I've just come from visiting with Navajo (Diné) farmers, also happens to be the site of a World War II Japanese Internment Isolation Center. The isolation center was a place where detained Japanese Americans were transferred if they were considered "undesirables or troublemakers" at their first internment camp.

This interesting thread ties two different lands and communities together. I follow this thread as I drive west to California to meet with third-generation Japanese American farmers who were able to hold onto their family land even through a time when their rights were taken from them during World War II.

❧

"This farm has been in my family for over 100 years," Gary Kozuki says as he begins to recount his family history while we sit together with his wife Kaye at their kitchen table. "My grandfather came from Hiroshima, Japan. In Hiroshima in the early 1900s, there were hard economic times, so he came looking for greener pastures. First he went to Hawai'i, to the Big Island, and he worked as a laborer in the fields. He then sent for my grandmother to come over. My father was born in Hawai'i,

but I think he was educated in Japan for elementary school. After Hawai'i, they all came to California as laborers. My grandfather was a cook in a labor camp."

Europeans had arrived in Hawai'i by the late 1700s, and the first sugarcane plantation there started soon after. The Hawaiian sugar industry grew rapidly, and plantation owners began importing labor from China and Japan amongst a few other countries. By 1925, over 180,000 Japanese workers were brought to work in the fields. According to the AFL-CIO, workers were put in segregated plantation camps and even paid different wages as a strategy to sow disunity among the various ethnicities of workers.[18] This would protect the plantation owners from a unionized workforce capable of challenging their working conditions and wages. Similar camps were started in California to provide labor to the growing fruit orchard and sugar beet industry. But workers unionized despite such underhanded practices; in fact, Japanese and Chinese workers were some of the first to form associations and strike for higher wages. By 1909, Japanese laborers comprised 42 percent of California's farm labor force, but they were still denied citizenship and therefore, land ownership.

"My grandfather was able to acquire land because my father was a citizen. He bought land by working and saving up," Gary continues. "But he was an alien, not an American citizen, and at that time the law stated that aliens couldn't own property here, so since my father was born in Hawai'i, they were able to buy the land and put it in his name. In fact, this would happen a lot as time went on; many people used my father and his citizenship to buy land. On paper, my father owned a lot of property even though he was just a kid," Gary chuckles.

This was a common method of gaining land ownership for many Japanese families at that time. In 1913, California passed the first of many Alien Land Acts prohibiting non-citizens from owning land. And citizenship was only granted to those deemed *eligible*, which was defined as "White or, at that time, of African descent." The Alien Land laws, passed in eight other states as well, and were upheld until 1952.

"My grandfather acquired 120 acres right here and began planting fruit trees and vines," Gary continues. "He ran the farm until my father took over, and then my brothers and I took it over after him. We expanded the land to over 800 acres and grow over 100 varieties of stone fruit as well as grapes. We've been very fortunate. We could have lost the land when our whole family was sent to camp."

"Camp" refers to the Japanese American internment camps, or war relocation camps, where over 120,000 people of Japanese heritage living on the Pacific coast were sent during World War II. The camps started in 1942, shortly after the attack on Pearl Harbor. Though over 62 percent of those incarcerated in the camps were American citizens, they were deported from their homes and held for almost three years in the camps. Many who were landowners, farmers, or tenants lost their land and their farms. Some were able to get their land back — if they had trustworthy neighbors, friends or workers to look after it until they returned.

"All of us went to camp," says Gary. "I was a young boy there, my wife was born there. My grandfather was no longer alive at that time, so my parents and my siblings and I were there. I have nine siblings, and we all lived in long barracks. They put three families in a barrack. They blocked it off, and each family had a section of the barrack. I remember there was a mess hall. I don't remember if there was a camp farm, I just remember the canal that we used to catch carp from. We were at the camp in Gila, Arizona. We were in the middle of nowhere. Even if people jumped the fence, the guards knew there was nowhere for us to go out in the desert."

"I don't remember a thing from camp," shares Kaye, Gary's wife. "I was born in camp. I was there with my whole family. Both my grandfathers came over here from Japan for economic reasons. My maternal grandfather was 20 years older than my grandmother, who was a picture bride.[19] They started here as farm laborers, then they lived and worked on a farm, but I don't think they ever owned it since they didn't have citizenship. When the war came, they were all sent to camp and after the war, my maternal grandparents weren't able to go back to the farm where they had worked and lived. So they went to Detroit to find work. I think my grandfather ended up working as a maintenance man at a candy factory. But my paternal grandparents had a farm near here in Fowler, and they were able to get it back. They were lucky and had Armenian neighbors who kept their land for them. So we all moved there, and that is where I grew up helping on the farm."

"We were also very fortunate," Gary continues. "At that point, my father had already taken over the farm, and there was a Mexican American guy that worked for my father who took over for us while we were gone. The military had a rating system for recruiting men for the war. For example 1A is perfectly fit, but if you were in college you would be a 1C, three down the list. During Vietnam, I was a 1Y because I was married and Kaye was pregnant. Well, the Mexican American who worked for my father must have had a medical condition or something because he was a 4F. And since he was not sent off to war, he could stay and keep our farm for us. It was about 120 acres at that time, and we were able to get it all back.

"A lot of the time you talk to older people that went to camp and had properties and when they came back, depending on how honest the person was who took care of their farm, they didn't always get all the land back or all of the income that was made on the farm while they were gone. And there were a lot of folks who couldn't get their land back at all. And when they did return, there was so much discrimination.

"My older brother can still tell you every neighbor that had it out for the Japanese. They signed a petition with the government to keep Japanese families from being able to return home," Gary recalls. "That means they signed a petition to make sure our families couldn't get our homes back. You don't forget that sort of thing. It causes a tension that never goes away for some people. My brother-in-law still refuses to buy a Chevrolet from the local dealer because when they came back from the war, trucks were hard to get and their name was put on a waiting list, but their name never came up. Everybody else's name came up, but not theirs. Why is that? He suspects discrimination. Now, that was two generations ago, but he still won't give them his business."

Similar to today's discrimination toward Muslim Americans after the attacks of 9/11, Japanese Americans experienced deep discrimination after World War II. The suspicion and hatred did not disappear with the closing of the internment camps. During the war, anti-Japanese groups formed up and down the West Coast opposing the resettlement of Japanese American families. One of the largest groups was the Pearl Harbor League, which was mainly comprised of farmers who wanted to keep Japanese landowners out so they could acquire their land.[20]

This makes me think about the many Japanese American farmers returning who must have struggled to gain a strong market of consumers again with that kind of community sentiment. Or the discrimination they encountered when they were in need of resources like tractors or trucks, as Gary mentioned, or loans to get their farms up and running again.

"There's always discrimination," says Kaye. "I don't think we'll ever get away from it. We luckily never experienced much with our business here and at the farmers market. But I always stayed around here, maybe if I had gone elsewhere, I would have.

"This is our home. We grew up here, both of us did, on farms. Like any other rural American kid, we grew up doing the same things, speaking the same language, eating the same food. Gary grew up wearing blue jeans and white t-shirts and staining them with juice from the peaches he ate running through these orchards. We have raised our kids here on this land. We have been here for over 50 years. We're proud of that."

Portrait 5:

Black Land Loss

Gary Grant, Black Farmers
and Agriculturists
Association (BFAA),
Tillery, North Carolina.

What's important for us to do is to understand the importance of land ownership. And to do that, we have to look at our own history and tell our own story.

— Gary Grant

T HE PRIDE AND VALUE of holding onto family land is priceless. But for many, that sacred inheritance has been slipping through family hands like loose earth. Land loss has impacted small family farmers all over the country, but Black farmers in the South have been some of the hardest hit. Back in Tillery, North Carolina, where I met with Mr. Whitaker (from the "Land Is Freedom" chapter), I also sat down with Mr. Gary Grant, of the Black Farmers and Agriculturists Association, who played an integral role in the discrimination lawsuit filed against the USDA by Black farmers from all parts of the country.

❧

Mr. Grant, like many long-time residents of Tillery, comes from a line of sharecroppers and family farmers. We sit together in his office at the Black Farmers and Agriculturists Association (BFAA), which he founded in Tillery, North Carolina. The office is a small building tucked away down a gravel road amongst the cotton fields and roadside markers for the historic Black Resettlement Project that existed here in the 1930s. Mr. Grant commands the room; as he speaks, his

voice carries the weight of the battles he has fought over decades of working to save Black-owned farms, including his own. "Land foreclosures here began on Black farmers in '75 and '76," Mr. Grant begins. "Ten years later the foreclosures reached White farmers in middle America. But when one White farmer shot and killed an FMA agent, it was at that point that we got a moratorium on farm foreclosures for five years.

"The foreclosures started again here when Black farmers would get into debt after bad hurricanes destroyed their crop. Remember the stories from Mrs. Hazel Hendricks about how the Black farms were put on low lands and more susceptible to storm flooding? Well those storms led to crop loss which led to farmer debt and a need to rely on loans. But Black farmers would receive loan payments too late in the season and fall victim to other discrimination-based delays in the system which caused farmers to lose out on the whole season. If you are getting your money to plant your crop in June and you were supposed to plant in early May, it means you've missed the window of opportunity. So your crop doesn't yield what it needed to, and then you aren't able to repay the loan at the end of the year. It just snowballs — you fall into debt and then become foreclosed on."

"Now these same storms were impacting White farmers too," Mr. Grant continues, "but they weren't going out of business. In fact, they were still operating and getting new tractors while Black farmers couldn't even get money to plant their crops. So how is it, when you have the same farmers in the same area under the same conditions that you've got this one segment of farmers failing while the other one is succeeding? There are mechanisms in place for supporting farmers in debt, there are ways to set aside debt and re-annuitize the loans. But none of these methods were used for Black farmers. If our ancestors, from slavery up until 1900, could manage to get almost 17 million acres of land, and we have lost almost 70 percent of it between 1920 and 1996, something's wrong. As my daddy would say, 'sumtin' wrong.' You have to remember that this is the South. Racism and discrimination are still alive and kicking. It's historically impacted Black farmers here, and this is no different."

The USDA's discrimination against Black farmers can be traced back to when White farmers became increasingly fearful of competing with freed slaves who had the stronger agricultural skills. In response, the government made USDA loans dependent on credit, a nonexistent asset for newly freed slaves. White farmers used credit to gain monopolistic control of agricultural production, and programs like the Resettlement Projects of the New Deal

Mr. Gary Grant.

era protected White farmers by shifting the risk to Black sharecropping tenants.[21] USDA discrimination became more blatant as racism in the South increased, with stories of officials telling Black farmers in need of equipment loans or disaster relief payments things like, "all you need is a mule and a plow" or "that's too much money for [your kind] to receive."

But more often, the USDA used paper-shuffling, delaying loans, approving only a fraction of loan requests, and denying crop-disaster payments for Black farmers, while White farmers routinely received them.[22] On average it took three times longer for the USDA to process a Black farmer's application than a White farmer's application.[23] The denial of credit and benefits to Black farmers and the preferential treatment of White farmers essentially forced Black farmers out of agriculture. By 1992, the number of Black farmers in America had declined by 98 percent.[24]

"We became involved in holding the USDA accountable when my parents' farm here was foreclosed on in the early '90s," Mr. Grant continues. "My family had records of late loan payments and other discrimination-based delays from them, and so we filed against them. During one of the hearings, the government loan agent walks in wearing a confederate neck tie. To a hearing on racial discrimination! I stopped the meeting and asked him how he would have felt had I walked in with a Black fist for Black Power on my t-shirt.

"These kinds of subtle messages were sent from government agents to farmers all throughout the South. We've heard stories of Black farmers walking into loan offices where a hangman's noose is displayed on the wall. Or the agent pulls open a drawer to reveal a gun in his desk. How are you supposed to apply for a loan in that sort of environment? So we fought hard, and in 1994 my family was approved for a settlement. But the Department of Justice stopped it because at that time Mr. Pigford's federal lawsuit against the USDA was beginning and they wanted to wait and see how that unfolded."

In 1996 Timothy Pigford, a Black farmer from North Carolina, along with 400 other Black farmer plaintiffs, filed against the USDA for the unfair treatment of Black farmers and for failing to process subsequent complaints about racial discrimination. With the Secretary of Agriculture

Dan Glickman as the defendant, the notorious lawsuit *Pigford v. Glickman* ensued. Over the course of the suit, thousands more Black farmers came forward with their stories, and the case grew until two settlements were finally processed under *Pigford* and *Pigford II* in 2013.

One of the farmers featured in this book (in the "Alabama Strong" chapter) shared with me her story of joining the *Pigford* lawsuit. Sandra Simone of Huckleberry Hill Farm told me about constantly being turned away for support. "A rep from the department sent me a letter saying they had funds available," Sandra recounted, "and that there was a minority program I qualified for. I just had to make an appointment and go down. I went down and when he saw me, well, I don't think he expected a Black female, and all of a sudden he said there were no funds and that it was such a long waiting list that I shouldn't even sign onto it. I was so confused and disheartened."

"I had been turned down over and over for loans," Sandra said, "and for other funded projects put into place to help beginning farms develop their land. You know, when you're in the process sometimes this stuff goes over your head, it's hard to see what's really going on. Finally I realized what was going on. I had to do a lot of research to prove the discrimination. I had to drive around and talk to White farmers who were doing what I was trying to do — dig a pond, put in a well, install fencing for my goats, etc. — and I found properties and farms that had the same shape and size pond or other projects that I applied for funding for, and I went to the courthouse and looked up records and could see that they were approved for funding for that project at the same time I was denied for the same project."

Sitting there with Mr. Grant, he begins telling me of many more farmers with stories like Sandra's. "We began talking to other farmers here going through what we'd gone through," Mr. Grant explains, "and since we were already working on our own settlements when *Pigford* came up, we decided to join together. We formed the Black Farmers and Agriculturists Association and began getting together and having hearings in communities all over the country. No matter where the hearings were held, all the Black farmers were telling the same story — in Mississippi, North Carolina, in California. They told us they weren't given the money, they weren't getting applications, they were told to get on waiting lists. Thousands of Black farmers all over the country were having the exact same experiences. That's when we knew it was a national crisis.

"But at this point, no national media coverage was picking it up. We could get state coverage, but we couldn't get national press. Then we had a demonstration in D.C. in 1996, and that finally got national attention, and that's when things got moving. Now you have thousands of Black farmers in court testifying and getting national coverage and real ugly stories begin to come forward. Then they offer a settlement, and what do you think that does? It stops the stories from coming out; it stops any stories from going into the record. The large settlement stops all of these smaller court cases, like my family's. They dropped our case after 30 years of fighting it. My parents died without any recompense for all they had been through.

"The $1 billion-plus settlement for all the farmers in the lawsuit ended up as a $50,000 award to each farmer — on which they also have to pay taxes. And the folks who think that's a good number are fooling themselves. Black farmers have lost so much more than that. For example, my family was going to lose 300 acres of land at $800/acre. That's a lot of money. This is back in the 1990s — that's almost $300,000. And that's just the land. We're not talking about what you can produce on all that land. $50,000 would not replace the tractor and the equipment that fell into disrepair while we couldn't get the loan to maintain it. My parents weren't the only ones to die waiting for their settlement. Many of the farmers in *Pigford* died before the case was closed. It was a 20-year battle, and the average age of the Black farmer is about 63.

"The settlement didn't even come close to restitution. We did not come to Washington for $50,000; we came to get our land back, and they have done everything but that. All that's happened since then is it started fighting amongst ourselves and sidetracked what the issue was all about. You've got families fighting over the money. You've got politicians and the media accusing us of fraudulent claims. But all in all, the damage is done. Black farmers are gone. We went from one million strong in 1920 to not much more than 15,000 today. We're not even a political mass to be dealt with. The USDA efficiently put us out of business. And the issues are still there."

Some of those issues include legal loopholes causing Black land loss, such as heir property laws — laws that govern the inheritance of family land. When multiple heirs inherit land and ownership is split up among them, some have an interest in using the land, some don't. Often, many relatives who have moved away are not even aware of the land inheritance. The land cannot be sold or even built on without the approval of all of the heirs. However, one or several heirs can buy out the other shares by petitioning the court to sell them the land and divide the money among the heirs. Often what ends up happening is an investor or developer comes along with an interest in buying the land, and they buy out *a share* from one of the heirs and use a process called "petition sales" to gain full ownership of the land, taking the land right from under the rest of the family.

Sandra of Huckleberry Hill Farm had this happen in her family. "Once land gets sub-divided so many ways, there's little you can do," she explained. "It happened here in my family. I had a very difficult time acquiring my portion of our family land. Members of the family divided the land among themselves and left some of the rightful heirs out of the division. It was a long legal procedure to correct the wrongful division. Also, my husband Harold had a strong vision of what the family could create with the land, which sat on the lakefront. He and his son, who is an architect in California, put together a plan for development of the lakefront property. They never wanted to sell but, instead, create income for generations of our family to come. We tried to get the family together so we could collectively develop the property, but they weren't interested. There was 250 acres surrounding the lake that belonged to five family members. And the other members sold that acreage for $250,000. There was nothing we could do. The land was gone, and for what? Five brothers, 250 acres, $50,000 each. After taxes, what did they really gain? Shortly after, it was developed just about the way we were trying to get the family to do. It was such a loss."

"What's important for us to do," says Gary Grant, as we discuss the fact that thousands of Black families in the South have stories like Sandra's, "is to understand the importance of land ownership. And to do that, we have to look at our own history and tell our own story." Mr. Grant stands up and motions for me to follow him into the adjacent room where stacks of binders and rows of filing cabinets sit holding decades of documentation on the history and struggle of Black farmers. "The Black community," Mr. Grant continues, "because of slavery, has a disdain for agriculture and no one wants to talk about farming or think about holding onto land they want to move on from. Because of our heritage and our current situation, we as Black people don't respect the Black farmer. It's something we have to overcome, especially Black urban folks who need to understand their roots. So I've realized you have to change the conversation. It's about land ownership and what that's allowed us to do. We start talking about the value of the land and what it has done for us as a people, and it helps to change that stigma a little bit."

Mr. Grant is also one of the founders of the Concerned Citizens of Tillery, a group that has created a History House (among many other projects), which documents and preserves the history of Tillery, including the history of sharecropping and the Resettlement Community. We drive over to the History House, a small house behind the Tillery Community Center where I had joined the elders of the community and met Mr. Whitaker the day before. The walls of the History House are lined with old black and white photos of farmers and families of Tillery plowing their fields or feeding their hogs.

Mr. Grant, who grew up as one of six children in Tillery, remembers being a happy child rolling tractor tires down the dirt road and going to the mill with his father to make flour and meal. He recalls most of the families of Tillery living happily, with food, shelter, health and an active, united community. We laugh together as he shares fond memories of his childhood. Mr. Grant laughs easily, and his laugh, along with his enduring spark of positivity and perseverance, is profoundly contagious.

"I think uncovering some of the history we had here helped us overcome some of the disdain toward agriculture and rural life," Mr. Grant continues. "It's our history and we should not allow anyone else to define it. We were poor, but nobody had told us, so our memories are what matter. If we talk about the drudgery of farming, we can also look at the fact that we had fresh vegetables, we had fresh fruit, we were canning and freezing, composting, reusing, recycling and all those things. We were self-sufficient. Those are pieces of our history to be proud of. And none of it would be possible without land."

Part 3:
Seeds of Resilience

 Through hardship, crisis and devastation, we begin
to see that community is the irreplaceable, resilient
infrastructure.

— Anonymous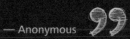

THE ROAD LUCILLE and I travel has begun to enter the beautiful forests of the West Coast. Giant redwoods, sequoias and cedar trees swallow us with their evergreen canopy, and Lucille's tires follow the gentle curves of the winding road. I roll the window down and breathe in the cool, fresh air emanating from these trees that have been standing tall for hundreds of years. For miles, I enjoy this scenery, until we round a corner and the landscape drops away completely. Suddenly the forest is gone. What lies before me instead is a barren land of charred stumps seemingly stretching on for miles.

This has been the hottest summer on record, and with the dry heat has come devastating wildfires.[25] I drive on, blinking back my shock as the burnt forest continues on longer than it should. I wonder how the forest will ever recover. Then, amidst all the ugly charred stumps and blackened earth, I spot tiny specks of vibrant green. Sprouting up strong and bright despite the devastation, I see seeds of resilience.

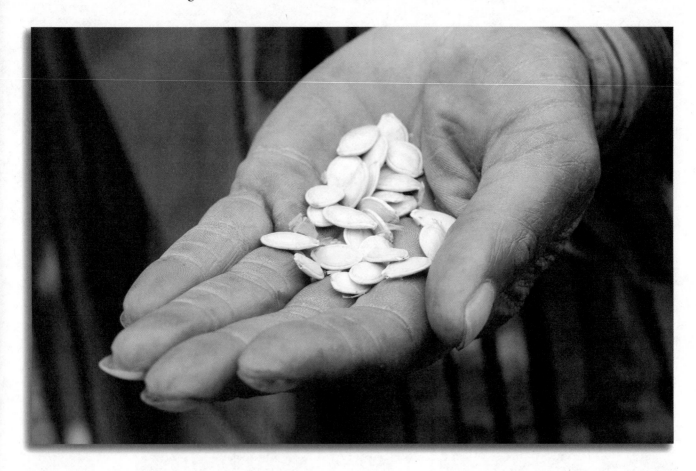

Resilience is a vital key to survival and is found in most living things. Forests grow back after wildfires, flowers re-bloom after harsh winters, communities strive to bounce back after disasters. It is what gives us hope and inspiration to push on no matter how dire it gets. This is why I look for signs of resilience wherever I go, particularly in agriculture. I look for signs of whether the soil can recover from our toxic pollution; whether the seeds can withstand our genetic modifications; whether the farmer can survive against the onslaught of corporatization or the rising challenges brought on by climate change.

Agriculture and climate change are inextricably linked. Not only has climate change begun affecting the global food supply, but it threatens to devastate agriculture from a multitude of angles. According to a recent USDA study, rising temperatures could cost farmers millions of dollars as they battle longer drought periods, new pests, faster weed growth and smaller yields.[26] Driving across the country, I am seeing the impacts of climate change with my own eyes. Farmers everywhere are dealing with what the National Climatic Data Center reports as the largest drought since the 1950s.[27] I have been meeting farmers who are being forced to make decisions like whether to cut down half their orchard to save on irrigation or what to do to meet the hefty costs of digging deeper wells as their water tables recede.

And it's not just about drought. Seasons are changing at different times. Frosts are coming earlier and staying later. Crops are wilting in extreme heat. The rising intensity and frequency of storms is flooding and wiping out entire farm fields. Especially for small farmers or communities with low food access, these storms have a direct impact on survival.

Yet, I am meeting farmers and communities who are resiliently pushing on. Farmers who are working tirelessly to prove that food can still be grown in abundance in the arid and drought-impacted deserts of southern New Mexico and California. Farmers who are picking up the pieces from one of our nation's most devastating hurricanes and using the experience as a wake-up call to become self-sustaining food producers.

However, our land and agricultural system are not the only victims of perpetual devastation. Our people have suffered just as much. Racial and ethnic groups in this country have faced hatred, injustice, oppression, abuse, humiliation, discrimination and blatant inequities in economic opportunity. Many communities' strength, culture and dignity as a people have come under threat and aggressive attempts to be razed to the ground. Yet, like the forest, seeds of resilience persist.

Despite a long history of injustice and discrimination, there is a growing community of Black farmers in the South who are resiliently coming up with ways to survive and thrive. They are transforming agriculture in the slow-moving South and innovating creative agricultural marketing strategies that are impacting the way we think about small farm and food entrepreneurship. Some of these farmers are even promoting agriculture as not just a way to grow food, but as a way to create lasting independence and wealth in the Black community.

Similarly, in the face of persecution and forced migration from their homelands, immigrants and refugees are arriving here and giving resilience a new meaning by planting their roots and their crops in unlikely climates and planting seeds of change and inspiration in their communities.

Despite the plight of many immigrants left with little choice but to join the unjust farm labor industry, workers are transitioning to owners, bringing back cooperatives, and sending a lesson to all beginning farmers on how it can be done.

I hold onto these seeds of resilience as I drive on through the charred forest toward the next farm, and soon the landscape comes back to life, and I'm once again surrounded by tall evergreen trees standing strong, defiant and beautiful.

Portrait 1:
Katrina to Chickens

Yard Bird Farm, Yasin and Elaine Muhaimin, Zachary, Louisiana.

> Hurricane Katrina was a wake-up call. It allowed us to see how close we are to dying. The hurricane is how I became a farmer.
>
> — Yasin Muhaimin

THINKING ABOUT THE RESILIENCE it takes to bounce back from struggle and trauma, I steer Lucille toward a region of the country that is still digging deep for the strength to overcome one of the worst hurricanes in our history. Hurricane Katrina impacted millions of lives in the South and dispersed families across states, leaving them with nothing to rebuild their lives. The Southeastern African American Farmers Organic Network put me in touch with a family who used their resilience, faith and passion for clean food to find new life after Katrina.

❧

The chicken in his hand clucks wildly as I ask Yasin Muhaimin about his farm. He swiftly puts the chicken's neck through the metal cone used to hold it in place upside down and expertly slices its neck. Three more birds with the same fate sit in the adjacent cones. Yasin recites a *takbir*, a required halal prayer, under his breath as he slaughters each bird:

Bismi Allah, Allahu Akbar
[With God's Name, God is Greater]

His cousin Booga then picks the chickens up and puts them into the hot water tank and then into the defeathering machine that spins the birds around until they are bald. We stand in this outdoor chicken slaughter facility in Yasin's expansive backyard. He continues working efficiently, and, over the sounds of clucking, he tells me the story of how he and his wife Elaine started Yard Bird Farm.

"We're from New Orleans. We're city people. We never would have dreamed that we would be farmers one day," Yasin chuckles. "I worked for the public school district in New Orleans. I had some real estate investments. We were doing well. Then Hurricane Katrina hit."

"We lost everything. We lost three homes. We lost 100 schools in the district due to damage. I had every intention of getting back to work to get back on our feet, but the governor called a freeze on hiring. Because of the loss of so many schools, there was no work, so they forced me into retirement.

"We had a family to feed, we needed to find work, and we needed a space for our family. There were six of us. We had no choice but to leave New Orleans. I had relatives up here, and they took us in for two months while we figured out what to do. Having all this land up here and being around farmers — my cousin raises goats near here — really got us thinking about farming to make a living, and also to have our own food.

"The hurricane was a wake-up call. It allowed us to see how close we are to dying. When the power went out in New Orleans, that meant no more food on the shelves. Even the city's food reserves and food in storage was ruined. There was something like a million chickens in cold storage that all went to waste. It was a scary time."

The Louisiana Farm Bureau Federation reported on Hurricane Katrina's damages to food storage and farmers, which included the dumping of thousands of gallons of milk and the entire contents of grain elevators along the Mississippi River. Katrina devastated dairy, timber, cattle, vegetable crops, sugarcane and the fishing industry with a financial loss of around $814 million.[28] But the hurricane also closed grocery stores, restaurants and routes for food to be transported into the city, quickly demonstrating how delicate the infrastructure of the food system we rely on really is.

"So when we found this house for sale and it had enough land," Yasin continues, "we thought maybe we could sustain ourselves on this land. Southern University is nearby, and they really got us into this. The Ag Center there provided some training and introduced me to other farmers in the area. At first we tried everything — from mushrooms to chickens. We were cutting logs and trying to inoculate; we learned so much. But there was some serious market interest in pastured poultry. So we decided to focus on that.

Yasin Muhaimin.

"We had to use all of our savings to get this land and start this. I'd lost my credit rating. Everything just went away with the hurricane. I couldn't borrow anything. I went to the USDA and had the same problem. They were very nice and helpful up to a point, but once they saw that I had all these judgments filed against me — I mean I had no money. There was nothing they could do, they couldn't loan me anything. So we took all we had in savings and put it into this."

One of the biggest challenges for beginning farmers is accessing capital, credit opportunities and affordable land. Though the USDA's Farm Service Agency (FSA) offers loans to beginning farmers, current loan rules often disqualify even experienced farmers with good credit, and small loans are hard to come by. And for real estate transactions, FSA loans take too long to process — up to 30 days to qualify and up to a year to receive funds.[29] And often the loan limits don't meet the high cost needs of buying land and funding the infrastructure needed (equipment, building materials, irrigation, etc.) to get started.

"I'm no longer interested in loans or credit at all," Yasin says, "I'm not interested in support programs. We try to do it all on our own. And it came out alright; we've been here now for seven years."

Yasin takes me on a tour of their small farm. In addition to the processing facility, they have a large brooder house, a large coop for their layers, a smoker where they smoke some of the chickens to sell, and a hoop house where they are growing vegetables for themselves and experimenting with specialty crops for market such as ginger, hibiscus and shiso, a Japanese herb that grows well in the area that they market for use in stir-fry.

"We're sustaining our own access to food, and we're also contributing to the clean food movement," Yasin says as he surveys everything on the farm. "We sell our chickens direct to consumers through farmers markets. We do the first and third Saturday of each month at the Red Stick farmers market in Baton Rouge. I also sell to a halal store. As Muslims, we process our chickens by halal standards."

Halal in Arabic means "permissible." In terms of food, it means food that is permissible according to Islamic law. For meat to be certified halal, it can't be forbidden (such as pork, carrion or blood). The slaughter of a halal animal is called *zabihah*, and there are certain guidelines to follow. Some of them include: pronouncing Allah's name during slaughter, using a very sharp knife to ensure a humane slaughter, and feeding the animal a natural diet without animal byproducts.

"All our consumers want is a clean chicken. We plant our own grass, and we know what goes into these chickens. The feed we supplement with has no animal byproducts. Our consumers don't want the antibiotics or the growth hormones. And we don't need them. It takes about seven weeks for them to grow to size naturally.

"People say grass-fed animals without growth hormones take too long. But seven weeks is not too long. Seven weeks is fast!" Yasin exclaims. "With layers, you know, we have to go almost 16 weeks before we can get an egg from a hen. And we can get meat in seven weeks, that's really great. Seven weeks is just 49 days. There are people out here with cattle farms, and they're grass feeding them for almost two years before they can make a profit. But that's the way it is if you don't want to mess with nature.

"Even if you're not worried about messing with nature, there is a direct correlation with the condition of our health and the food that we eat. If we're eating growth hormones, it has a direct effect. If we're eating excessive amounts of antibiotics and all the other chemicals they put into the food, then that has a direct effect on us. It affects us spiritually too. It's just not necessary. There are models for running these chicken farms on grass without a problem at high levels of production. Chickens are foragers. They live on grass — that's how they're supposed to live."

Yasin takes me into the brooder house where there are 100 chicks chirping under a warming red light. It is a large space, portioned off for the baby chicks in the brooder and the adolescent chicks wandering around on the ground. "We slaughter 100 chickens every two weeks," he explains. "We do it staggered. We have 100 chicks in the brooder, 100 older ones on the floor, and we always have 100 adults out here on the grass. And we just rotate them through until they are ready for slaughter."

"Slaughter laws are different in every state," Yasin explains. "We can slaughter here on site. I have a state permit, and my limit is 20,000/year. We had to learn the whole process and set up our own facility. At first we started in our carport, but the inspectors said we couldn't do it there. So we got this portable building for the cleaning room and built this open-air processing area. It takes about three minutes to process the chicken from slaughter to bald. We can do about five chickens at a time. We usually do about 40 a day on slaughter days. Then they go to the cleaning room and Elaine does the evisceration. We had to learn that whole process too."

I head into the cleaning room where Elaine is doing the processing. "Careful while you walk," she calls out as I enter the little room with slick linoleum floors that is adjacent to the open-air slaughter area. There's just about enough room for four people to work inside; there's a large, clean countertop where Elaine works and a large metal sink beside her. She's wielding a sharp knife and has a bandana over her hair. As she expertly eviscerates each chicken, I ask her what her first thoughts were about learning the process.

"There's things that I'm doing now that when I came here I never thought I'd be doing," Elaine answers. "Sitting on a lawn mower cutting grass, up here in the woods, pulling weeds out of a big old garden like that, walking through the woods in the day and in the night — I come from the middle of the city!

"But I thought about the fact that I had to do it and thought I didn't want to do this, but if he could do it, I could do it. And he knows it. Most of the things we both do I know we both have to do, and I might feel a little intimidated the first time, but once I see how it's done and know it's something that has to be done, I'll do it."

She reaches down and pulls out the chicken's innards. "We use and sell every part of the chicken," she explains, "the head, the feet, the liver, everything but the viscera. That we give to our neighbors who feed it to their pigs. We're very careful when removing certain things like the gallbladder, to avoid contamination. We try our best to keep it as clean as we can. We have inspectors that come, they just drop by, we never know when they're gonna come. Matter of fact they came last week. They really like what we do. They recommend other farmers to come here and see how we do it. We've had people call and ask if they can come learn from us. The inspector recommended us as an example,

*Elaine processing
a chicken.*

and these are people that have been processing longer than we have. I don't know what we're doing differently, but we get a lot of compliments.

"We do a special hand plucking and deskinning of the chicken that gives the meat a better flavor and color that is not lost in the hot boil. We take the skin completely off the chicken, which is something popular among our Muslim customers. They say there's too much fat in the skin and that a lot of bad stuff could be in the skin. We don't eat the skin either. We've been eating skinless for years, even before we became farmers. We've always eaten clean, healthy food. It's part of our religion. I've been a Muslim for 39 years and have always eaten clean, no pork, and very conscientious of what goes into our food and how we handle it."

As I look down at the chickens she's cleaned, I notice how pristine they look.

I can't help but think about whether I would see the same attention and care in the processing room of say, Tyson. And I know the answer. While I was interviewing Yasin and Elaine, a student from Southern University was there to run tests on their chickens because of Yard Bird Farm's high quality standards in cleanliness and natural diet. Yasin told me they wanted to be able to scientifically prove that their chickens are toxin free, antibiotic free, and more nutritious. So the university came out to take samples from the chicken carcasses and also of the compost where they put the chicken litter.

"I don't eat chicken from anywhere else," Elaine says. "I can't. And people depend on our chicken. On hard days here, when the price of feed goes up and I want to quit, I don't, because even when we miss one day at the farmers market, people call up and beg us for our chicken. We've created a big demand."

"We sell an average of 6,000–8,000 birds a year," Yasin chimes in, "We're doing well. I just bought my wife a new car," he smiles. "We don't do outside work, this is it."

"And we love it here," Elaine adds. "Our children, our grandkids, they love it here. They can't wait to get here. When they come, they go swimming, horseback riding, airgun shooting, tour different farms — they never want to leave. We couldn't have had this life in New Orleans. We're fully sustaining ourselves here. We have survived."

Portrait 2:
Transitioning to Sovereignty

Luis Castañeda,
SOLAR Farm,
Chapparal, New Mexico.

> Empowerment is a word that has been so overused that nobody believes in it anymore, but that's what we have to do. We need to empower immigrant farmers to lead the way in creating new livelihoods for themselves.
>
> — Rigoberto Delgado, National Immigrant Farming Initiative

S URVIVAL FOR A COMMUNITY after devastation takes on many forms. As discussed in the chapter "Forced Migration," immigrant communities often start over with nothing after migrating to the U.S., with the added complications of language barriers, legalities and new systems in which to operate. In a region where many immigrant communities are left with low-wage and oppressive agricultural work to survive, I met with resilient families working to transition from merely surviving to having sovereignty over their lives, their opportunities and their food.

❧

I steer Lucille down a long, dusty road in the dry, hot desert of Chaparral, a small town in southern New Mexico. I see nothing but a few houses sprawled along the blacktop road, then suddenly there's an oasis of green and purple on the side of the road. I pull in and see about half an acre overflowing with neat rows of vibrantly healthy produce growing under the desert sun. I get out of my car and am greeted first by a wave of heat and then a warm smile from Luis Castañeda, one of the farm owners here at the cooperative farm they call SOLAR. With him is Rigoberto Delgado, one of the supporters of the farm from the National Immigrant Farming Initiative (NIFI).

"In Spanish, 'solar' means your property — your farm — because we don't really have a specific word for farm in Spanish," Luis explains in Spanish as he walks me through the rows of broccoli, peppers and *calabaza* (squash or pumpkin), "You can say *granja* but *granja* is like for animals, or *rancho* is for livestock; *huerta* is like a garden, but for a small family farm next to the house — like we called it in my childhood — it is *solar*. Sometimes it's referred to as just a backyard, but we use it with an agricultural meaning."

SOLAR is run by Luis, his wife Irma and two other families: the Gallardo and Ramirez families. All of them worked as farm laborers alongside many other Mexican American farm workers in the region. But they are now working to transition to running their own small farms and starting added-value food businesses. They have partnered with a group of women from Chiapas, Mexico, who run an artisan craft business called Cassava Creations, and together they hope to start their own market where they can sell these handmade crafts along with the farm's produce and food products. SOLAR has plans to create a commercial kitchen where they can make and sell foods like *asadero* cheese, tortillas, quesadillas and *cubiertos.*

"*Cubiertos* are traditional Mexican candies made from *calabaza,* sweet potato or *biznaga* [a barrel cactus plant]," Luis explains. "We grew up with these candies and now we could make them and sell them. Also our quesadillas may not be what you think. We make our quesadillas with the squash blossom. They are like a flower taco or blossom taco mixed with corn tortilla. Many people have already lost the memory of this traditional food. We could bring it back."

"Food is so important to us, it's how we grew up, it's our history," Rigoberto adds. Rigo, as he likes to be called, grew up farming in southern New Mexico. He tells me that his family didn't have much but they were never hungry. They grew everything they needed. "I remember eating *calabaza* like a breakfast meal. My mom would cut the pumpkin in big chunks — with shell and everything — and then kind of steam them. She put brown sugar in it as it cooked. You would get the hard shell and cut the meat off of it and put it in your bowl and put milk on it and that was your cereal — *calabaza con leche.*"

"There is a nostalgia for these foods," Rigo affirms, "and the farmers are remembering and wanting to bring them back, and so they are beginning to grow them again."

Luis continues to show me around the farm, excitedly showing off the healthy vegetables; describing the farm's salty, sandy soil; pointing out the drip-tape irrigation pumped in from the municipal water supply; and informing me of the secret to such beautiful plants: *gallinaza* — chicken waste fertilizer. As Luis picked one of everything on the farm to fill up a basket for both me and Rigo to take home, we munched on sandy carrots and talked about the success and future for SOLAR. Other families have begun to take notice of this farm and are tapping into the knowledge being offered about how to grow food. Other families, like the Briones, who we visited later that afternoon, have been quietly growing on abandoned plots and are now contributing their skills and knowledge to SOLAR.

Together, we drive over to visit the Briones farm and as we drive we talk about how the idea of food sovereignty seems to be spreading and growing in this farmworker community. And Luis says that they owe it all to the help of Rigoberto and his organization NIFI, an organization that knows all too well the barriers of the system that keep many farm laborers and immigrant farmers from success.

"Our agricultural system is difficult to navigate for the average family farmer, let alone for those that don't speak English, or are unfamiliar with the system in this country," says Rigo, "Those farmers that do speak English, but with an accent, are often considered ignorant by the authority and therefore are discriminated against. So

they carry their well-founded fears of institutions and public agencies and tend to
avoid seeking support from them. In addition, many immigrant farmers lack capital.
They come here and have not yet had the
chance to establish credit. Without credit,
you are nobody right? So for many immigrants, they are simply not taken seriously
as producers.

"That's where NIFI comes in. Our job
is to ensure the system not only knows
about this population of producers, but
we work to ensure they are receiving the
support they need. We started the initiative
in 2002, and since then have been working
to interpret the U.S. farming system for
immigrant farmers, refugee farmers, and
farmworkers through outreach and technical assistance, as well as training and
mentoring. We also bring local organizations together to work as a network
supporting other 'socially disadvantaged
farmers.' That's what they call us, which
we don't like, but that is our official term."

Socially disadvantaged farmers are
defined by the USDA as "a group whose
members have been subjected to racial or
ethnic prejudice because of their identity as a members of that group." But they
leave out gender discrimination. Women
farmers are socially disadvantaged too, and
NIFI works with women farmer groups as
well.

"Despite the fact that these farmers are
'disadvantaged,' 30 percent of producers in
the U.S. are women," Rigo explains, "and
the number of immigrant farm operators
continues to rise, especially for Latinos,

who are currently the fastest growing
population of farm operators. What does
this mean? They are our next wave of
farmers. With the current farming population aging out and family farms facing
unprecedented challenges in the struggle
for viability and a place in contempo-
rary agriculture, our country is losing its
farmers. Some estimate that one third
to one half of all the small farms in the
country will disappear or the operator will
retire within the next decade.

"Meanwhile, you have a growing population of immigrant farmers and farm
workers who want to be farm owners and
work for themselves. Farming is a dream
for many of the immigrants, refugees and
farm workers we work with. They often
come from rural and agricultural countries and bring skills and unique crops that
are in demand at the markets here. They
bring the experience, the know-how and
the passion for it. But this passion in most
cases is not enough to succeed.

"For those of us that care about community food security, family farmers and
social justice, we have a tremendous opportunity right now to support these farmers.
This is a time to link immigrant farmers'
passion with the resources, knowledge and
information they need, so they can survive
and thrive."

Rigo continues to tell me about all of
the work they do to support the transition
of struggling immigrant farmers or farm
workers to successful farm operators and
food production business owners. Their
main focus is training farmers in groups

and encouraging group development and cooperative business management.

"It's all about the multiplying effect," says Rigo. "Working with a group not only has a broader impact on community change, but it encourages cooperative farming which has many benefits, but also challenges."

"Cooperatives" in agriculture is a loose term. A couple of the common types of cooperatives we see in the U.S. ag system consist of groups of farmers pooling their land, labor and resources together to farm jointly on a large or small scale, or groups of farmers pooling their products together and marketing them cooperatively. We have a rich history of cooperatives in this country, particularly in the South, with groups like the Federation of Southern Cooperatives who have been around for over 40 years developing cooperatives within the African American farmer community. The Federation believes cooperatives simply give people a way to have a business of their own and keep the money they make in their own community. They emphasize that only when we begin to control our own businesses will we be able to have some control over what happens to our community. It's about empowerment.

"Empowerment is a word that has been so overused that nobody believes in it anymore," Rigo continues, "but that's what we have to do. We need immigrant farmers to lead the way in creating new livelihoods for themselves. But the prep work even before the farm set-up is so important. Organizing and getting groups

to collaborate is a lot of work. It's new to many of our folks. They've never belonged to a group before. But they come together and develop leaders and vision and create their strategic planning. They enhance their feeling of belonging to a group. It can be powerful.

"But organizational development as a group is so vital, it has to be done before doing anything else. That's why so many cooperatives have failed — they haven't focused on developing that collaboration. We help facilitate that and then support the innovators and leaders and connect them to mentors and leadership training.

"Take Luis and his group for example. He is currently training with an agricultural

Rigoberto and Luis.

training program started by the American Friends Service Committee (AFSC) and hosted here by the local group La Semilla—both groups that we work with. And AFSC is doing this kind of training up and down the state, even in other parts of the country. And we work in over eight states as well.

"But developing new farms and farm cooperatives is a time-consuming process. It's expensive to organize, and the federal support is not there for the training and resources, so not a lot of groups do it. We need support to do this work effectively. We need the resources to provide resources. When the economic downturn hit, we had to lose most of our field coordinators. We can't support them if we don't have the support.

"This is a resilient community, continuing to fight after migration from their own countries, working in oppressive conditions here, and navigating our system with limited knowledge. Now, they have the opportunity to do great things in agriculture, but we have to bounce back with them."

Portrait 3:
Bucking
Dependence

Renard "Azibo" Turner,
Vanguard Ranch,
Gordonsville, Virginia.

Self-sufficiency is at the core of all I do. I don't like being dependent. There's a political component to being dependent. Being a descendant of enslaved Africans, we never had the freedom to be independent. We were property.

— Renard "Azibo" Turner

WHEN REFLECTING ON AFRICAN American history, the resilience in overcoming centuries of slavery, trauma and oppression is undeniable. That same resilience, coupled with a drive for independence is what many Black farmers would say is a key to their survival against the odds of deep-rooted discrimination and shrinking opportunity in the agricultural industry. I met with one such farmer who is creating his own opportunities and advocating for farming as a tool for self-sufficiency.

Renard is a compact bundle of energy as he swiftly moves from one part of his 94-acre farm to the other. During my three-day stay with him and his wife Chinette on their goat farm, I run around, juggling my tape recorder, camera and whatever farm tool he has me carrying as I try to keep up with him. He is a machine, a very methodical man who never stops working. There's always something to do on the farm. He starts each day with just five hours of sleep and a cup of coffee and doesn't stop working until supper.

In the early morning mist, we work together pushing bean seeds down into the clay soil in the garden patch, just beyond the fence that divides the crops from the goat pasture. Renard grows just about everything, from radishes to kale and lettuce to beans. He sells his produce to the Local Food Hub, an innovative non-profit distributor in the foodie town of Charlottesville, Virginia, that connects small farmers to market. He grows organically with just goat manure and lime added to the soil and Neptune Harvest's seaweed fertilizer for all the crops. He has a high-tunnel hoop house and a greenhouse. Food is growing everywhere.

But produce is just a part of this farm. Chickens peck their way around pasture in chicken tractors that keep them mobile yet fenced in, while heirloom hens are busy laying chocolate brown eggs in the coop, and a herd of about 50 Myotonic goats (the fainting goats) graze over 50 acres. It is a picturesque scene, and Renard keeps it all running pretty much on his own, while Chinette helps and works at her off-farm job.

"I wear many hats," Renard says as we move from seeding to fixing the goat fencing. "I'm required to be a marketing person, an agronomist, a weatherman, a mechanic. I gotta work smart, either work smarter or work harder. I choose to work smarter. We have many streams of income by having such a diverse farm. If you're just gonna sell produce, you have to have a lot more labor, and then you're not getting the same profit. We are a value-added producer. We raise goats, cook the meat, and sell our goat meat products. We sell our eggs, our produce, and we sell to a wide range of markets. Any small family farm has to look at ways to maximize their profits and one of the ways you do that is by retaining ownership of your product throughout the whole process."

Vanguard Ranch is well known in Virginia for their goat meat. They have a certified mobile kitchen that they drive to festivals throughout the state and sell goat burgers, goat kabobs and curried goat to festival goers. They also sell their meat to local restaurants and have created a high demand for their product over the past eight years.

"I can get $38/lb with my goat meat, and people wonder how we do it. Well, look at the work that goes into it. We work 15–16 hour days. We had to buy the mobile unit, take these food safety classes, get certified, get insured, take care of all the paperwork, put up a website, pay festival fees. That's just before you can do anything. Now, for each festival, we're up 2–3 days prepping and cooking the meat, then hauling the unit around the state, running the generator at the festival all day, making sure we're meeting all the health department requirements. So by the time we get

that money, we deserve it because we've gone through all that work. And we're never really separate from it. This is full time, we're always running. Really, we're restaurateurs as well as farmers; there's a lot of layers to what we do.

"And it pays off. The farm pretty much pays for itself. Chinette only needs to work off the farm because start-up is expensive, and we're still paying off the loans we took out for that. And also because of insurance. But it shouldn't be much longer. The farm exceeds her income off the farm. This year it should double, and by the time it gets to triple she should be able to stop.

"We just want to get out of debt. To start up, we worked and we took loans. It was hard getting loans — it was very difficult. It took us 11 years to get a Farm Service Agency (FSA) loan, and now we're still paying it all back. We didn't get anyone, literally, anyone listening to us 11 years ago when we started. I went with plans that I spent six months working out and I might as well have spent six minutes on it. We had to do it pretty much all by ourselves, over time and then find ways to fund it. It took every penny to do what we did."

Renard and Chinette first had their dream of farming while living in Washington, D.C., in the '70s. They were part of an Afro-centric circle of back-to-the-landers, but the circle seemed to be all talk, and Renard and Chinette ended up alone on land in rural Virginia that they had hoped would be a Black community for sustainability. They had to learn everything because neither of them came from an agricultural background. Renard grew up in California as the only Black kid in his school's Future Farmers of America (FFA) program, but their conventional teachings didn't prepare him for this kind of agrarian life. The couple subscribed to resources like *Mother Earth News* and learned over a number of years through growing for themselves, and when they reached an excess harvest, they began to sell their produce. Their dream was to sell to the African American communities of Richmond and D.C., but they struggled with transportation costs and finding consistent customers.

"We tried to do a CSA, with a work-share for members to balance out our cost of driving into the city to distribute and sell. But that posed a problem for transportation for our customers as well. You have to be within a reasonable distance to a city to successfully market that way. And finding local people of color to support us out here has been painfully slow. In fact, in our experience, we have found no African American folks in our area that are willing to come work on our farm in exchange for fresh produce. It's either because they have enough space to grow their own garden or it's because they want nothing to do with the farm. It's an uphill battle to find people of color that have an interest in farming. I think it gets back to what I call the 'anti-agricultural Blacklash' where Black folks are still equating farming with slavery. But nothing could be further from the truth. Yes it is hard work, but at least we are doing for self."

"I align with Dr. Ridgley's belief of 'Do For Self,'"[30] Renard continues. "I believe what we are advocating for is larger than just farming; it's a return to agrarianism. A lifestyle that is about choice and is the basis for restructuring the African American community in a way that will create value and be lasting and inheritable, passing that wealth on.

"We've become too dependent as a society. We are trading our time to work for someone else and not be fulfilled. We have to reconnect with our own abilities, and we have to maintain our own communities and food systems. We need to have stores, we need to have farms that supply those stores, we need to control and own those farms and stores and have a lot more control over the destiny of our own lives. It's a major issue because we've stopped being our own providers and producers. We now provide by trading time for dollars, which we pay to have someone else produce and provide everything for us. It creates a cultural tradition of not being productive and self-sufficient, and I think that's a problem.

"We need a paradigm shift in who we are and where we want to get to. And I don't think it's possible to make those types of changes without returning to the land. It's just not possible. Living closer to natural cycles and the earth is very important. Indigenous people always knew this, in whatever part of the world they lived, they knew. Now we have people living in boxes and cubicles, we've lost our way — we're not connected. Yet we call it progress. I call it *regress*. The answers are there for us in Indigenous culture and nature but we're shunning it. People say to us, people from our community, the Black community, 'what's all that natural stuff you're eating, y'all are too natural for me.' It doesn't make any sense.

"Even with folks who are farming — Black farmers in the South who continue to grow conventionally and stay trapped in the large farm industry. There are many who are not switching over to organic, they are not diversifying their businesses. I get it — humans are creatures of habit, we do what we know. We're not going to try something new because we're not comfortable stepping out of the zone of what we know and of what's already bringing in money. Also how do you make the conversion to organic or evolving your farm business, and how long does it take, and how do you continue making money in the meantime? These are all valid issues, and it's not so easy. But you don't want to end up like the chicken slaves to Tyson over in the valley.[31] As Black farmers we are going to have to really reinvent ourselves to meet the demands of the times we're living in. I think not going into the natural food production sector is a huge mistake.

"What I would like to see African American farmers do, and prospective farmers, is we gotta network more and have think tanks and sit down and talk to each other about what we really want to do. We have to know the things to do to make profit possible. You're not gonna do it with peanuts and soybeans and corn. You have to find a niche market. You have to continuously be learning. Not a week goes by that I'm not studying something

Renard and Chinette Turner.

or reading up on something on food and agriculture. I've been doing that for 40 years.

"And we have to stop looking at federal support programs as the way to do it. An effective food system is on us as producers and communities, not federal support programs. Number one, it's because it's not easy to get that support. Many minority farmers don't even know the programs are out there and when we do, we go and there aren't people in the office that look like us. This leaves room for problems of discrimination or no one who will take the time to walk us through the paperwork and processes. That's still a major issue with the USDA, and I don't think it's necessarily going to go away, because discrimination is ingrained in our society. I think it'll take a long time if it ever does go away.

"We talked earlier about the need for our communities to pass on our wealth. Well, had things been on a fair and equitable basis from the start of USDA support programs for minority farmers, those farms would now be in a totally different socio-economic status than they are now, and their descendants would have been able to inherit that wealth. That could have changed the whole equation for a lot of families and communities in this country.

"Agrarianism is about not getting caught up with the government agencies. You can use their programs as a tool, but it is ultimately so that we can stand apart from that on our own. It's not sustainable to rely on the federal support programs and go into debt; you'll end up in foreclosure. That's why I'm a staunch do-it-yourselfer. Self-sufficiency is at the core of all that I do. I don't like being dependent. There's a political component to being dependent. Being a descendant of enslaved Africans, we never had the freedom to be independent. We were property. The only way you can be in charge of your own food is by growing your own, and the only way you can do that is to become a landowner. We have to find proactive ways to get there and help ourselves.

"But we can't be afraid to step out there. We are afraid to take that risk, afraid we won't be successful. Because we really haven't been conditioned to think successfully, we've been conditioned to think quite the opposite. But we have the opportunity to grow that wealth. We have been and still are an agricultural people. We need to embrace that instead of trying to live in someone else's reality and be dependent. We are limited by a lack of knowledge of our true selves and our own people, and so we live in someone else's reality, and I personally think that stops us from being all that we can be."

Portrait 4:
Surviving as Transplants

Pang Chang,
PEC Tropical Farm,
Fresno, California.

"

A lot of people ask me how I do what I do here. I tell them I went to no school. For Hmong people, the knowledge of farming is passed on. We just learn by doing what generations before us have done.

— Pang Chang

"

ON A 101-DEGREE AFTERNOON in the heart of California's Central Valley, an agricultural extension agent, whom I'd just been introduced to by phone a few days prior, graciously offers to meet me at a tropical farm in the middle of the arid valley plains. It may sound surreal, but it has nothing on the unbelievable story of the family I was to meet with, and many more stories like theirs — stories in which resilience and passion aid a refugee immigrant community in starting over in a new place.

❧

Imagine living in the rural mountains of Laos: climbing papaya trees, growing lemongrass, and living in peace. Imagine that peace disrupted as your community is attacked and forced to flee, cross rivers and jungles on foot, and dodge bullets and starvation. Then picture finding refuge in a foreign country with a foreign language and culture where you have to start over and try to survive. This picture is a reality for many Hmong refugees living in the U.S., and their harrowing stories are often too painful to recount.

Hmong people have thrived in agricultural, mountainous regions throughout China, Laos, Vietnam and Thailand for over 2,000 years. Targeted as ethnic minorities, they came under attack in Laos and Vietnam after their mountain tribes were recruited by the CIA to fight in the Vietnam War. They were forced to flee to refugee camps in Thailand by crossing the Mekong river, and many then fled to the U.S., France, Canada and Australia. Today, the U.S. is home to the largest Hmong population outside of China, with over 200,000 people. The majority of the American Hmong population came from Laos and are concentrated in California, Minnesota and Wisconsin. In California, the Hmong population is concentrated in the Central Valley, the top-producing agricultural area in the nation.

Agriculture is a strong facet of Hmong culture, and many have turned to farming as a way to survive here. However, as with many immigrants, accessing land, capital and an agricultural system in another language is extremely difficult. Yet farmers like Pang Chang have managed to overcome the challenges of being transplanted into another world, much like the trees he grows.

Walking through Pang's 12-acre orchard in Fresno County, California, was like walking into the lush tropical jungles of Southeast Asia, with the sweet smell of papaya and guava hanging in the humid air of the greenhouse. In a dry region suffering from drought and known for its expansive cotton and grape farms, the sight of guava, papaya, mango and jujube trees (known as Chinese dates) is a true oasis — you almost can't believe your eyes.

A farmer who fled Laos and settled in Fresno to do the only thing he knew how, Pang is one of the only growers in his region successfully producing tropical fruits. He started out growing vegetables like tomatoes and daikon, but decided to plant trees with his father's advice that "vegetables allow you to survive year to year, but long-term wealth comes from trees." It turned out to be the right decision. With many other farmers in the area competing with the same vegetable crops, Pang enjoys the lack of competition and high demand for his tropical fruit.

However, non-native tropical trees aren't easy to grow in Fresno's climate, so with a hunger to learn and thrive in a niche market, Pang sought help from the University of California's Agricultural Extension office. There he found a friend and advisor who shared not only his passion for growing but also his connection back to his homeland in Laos.

Michael Yang is a Hmong farmer and agricultural agent with the university who works with Asian American farmers throughout the Central Valley of California. He remembers fleeing Laos as a seven-year-old boy carrying a rifle on one shoulder and a grenade in his pocket. His memories of escaping with his mother and brother through the dangerous jungles of the Mekong are reminders of survival, something he shares with many of the farmers he now supports.

"Pang is determined to survive in this market," says Michael as we walk through Pang's orchard, PEC Tropical Farm, and head back to the greenhouse where Pang grows his mango, papaya and guava trees in a controlled environment. "He wants to learn. He comes to all of our workshops and then he comes back here and does better than what we do at the extension.

"We host workshops on new crops and varieties trying to encourage our farmers to branch out from commonly grown Asian vegetables like daikon to rarely grown fruits like papaya in order to meet the rising demands in Asian markets. We teach farmers about how to create the right climate for these trees and how to avoid the common pests and viruses that infect these varieties. He's always the first one to come to the workshops, and he's making it work here."

We enter the humid greenhouse and are transported into another world, dense and vivid green. Trees, plants and herbs seem to be growing on every square inch, all vibrant and healthy, many foreign to American soil such as the Filipino Moringa tree, dragon fruit, ginger and lemongrass. Pang and his wife May greet us and begin walking us through the trees, ducking under heavy limbs swollen with fruit and handing us one of each variety to bite into.

"We've been living on this land for six years," Pang says in Hmong as he cuts open a papaya to share with us. "We first rented land and worked for many years to save until we could buy this land. When I first arrived from Laos, my only language was Hmong. I had no English and no education. Language was a barrier, so I had to attend school — ESL classes to get the basic understanding and to communicate here. I was farming all my life in Laos. It's what I did, and once I settled here the first thing I knew to do was what I know best: farming."

This is the case for many Hmong farmers in the U.S. And with so many Hmong immigrants in agriculture, two Hmong brothers who came here as children and grew up on their parents' strawberry farm in Fresno County started an organization that could be a voice for this growing population. The National Hmong American Farmers (NHAF) was started in 2003 by Chukou and Thulo Thao and is now run by Chukou and his son Jon.

In addition to advocating for the Hmong farmer population on the political stage in Washington, D.C., NHAF has worked closely with the USDA to make programs more accessible to Hmong farmers, sending in translators to help with outreach material and loan applications. NHAF also works locally to support and connect small Hmong farmers (and other underrepresented farmers) to USDA programs, and it assists in reading and filling out translated paperwork for elder farmers who often speak Hmong but cannot read it.

Working to reach the small farmers and farmworkers of the nearly 100,000 Hmong living in California, as well as the Hmong farming communities of Minnesota, Wisconsin and North Carolina, NHAF has their hands full. They focus on connecting farmers to markets, helping them to understand rules and regulations and helping to further their knowledge and skills through training — though many Hmong farmers bring deep agricultural knowledge that just can't be found in an institution.

"A lot of people ask me how I do what I do here," Pang continues as we walk along the 11 acres of jujube trees growing outside of the greenhouse. "It's so beautiful and healthy and people can't believe everything I have growing here. They ask me what university or school I attended to learn this. I tell them I went to no school. For Hmong people, from generation to generation, the knowledge of farming is passed on. My parents learned from their parents, and I learned from my parents. I grew up soaking in their knowledge as they grew rice and vegetables. Hmong people, we don't have much technology or education, so we just learn by doing what generations before us have done.

"But the extension workshops do help me to learn new things. I just continue to work at it until I get it right. You have to have a passion for this. You have to love it. When you start farming, it's a lifetime job. A lot of people want to get to the result and just get there quickly, and it doesn't happen that way. You have to start from the bottom up, and it's hard work. You

have to continue through the mistakes you will make, try to correct them and always constantly put in the effort. That's how I became what I am today."

Pang and May now support their family on the farm's income, selling their fruit to wholesale distributors who supply markets throughout California. Pang and May raised 12 children on the farm, sending many of them through college.

But it hasn't all been easy. With severe drought in California, many farmers have been hit with hard times, losing their water as water tables recede or losing their crops to the harsh heat. Pang's trees were under threat in the last few years when his water table ran low and everything began to dry up. The only solution was to dig a deeper well on his property, which meant paying $26,000 to have it done. That's no small change for a small farmer. And though USDA support programs exist to help farmers front this cost, there are many hoops to jump through to be qualified for such a loan.

Pang Chang and Michael Yang.

Pang had to come up with the money on his own and was able to dig a deeper well and save his trees, which he claims bear fruit sweeter than any that you'll find in the store. I like to think his fruit is sweeter and his trees stronger for having survived near-death and the fight to live on foreign soil, much like Pang has.

Cynthia Hayes,
Southeastern African
American Farmers Organic
Network,
Savannah, Georgia.

66

With all the obstacles and land loss impacting Black farmers, those who are still here are the ones that have a level of resourcefulness. We're simply helping farmers to maximize and expand on that resourcefulness and access even more resources to stay alive.

— Dr. Owusu Bandele

99

SOME MIGHT SAY with the plummeting number of Black farmers over the last century that there is little hope for reviving the Black farmer community. But some, like Cynthia Hayes of the Southeastern African American Farmers Organic Network (SAAFON), are standing up to that and proving quite the opposite. With a transition to organic farming and a strong network across the South to support Black farmers, Cynthia Hayes, Dr. Owusu Bandele, and the rest of SAAFON are planting seeds of survival and proving just how resilient their communities are.

Before I even started this journey, I was connected online with Cynthia Hayes, who I now fondly call *Mama C.* She was immediately supportive of my project and got right to work helping me to fundraise and reach out to farmers in her network who were willing to participate in interviews. As I drove all over the Southeast, the majority of the farmers I interviewed were SAAFON farmers and were thrilled that Cynthia had sent me their way. When I finally got closer to Savannah, Georgia, where SAAFON is headquartered, I couldn't wait to finally meet this inspirational advocate for Black farmers and invaluable supporter of my work.

❦

I've picked up a hitchhiker on this journey: a small kitten whom I've named Low Country after the coastal area of South Carolina where I found him lost and alone on the side of the road. I'm not sure yet what I will do with the kitten, but for now he is living with me in Lucille where he has a homemade litter box with sand from the beach and plenty of space to frolic and play as we head south to Savannah. I'm on my way to meet and stay with the executive director of SAAFON and though I've never met her in person before, I'm hoping she doesn't mind an extra, furry houseguest.

As I walk up to meet Cynthia and her husband Mr. Hayes at the farmers market that they, in partnership with three other women, started in Forsyth Park (a park where people of color were banned from walking until the mid-1960s). I am holding this little kitten in my arms in the heat of the summer sun. Cynthia is perplexed as she tries to register the furry orange object in my arms, then her face lights up and before I know it she is holding Low Country on her lap, gingerly running an ice cube over his fur, while Mr. Hayes pours me a cup of his famous watermelon juice. The kitten and I are both instantly refreshed, and I have no doubt that my new, kind hosts are the giving, generous people who have decided to dedicate their time to refreshing the lives and livelihood of Black farmers across the South.

"I saw a need to find a way for Black farmers to save their land," Cynthia says later when we are back at her house talking about SAAFON and watching Low Country jump happily around the room, "and I knew that the organic industry was booming, so it just made sense."

Converting to organic can most definitely boost the survival of a farm. According to a 30-year side-by-side comparison study at the Rodale Institute, organic plots of corn and soybeans were almost three times as profitable as conventional plots, with the average net return for the organic farms at $558 per acre per year versus $190 per acre per year for conventional farms.[32] Though the figures might be skewed due to higher prices farmers charge for organic, that alone doesn't account for the difference in profit.

The hidden costs of commercial agribusiness could be the main culprit in the difference of profitability for conventional and organic farmers. Though organic production is often more labor intensive, resulting in higher labor costs than conventional systems, overall input costs can be greater for conventional growers because of their heavy dependency on chemical fertilizers and pesticides. Also, soil depletion due to the use of chemical fertilizers decreases water retention, which directly affects irrigation costs for conventional farmers. Thus, the practices utilized by organic growers become more sustainable over time.

These are just a few of the reasons these SAAFON farmers have made the switch to organic. But the transition isn't easy. With so much paperwork and the many fees required to become certified, support for transitioning conventional farmers to organic farmers is vital. This is why many sustainably minded farmers today are simply opting not to get the certification, though they are growing "organically." But, according to Cynthia, many Black farmers don't have that option.

"Some farmers out there at market are choosing not to go USDA Certified

Dr. Owusu Bandele.

Organic, for various reasons," Cynthia explains, "they instead simply put up a 'grown chemical free' or 'natural' sign at their table. When SAAFON was launched, our farmers could not do that. There was a trust issue. Black farmers growing organically was a very new concept for both the White and Black consumer at markets. Just telling their customers it was organic wasn't enough. They needed to have that USDA Certified Organic stamp. So they came to us and we helped them get it.

"SAAFON farmers come to us to get training, to get support on the organic certification process — the application is a really spooky thing. It's like 19 pages. And we help them work through the application process. They are then asked to be a part of our program for three years. During those three years we ask them to also serve as mentors to new farmers coming into the network. Resources and trainings they were left out of in the past — we make sure that that doesn't happen anymore. When they come to us, they spend about three days in trainings and orientation: Organics 101, Farm Planning, etc. They have to come to the training with soil samples, sketches of their farm, all of it. And when they leave the training, their organic certification paperwork is complete. We pay the first fee to submit their organic certification application to help jump-start them. After that, we make sure they get where they need to go. If it's a Southern Sustainable Agriculture Working Group (SSAWG) conference, or a Growing Power gathering with Will Allen, we make sure they get a

scholarship to go. If they need to speak to the National Organics Standards Board, we find somebody to make that happen.

"We look over the whole experience of farming and think in terms of how to create a sustainable system for them, which means they have a product and a location to sell it for a fair trade price. This allows them to make a good living so they can pay their taxes, the note on their truck, etc. *That* is sustainable agriculture. And that's what we're all about. At the same time, we tell the story behind the significant role Black farmers have played in the agricultural industry so we connect to stories and the economics of it all.

"I come from a family of Black farmers," Cynthia continues, "I come from a long line of farmers. Mr. Hayes does kind of too, but I am a generation closer to farming than he is. My family were tobacco growers in Kentucky, and every summer, part of their labor force was the grandchildren. So up until I was about 16 years old I went to the farm to work. I can trace my family all the way back, because they all resided in the same place, farming in the same county of Kentucky for generations. So I tell our farmers: 'Trust me, I know all about everything y'all are going through because farming is in my blood.'"

Later on in my journey, I have the opportunity to sit down with Dr. Owusu Bandele, agricultural professor emeritus from the Southern University Ag Center in Baton Rouge, Louisiana. Dr. Bandele is a monumental figure in the Black farmers movement and Cynthia's partner in founding SAAFON. And we have a very similar conversation about the significance of understanding the story of Black farmers in our history. "Sometimes I don't think Black farmers themselves even appreciate that family legacy and their historical significance," Dr. Bandele comments. "A lot of folks don't realize their historical importance. It's easy to get caught up in the present-day problems with what's going on today and forget the history and appreciate where we are, who we are.

"In 1920, Black farmers owned about 16 million acres of land," Dr. Bandele says. "That's a heck of an accomplishment in the face of extreme oppression and racism. With all the obstacles and land loss impacting Black farmers, those who are still here are the ones that have a level of resourcefulness. We're simply helping farmers to maximize and expand on that resourcefulness and access even more resources to stay alive."

Back in Savannah with Cynthia, we continue the discussion on how hard it is for farmers to stay in production. There are so many factors farmers are affected by. Not just in this country, but globally, with changing economies and international trade. She and Mr. Hayes spent ten years living in Jamaica where they bought 18 acres and started a bed and breakfast and a farm. They left because the economy went down in a snowball effect that began with international trade policies flooding the markets and squandering local industries. Cynthia and Mr. Hayes were living in Jamaica when the banana industry went

under. Unable to compete once monopolies like Chiquita Banana came in, small banana farms were put out of business. This is all it takes in the agricultural industry to wipe out generations of farmers.

But farmers are resourceful, and for many, transitioning to organic to join the growing industry is just reverting back to what they've always done. "Growing organic and growing smart on a small scale is tapping into that resourcefulness," says Dr. Bandele who has been growing organically since the '70s. Dr. Bandele went back to school for agronomy after first receiving a history degree, then teaching in public schools in Baltimore and starting the Timbuktu Educational Center, an Afro-centric center there. In 1978 he moved to Louisiana to work for the Emergency Land Fund in the South, assisting farmers and landowners in holding on to their land. He later went to Tuskegee University in Alabama to study under Dr. Booker T. Whatley, one of the most important agricultural scientists since George Washington Carver. Dr. Whatley encouraged farmers throughout the South to produce a variety of vegetables and fruits that were better suited for small-scale operations than field crops such as soybeans and cotton. After obtaining a Master's degree from Tuskegee and a Ph.D. in horticultural science from North Carolina State University, Dr. Bandele became an agricultural professor at Southern University where he pushed sustainable and organic agriculture. "I thought it was ironic," says Dr. Bandele, "that in the beginning, with little agricultural knowledge, I was growing organically, and now after several degrees in agriculture, I'm still right back here with organics."

Dr. Bandele and his wife, Efuru, established the 4.2-acre Food for Thought Organic Farm in 1997. "We didn't set up the farm to make money, although it was profitable," Dr. Bandele explains, "we wanted to show that it was possible to grow organically in the South, where many farmers and agricultural professionals didn't think it was possible due to greater insect and disease pressure in our subtropical environment." Dr. Bandele became the first African American organic-certified farmer in his state of Louisiana. He decided he wanted to change that notion about organics in the South, and he sought ways to provide organic certification training.

Funds to provide that training across state lines came with one component of a collaborative grant obtained by the Southern Food Systems Education Consortium (SOFSEC). The SOFSEC includes nine Historically Black Land Grant Universities. Dr. Bandele, under the auspices of the Southern University Ag Center, was responsible for developing the organic component and conducting the certification training. "I really needed a lot of assistance in identifying candidates for training in states other than Louisiana," said Dr. Bandele. He was soon introduced to Cynthia, and SAAFON was born. "Cynthia did an outstanding job in recruiting interested farmers who were willing to stay with the program until being certified." Although the training was available to all farmers, particular emphasis was placed on increasing African American participation in organic production since they were greatly underrepresented in the organic arena.

SAAFON now works with over 122 farmers in eight states and the Virgin Islands. They are also working internationally to train and support farmers abroad and connect Black farmers here in the U.S. with farmers from all parts of the African Diaspora to exchange knowledge and information and celebrate the culture of food. SAAFON has served as a representative of the African American farmer at Slow Food International's biannual Terra Madre/Salone Del Gusto gatherings where farmers and food culturists from around the world gather, connect and share. Now, farmers who were pushed to the brink are pressing forward and galvanizing strength through an expanding network that is not only teaching us how to grow and survive, but how to thrive.

Part 4:
Preserving Culture and Community

A people without the knowledge of their past
history, origin and culture is like a tree without roots.

— Marcus Garvey

AMERICA LOVES ITS FOOD. Our food culture scene is exploding, with foodies drooling over fusions like pulled pork sliders with watermelon relish, green chile and goat cheese empanadas, or banh mi with candied bacon. But few want to recognize the communities where each food culture is rooted. Folks don't want to ask how that food came to be or how these communities and the culture they are fighting to preserve are under threat.

On my way out of the South, with a delicious memory of Mr. Hayes' watermelon juice on my tongue, I think about where Southern Black food culture originated and how it has managed to be preserved. I think about the chitlins, collards and black-eyed peas my great grandmother Eliza, or "Lala" as we called her, would make in South Carolina. And how that food stems back to the days her mother

and her mother's mother cooked with what they had and created the delicious food culture we all strive to recreate today. Soul food became a staple not just in the lives of Southern Black families, but in the lives of White families across the South as well. Black slaves and cooks introduced their own food culture into the kitchens they worked in, like my Lala who worked as a cook in the homes of wealthy White families in Greenville up until the 1960s. This delicious food culture has continued to be adopted around the world.

With roots in many countries across Africa and the complex impact of Southern history, America's Black food culture and the stories it carries is vast and deep. And this section doesn't even begin to cover the rich array of foods and varying food cultures that exist or who introduced them to us. Instead it attempts to spark thought about some of our most familiar foods and the stories they carry.

Watermelon alone has endured an incredible journey from Africa, arriving in the Americas with African slaves, becoming a widely grown crop among many communities, including Native Americans throughout Florida and the Mississippi Valley. It has lived on as a traditionally grown crop in the Black South, along with sweet potatoes, peanuts, cotton and soybeans. We all know the history of cotton in the South, but the introduction of sweet potatoes and peanuts — two staples of Southern food culture — as well as soybeans (one of this country's top three agricultural crops) was partly the product of Dr. George Washington Carver's work to promote alternative crops to cotton for the survival and health of Black farmers across the South.

We can similarly thank ancient Indigenous farmers, from what is now known as central Mexico, for the introduction of the biggest agricultural staple and influence on American food culture in history: corn. Corn or maize, domesticated from wild grass at the dawn of human agriculture over 7,000 years ago, has now been adopted the world over, feeding humans as well as animals. This would be an evolution to celebrate if it weren't for the fact that it has been modified, overused and abused. Corn is now used in 75 percent of processed foods directly linked to nutritional health epidemics in this country, including the need for antibiotics in livestock. And it is one of the top GMO crops around the world.[33]

This evolution of corn speaks to the dire need to understand and preserve food culture. Today's modification of corn threatens the very culture of Indigenous, Native and Latin American communities that have grown and used hundreds of varieties of corn in traditional foodways and sacred ceremonies for thousands of years. With the introduction of the GMO and food processing industry, corn as it has been known for thousands of years could be wiped off the face of the earth.

Ancient and heirloom seeds are under threat of disappearing for good, with many already gone. Our wild foods and the food culture they have provided for Native communities for thousands of years are also under threat. Wild berries, game and fish are at risk of depletion due to development, toxic pollution, genetic modification and conservation laws that prohibit communities from hunting and harvesting.

Gentrification, assimilation and corporatization have also been big factors in the loss of traditional food culture for many communities. I have encountered many stories of farmers who are trying to keep their food culture alive as children of their community choose today's food products off the shelf over their ancestors' foods. Or who are trying to preserve the authenticity of taste as foods are processed or crops are altered. Gentrification and corporatization has also affected neighborhood dining and shopping options; new foodie restaurants or corporate food stores often put the mom-and-pop shops and restaurants out of business. And the pressure to assimilate often results in young people feeling ashamed and giving up eating traditional meals from home in order to fit in — to avoid the discrimination of "smelling like curry" or "bringing weird food" for lunch.

That lack of a sense of belonging, or solidarity, is so detrimental. And it carries over into today's food movement, where food cultures are excluded at farmers markets and nutrition campaigns. Cultural solidarity is also important in engaging communities in urban farm projects or garden education. When garden projects and classes are missing that person that relates to or represents the community, it erodes that sense of belonging; that sense that this is for the community.

The devolution of the family dinner and the communal tradition of agriculture has also eroded food culture and the sense of community that is supposed to a part of it. Like the Sunday dinners after church in the Black South, the communal potlatch feasts in the Native Northwest or the Nian Ye Fan dinners hosted by elders to pass the Chinese New Year, or just the daily dinner at the table with family after a long day. Many farmers I have talked to reflect on the loss of that vital shared meal that keeps the family and community together. It provided a space in which to pass our foodways onto the next generation.

This lack of preservation of foodways has left a large impact. Many from this generation fail to recognize or have forgotten the foods of our ancestors or how to grow those foods. Many of our elders used to garden in their yards, harvest fruit and wild foods, or fish right in the neighborhood. They use to grow food in cooperation with natural systems, a method that is now referred to by all kinds of new terms as if they're new concepts, but they are simply practices our ancestors carried as part of the culture of their time. They used to cook for each other and share food across the community during hard times. Our ancestors used to work cooperatively in many ways. And there are signs that we as a society are beginning to miss that sense of community, particularly around food.

The cooperative and shared economy is coming back. With farmer cooperatives, cooperative markets, restaurants and food hubs, community kitchens and community gardens on the rise, it's clear we want to revert back to having community. With development and climate change rearing its ugly head, society is also yearning for the old culture of living sustainably. These concepts aren't new. Humans are communal in nature and lived holistically with the earth for thousands of years. We have old roots in community building and cooperation. And there are powerful tools being held in the back pockets of our ancestors that can help us revert back to sustainability, preserve culture and bring back community.

I like to think that our ancestors have sent us people to unearth and carry those tools forward — people who are dedicating their days to sustaining the soil and ensuring the survival of community and food culture. They're called farmers.

66

Our heritage lives in these seeds, so when we give these
seeds to people, we are empowering them not only
to grow but to revive culture.

— Kevin Welch 99

MY FIRST STOP FOR EXPLORING the preservation of culture and community through food and farming is a place that is the sacred foundation for some of the first peoples of this land, a people who some might say were the first agriculturists of this country.

⁕

The sky is a brilliant blue as my partner Crosby — who has joined me on the road for a while — and I drive onto Cherokee land in the Great Smoky Mountains along the North Carolina–Tennessee border. This Eastern Band of Cherokee is the only federally recognized tribe of Native Americans in North Carolina (though many other tribes live in the state). They are called the Eastern Band, with the larger Western Cherokee Band of the Cherokee Nation based in Oklahoma, where the Cherokee were forced to relocate in the 1800s during what became known as the "Trail of Tears."

The Eastern Cherokee land in the mountains of North Carolina is considered the original homeland of the Cherokee, and the tribal members there are said to be descendants of those who resisted the U.S. Army and evaded capture and removal from the land. Lands claimed by the Cherokee

Nation encompassed parts of what are now eight states: Kentucky, Tennessee, Alabama, Georgia, South Carolina, North Carolina, Virginia and West Virginia. The total land area was estimated to be about 135,000 square miles; today only 56,000 acres of their original homeland comprise the Qualla Boundary, commonly referred to as Cherokee, in western North Carolina near the Great Smoky Mountain National Park. When visitors arrive on the reservation, they are entering a sovereign land held in trust specifically for the tribe by the United States government and purchased using funds raised by the Cherokee through Will Thomas, a Cherokee chief who was adopted and raised by the tribe. The Cherokee population there is about 10,000–14,000.

We drive through the green valley of this Cherokee homeland and pull into a small driveway leading up to a modest house with a sign out front that reads "The Center for Cherokee Plants." It's where Kevin Welch and Sarah McClellan work to save seeds and propagate plants significant to Cherokee culture. We are met with a friendly greeting from Sarah, and she leads us through the house (that's been converted into an office) and out the back door to meet Kevin. Kevin is a gentle, yet serious man, and I can feel his guarded demeanor as he explains that we will not be able to photograph some of the plants or gather detailed information on the seeds they save, as they are sacred and to be preserved and protected within Cherokee culture.

Native tribes have been exploited for hundreds of years, with their cultural traditions not only taken away from them but commercialized for entertainment, diluted and disrespected. So in an effort to preserve and honor culture and protect the tribe, many are beginning to close their doors or share more cautiously outside of the community.

We sit together in a circle under the shade of the carport where piles of farming equipment are stored, and Kevin begins speaking so softly that we have to pull our chairs in closer to hear him clearly. The only other sound is the beautiful birdsong from the nearby trees.

"One of the things a lot of people don't realize is that the Cherokee are the original agriculturists of this region," Kevin begins. "We've been growing food here for 6,000 years. Agriculture developed for us as it does for many cultural groups: once our resources were stable enough and we didn't need to spend our time searching for those resources, we started cultivating. We started raising squash several thousand years ago and beans and corn in the last 1,400 years. But agriculture for us still includes wild gathering. We collect our food from plants, either what we cultivate or what we gather from the woods. I tell the kids we work with, we're not horse people like the Plains Indians, we're not salmon people or fish people like the Northwest tribes, we're not desert people like the folks in the Southwest. We came out of the woodland. We're agriculturists.

"We believe in the power of the plants that grow all around us. It's part of Cherokee folklore that plants are sacred and not only feed us but have healing powers. An old Cherokee story is that when animals were being over-hunted by men, the animals decided to get together and hold a counsel, and they decided to infect man with disease, and each animal came up with a disease. But the plants were still friendly toward men, so each plant came up with the cure for each disease that infected man. This story teaches us that if you look around, the cure for what ails you is always growing close by. Cherokee people have a holistic approach, and many Native peoples all over the world have always believed that the things we need to maintain our lives are out there, surrounding us.

"But our people have gotten away from who we are. The younger generation has lost their heritage and forgotten how to garden as our elders did. Our diets and health as a community have changed drastically. Native Americans have the highest rates of diabetes, heart disease and psychological illness, like depression and alcoholism. Up until the last few decades, we never ate all the processed foods introduced to us from outside of our culture. We're only 600 years removed from never even seeing you guys before. This has had a huge impact on us."

About 60 percent of Eastern Cherokee children are overweight or obese. About 35 percent of Eastern Cherokee adults are diagnosed with diabetes, and almost 25 percent of their enrolled members live at or below the poverty level.[34]

"If we can bring back our cultural foods," Kevin continues, "and put them into the hands of the person that's putting food on their tables, then we can change things. That's what we do here at the Center, we collect and propagate culturally relevant plants that Cherokees have historically used and give them to Cherokee families while re-teaching them the skills to grow their own. We find and save heirloom seed varieties or develop them if we can no longer find them. We're a seed bank, but our goal is not to keep seeds here; our job is to get them out there to the enrolled Cherokee members. The best way to save an heirloom seed is to share it."

The Cherokee tribal leaders recognized the need to put agriculture back in the community, so the chief started a garden kit giveaway program which Kevin and Sarah provide seeds and seedlings for. They give away 700 garden kits every year, with the seeds and seedlings ready to put in the ground. They've been doing this for about nine years and have given away over 6,000 garden kits to enrolled Cherokee members. Kevin and Sarah also have a youth gardening program and a mobile classroom which they use around the state to give workshops on gardening, health and the cultural history of Cherokee plants and foods.

"We can pull up to any group or place, and in 10 to 15 minutes we can have a classroom," says Sarah. "We can go from standing out in the hot sun in a field with a group, to setting out a really nice and fun environment to learn in. It's really amazing. We have books, farming tools, coolers for drinks, shade and chairs for elders. We even have blankets and games for the children to stay busy while the parents get into the workshop with Kevin."

"We don't want people not to participate because of lack of resources," Kevin says, "so we go to them. We can do so much more with both the adults and the kids. We teach the kids how growing food is a part of their culture, and we reinforce that by talking about how that particular bean or corn is connected to their people. We teach the adults how to use and make compost and other best management practices and techniques.

"We use the term 'best management practices.' We don't use the term 'organic.' Organic is a government-produced word. Labeling your stuff organic is what people do to sell. Commercial growers use the word for marketing. But for a lot of small growers, we can't afford not to be 'organic.' Have you seen the prices of all those chemicals? We just plant complementary plants; we use pepper spray; we make our own compost; we can run that compost through water and make a tea to apply to the plants and soil. This is just wise and the best thing to do good for your plants and the environment.

"That's how the old folks have always done it. You talk to the old timers around here and they don't have any idea what 'organic' is, but they do know how to till under and get nitrogen back in the soil. They know how to compost and grow healthy plants without chemicals. They may not know the scientific terms, but they are doing it. All this academic theory and these weird terms create a disconnect from the land and from the people. I stay away from all that when I teach."

"From my perspective, the really effective teaching that Kevin does is with Cherokee people," says Sarah. "There's a whole different dynamic when Kevin is teaching, no matter what the age, because he is part of the community and of the culture, and that really makes a difference. Education happens so differently then, as opposed to when agricultural workshops are taught from people like me from outside of the community. Having a Cherokee teaching Cherokee people creates a connection that couldn't happen with a written curriculum that comes from a national gardening program. A government or outside agency just truly can't be that effective when doing this work because it's not of the culture."

"That culture is what we're keeping alive here, aside from these plants," Kevin emphasizes. "The plants that we collect and cultivate each have a story behind them, and that story is what makes them relevant to our culture. That concept applies to any group of people. Just like storytelling, song and art, agriculture is a part of culture, it enriches culture. When we talk about getting back to our roots, food really is the basis of that.

"To bring back the history of our plants and our people, we interview elders and do memory banking, collecting oral histories. It's like being Sherlock Holmes, discovering so many unknown stories about every seed. You can take a handful of seeds, and it just looks like a handful of seeds, or you can take it and see that these seeds were grown by a family for survival at one point through the Depression, or they were hidden in the long skirts of Cherokee women during their walk from here to Oklahoma.

"Our heritage lives in these seeds, so when we give them to people we are empowering them not only to grow but to revive culture. And when we teach kids the skills to grow, we're giving them ownership over their gardens and their heritage. They are being empowered too. They've learned a life skill that they can use and pass on to the next generation. To me, that's the success story because our ways have been changing with each new generation.

"We've lost much of our agricultural land because of generational change. We live in the mountains. We don't have much flat land good for farming. But if you go back through time and look at where the elders built their homes, they built on the most unusable land they had. They gardened all the way up to their doorstep. They didn't have yards; they gardened everywhere they could plant food. But when the younger folks started building their homes, instead of going up on the mountain to clear land to build their houses, they put their houses on the flat land where the old gardens and farms had been.

"But even with this loss of agricultural land, many of our people still collect and eat traditional foods. However, we've also lost much of our wild gathering lands. Our whole tribal land base is about 56,000 acres, the national park we live right next to is about 11 million acres. The national park doesn't allow us to go into what were our traditional gathering areas to gather our wild foods. The mentality is conservation, but the misunderstanding is that Cherokee harvest with a philosophy of conservation. It's a simple philosophy: if you destroy your resource, you have to move somewhere else to find another resource. If you want to have your home here and keep your resources, you don't destroy them. It's the philosophy of not taking more than you need, it's actually really simple.

"Our people never took more than we needed. The White attitude was get it all before somebody else gets it. That's not the Cherokee attitude. If we're gathering from a plant for the green, we don't take the whole plant. We'll take some of the leaves off of it, and move on to the next one. We know the proper way to harvest without depleting growth. Like with ramps, a wild scallion that only became popular when someone called it gourmet, and everybody started going out to dig up as many as they could to sell them and devastated a ramp population that native peoples have been harvesting and conserving for thousands of years.

"All of this really created a need for us to bring these kinds of plants back. With the loss of access to wild gathering and agricultural land, propagating these plants ourselves and putting them back into the community became our solution."

And their solution has been a huge success. They've seen a 70 percent increase in the number of gardens within the Cherokee community, and they have garnered a lot of interest from within and outside the community, including other Native American tribes around the country. Kevin travels all over to speak and teach about their seed bank and propagation program. He has provided support to the Sac and Fox Nation (Sauk and Meskwaki Native Americans) as they started their gardening program, and he's provided seeds to the Western Cherokee in Oklahoma who are starting a similar seed-banking project.

"We really enjoy working with other tribes. We, as Native Americans, get exploited enough in life. We're not trying to create traditions, we're just trying to save the ones that we have."

Portrait 2:
Sustaining Community

Jenga Mwendo, Backyard Gardeners Network, Lower Ninth Ward, New Orleans, Louisiana.

Gardening for us is a cultural tradition and cultural traditions don't just sustain themselves, they need community and support.

— Jenga Mwendo

From Cherokee land in North Carolina, I head as far south as I can get before reaching the Gulf of Mexico. In the Lower Ninth Ward of New Orleans — a community also familiar with exploitation and fighting to save their way of life — I meet with a woman who is passionately working to preserve the cultural traditions of her community through food and gardening.

❧

"I was born here in the Lower Ninth Ward," says Jenga as we sit in her home in the Lower Ninth neighborhood and rain trickles down outside the screened front door, "literally, it was a home birth, so I was literally born here in the neighborhood. I'm proud of that."

The Lower Ninth Ward is the neighborhood in New Orleans that was put on the national stage after Hurricane Katrina. No place in the city suffered greater devastation from the hurricane than the Lower Ninth. The neighborhood sits lower than the rest of the city geographically, at the mouth of the Mississippi River. (The area's low coastal lands were once sugar cane plantations.) The Lower Ninth Ward is flanked by two more waterways dredged

for shipping routes: the Industrial Canal to the west and the Bayou Bienvenue to the north. These surrounding waterways with poorly engineered levees, in addition to the loss of tens of thousands of acres of protective coastal wetlands (which acted as a buffer for storm surges) during the construction of deep cargo shipping lanes, left the Lower Ninth extremely vulnerable to flooding and storm surge.

Hurricane Katrina caused over 50 breaches of canal levees in New Orleans, including one that sent a cargo shipping barge over the levee wall and directly into the Lower Ninth Ward, leveling homes in its path. Eighty percent of the entire city of New Orleans was flooded, with some areas under 15 feet of water, while others (like the touristy French Quarter) managed to escape heavy damage. The destruction in areas like the Lower Ninth was unfathomable, and residents still today have not been able to return to what was once their home.

"We lost 75 percent of our population after the hurricane," Jenga says. "Due to displacement or various reasons of loss, they are not able to come back. Seventy-five percent gone in the Lower Ninth." According to the 2000 Federal Census, the

Lower Ninth had over 14,000 residents, and in 2010 the number was just at about 5,500.

"There was a lot of instability and fear about coming back for a lot of people," Jenga continues. "It's still difficult for people because once you move away and start establishing your life somewhere else, it becomes harder to come back. To come back is to commit to a place that is not stable. For my family, we used to all be here for the most part. Suddenly, we were all dispersed around the country, and we didn't know what was going to happen to the city. It was one of those moments where we had to ask: where is our home now? What is home anymore when all the physical structures you know are not there anymore, all the people that you know are not there anymore, and you just don't know what's gonna happen?"

Jenga, who left New Orleans after high school to study computer animation, was living and working in New York with her one-year-old daughter Azana when Katrina hit. She decided to return to the Lower Ninth despite the fear and find a way to help rebuild her community.

"I was raised in an Afro-centric household with my parents as activists, and we tried to live by the *Nguzo Saba,* the Seven Principles," Jenga explains. "Principles like *Umoja* [Unity] and *Ujima* [Collective Work and Responsibility] and others that all teach the importance of community, our responsibility as part of a community, and working together to make that community beautiful and strong. So when

Katrina hit, it was just that catalyst where I knew I needed to come home and contribute somehow.

"From New York, I sprang into action and became the organizer of my family, trying to keep track of everybody, raising money to send, and collecting clothes. It was a crazy time. My father was a first responder, so he never left. He is a firefighter, so he was here through the entire thing. My grandmother died a week or two after Katrina hit. There was just so much. I started putting things into motion to leave my job and leave New York.

"I already owned this house while I was living in New York, because I wanted to invest in the neighborhood and keep roots here, always thinking I would move back one day to raise my daughter close to family. So when I came back, my first goal was to fix up the house. I had to gut the entire house. There was about 3–4 feet of water in here. You could see the water line around the windowsill, so you can imagine what it must have been outside because the house was already raised two feet off the ground. This whole area was just covered in water. There were scares about mold; I didn't want to bring my daughter into that kind of environment. So we had to stay with my mom for 18 months while I worked on the house."

Jenga, a fierce single mother, rebuilt the house herself. With the high cost of contractors and so many of them taking advantage of residents' needs after Katrina, many folks were left with no trustworthy support to rebuild their homes. Others simply could not put money into homes that were now worth far less than what was owed on them or what it would cost to rebuild. Even with so many "free rebuild" programs coming into the city, there were a lot of empty promises and suspicious requirements, such as having to be finger-printed to qualify, which kept people from applying.

"It was difficult. But I was determined to do it myself," Jenga continues as we sit in the living room she gutted and reframed. "It actually fell in line with a long-time dream of mine anyway. I had spent all these years creating on the computer, which is fascinating in a way, but it wasn't real; I wanted to know that I could do something real. That I could build things with my hands. So I just learned how to do it. I started not knowing any-thing; the most experience I had with a hammer was hanging pictures in my house or assembling something from Ikea. I had to learn how to do framing — I framed

out my bathroom, I tiled my kitchen floor, hung my cabinets. The only thing I didn't do is plumbing and electrical.

"So while I was doing all that, I kept looking for ways to make a contribution to the community. I was the only one on this block when I came back; only 40 percent of the homes in this neighborhood were occupied. I felt like my job was to find out who else was here and what folks needed to come back. I thought the least I could do was help make the neighborhood somewhere people would want to come back to. I thought a community garden would bring us together and inspire hope and beauty and productivity in a neighborhood that was robbed of all that.

"It became my focus. I started organizing and going to neighborhood association meetings to ask if people were interested and recruit people who wanted to be involved. There was one weekend when 12 of us got together and chopped all the weeds down in this abandoned community garden; the weeds had gotten to above my head. It looked like a jungle. We started planting; we formed a garden committee. And I started to see the power of a community garden to bring unity to a place that had been separated so traumatically. This was a project that allowed us to feel good about our neighborhood and just start growing, literally and figuratively."

That growth sprouted into what is now the Backyard Gardeners Network, an organization Jenga started that supports gardeners of the Lower Ninth Ward and brings the neighborhood together around two community gardens that host neighborhood activities and provide resources for gardeners.

"The gardens are our community centers," Jenga explains. "It's really about the people first. The space needs to serve the people. It's not about the number of gardens or trying to turn everyone into an urban farmer. What I'm focused on is increasing the capacity of these gardens to serve our people and be effective community-building tools. And it's working. We are building community and replenishing old cultural traditions of our neighborhood. There was a time when everyone here had their own backyard gardens, when it was just something that they did, sharing produce and helping one another, harvesting from fruit trees that grew around the neighborhood.

"We decided to do a mini oral history project in the neighborhood, and many of the stories were about how gardening and growing your own food was just a part of the life in the Lower Nine. People would forage in the bayou for wild onions and pepper grass or take their dogs out to hunt or catch crawfish when the rivers would flood. People in this neighborhood have always been more connected with the land — hunting and fishing in the river — because the Lower Ninth Ward was kind of rural and cut off from the rest of the city when they dug the Industrial Canal in the 1920s. Despite that connection to the land, folks never really think about themselves as gardeners or part of urban agriculture — nobody uses those terms, it's just what they do. It's a cultural tradition, and this work is about encouraging and supporting that. That is the way to make culture most sustainable — cultural traditions don't just sustain themselves, they need community and support.

"Even though it's traditional in our neighborhood, I did have to be very intentional at branding this as something that Black people do, since urban agriculture is nationally seen as a White thing and since a lot of people coming into New Orleans since Katrina interested in urban ag are White. It's not that I don't want them at the gardens, but the leadership here has to be Black. I feel very strongly about that. This has to be a space that is safe for people who have felt disenfranchised and overlooked. So that as a community we know these gardens and projects are not about other folks coming here and deciding what should happen — that this is ours.

"We started a Garden Walk program where we walk the neighborhood visiting all the gardens, and other than being great exercise for our elders, it's also a way to say 'this is still our neighborhood, we are still here.' We have to claim our neighborhood. Gentrification is becoming a big issue here. This area used to be one of the few places during segregation where Black people could come and buy property and build communities; it was like a safe little bubble for Black people to grow and prosper. Folks literally built their own houses here, and before Katrina, we had a 65 percent ownership rate, which is higher than anywhere else in the city. Of course

now, that is not the case. There is a lot of vacant land and empty houses to be renovated. The city is trying to get rid of these properties so they don't have to continue maintaining them, so they're doing these auctions. This creates an opportunity for people, but only if you are in the position to take advantage of that opportunity. That's where racial inequity comes in. The predominantly Black population that used to live here didn't get the proper support to come back, and now people who have more resources and support because of their privilege are able to move in — to take advantage of our disadvantage.

"Corporate food stores are also trying to come in on the opportunity. Before Katrina, there wasn't a grocery store in the neighborhood; there hadn't been a grocery store here since maybe the '80s. After Katrina, half the grocery stores in New Orleans closed and never reopened, and for a while the closest place for us to go was about four miles away, which is a lot for an urban area where stores should be at least a mile from where you live and 30 percent of residents don't have their own transportation. So we're considered a food desert, and in 2011 a Walmart opened up to 'solve that problem' for us.

"But that's not the kind of solution we want. It really bothers me to hear people talk about solutions to problems in neighborhoods like the Lower Nine as just a quick fix. Like 'here's a store, any store.' As if we'll just accept anything that you give us because we're so poor. It's not the case. It's not that people don't appreciate the effort, but it's important that these efforts are actually supportive, instead of imposing what a few decide onto a whole community. One thing I've been doing is having visioning meetings with the neighborhood to create a food action plan that outlines exactly what we want for our community. And we have certain standards of what we want for ourselves. Residents want a community-owned store, Black-owned businesses, a return to the mom-and-pop shops that used to be here, fresh quality produce, quality meats, seafood and bakeries. It's really important to us who owns the store and that the money stays in the community. The Walmart they opened is in the adjacent parish, so the tax dollars aren't even staying in our neighborhood.

"I am determined to fight for everything that we want. In a neighborhood where people feel ignored and neglected and defeated, especially after Katrina, it's hard to envision when we're focused on what we can't have and can't do, what's not possible. We deserve to have these things, just like any other community. We deserve to have a clean, beautiful and thriving community, to feel good about where we live. To feel powerful.

"I like to think that what we are doing as a community to come together around such a strong cultural tradition as food and rebuild our vision for the future is taking us one step closer to that."

Portrait 3:
Acequia Culture

Don Bustos,
Santa Cruz Farm,
Española, New Mexico.

> We're working to change community food systems from the bottom up, and we're starting to see the results already in the form of community cooperation. It's the tradition of our ancestors to work cooperatively. They've been working together through acequia systems for generations.
>
> — Don Bustos

I DRIVE WEST from New Orleans thinking about communities coming together around cultural traditions to find solutions for a better future. And while there are many examples of communities working cooperatively to preserve culture and build success, I am drawn to one of the oldest systems for cooperative opportunity in our history. It's a system steeped in the cultures of the Middle East and Africa and spread to Spain and the Pueblo communities of the Americas. I head to New Mexico to learn more about this system from a farmer whose ancestors began using it to literally give life to agriculture.

❦

"I farm the same land my ancestors farmed," says Don Bustos as we walk through the fields of his farm in the hills of Española, New Mexico, "I still use the same rituals and traditions that they did; all we do is incorporate a little bit of new technology that allows us to be economically viable. So, when you walk on the footsteps like you did coming down to the field, you can imagine 14 generations of men and women doing the same thing:

walking down there, harvesting beans, squash and corn, and then walking back up to where we just did underneath the trees cleaning [the crops], washing them with the same water from the acequias as our ancestors did.

"Nothing has changed. Maybe some politics and governments have changed, but the way we grow food here and the way we honor the earth has always been the same."

Don Bustos is a New Mexican farmer who comes from a long line of Indo-Hispano farmers who migrated up to the Santa Cruz area from Central America over 350 years ago. He named his farm after the Santa Cruz church just a mile from his land. The church was named after the Santa Cruz de la Cañada land grant, which granted over 4,000 acres of land to the 16 families who migrated here. These families introduced to the area the acequia system, which is still in operation now. The acequia system is a democratic, cooperatively owned irrigation system of small canals engineered to carry water from the mountains to the fields, making water a commons. The system has ancient origins in Arabic and Muslim culture in the high deserts of the Middle East and northern Africa. It spread from north Africa to Spain with the Arabic Muslim community of Moors and was integrated with Pueblo Indian irrigation systems when the Spaniards came to the Americas.

"There are so many different cultures that influence how we do things today," Don continues as we stand near the acequia that divides his land in half. "It's important to remember that. All of that history came together and took place on this land right here. As a matter of fact, I have a historical document that traces our family's names, down to how many chickens people owned. It's pretty cool to see. This piece of land here was in my mom's side of the family, the Valdezes; it's always been passed down to the women in our family. It was passed down from one generation to the next, and hopefully I'll be able to pass it on to a niece a little bit later on. The women of my family lived here outside of the main village of Santa Cruz because they were a bit ostracized from the community — they were *curanderos,* [healers]. And this Indigenous way of healing wasn't always accepted by the community. But they had a special gift with herbs and how to use them in medicinal ways, so they were embraced by those they were healing within the community.

"Our ancestors have always looked to the earth for remedies and guidance. Even in the way they farmed. We continue many of these traditional practices here on the farm now. We still plant with the moon cycles; the new moon and the waning moon have a lot of influence on how we plant our crops and which crops we plant when. Like the above-ground crops are supposed to be planted according to the full moon so that they pull from the moon's energy, pulling the plant taller and stronger above the ground. When the moon is waning and it's getting darker, those are good times for the below-ground crops, because that energy is instead pulling them down.

"It's also our cultural tradition to plant according to our saints' days, like *Día de Santa Clara* is the day we're supposed to be harvesting chile and corn, and *Día de San Juan* is the day the waters are blessed so it's OK to use the waters. *Día de San Isidro* is the farmer's day when you're supposed to start planting your crops. We also of course watch the weather and everything in our environment. My mom would always tell me 'always plant when the snow melts over there in the Chacoma, if you plant before that day it will freeze *mi'jito.*' So we always look at the mountains, the trees, the environment and how that will impact when you grow and what you grow that season. It's about cooperation with natural systems. This wisdom is being forgotten. While it's important to recognize that it's a cultural tradition, it's also important to remember that it's simply a sustainable method."

Don Bustos is all about sustainability, not just in agricultural techniques, but in creating viable farm and food businesses. In fact, he has dedicated his work to training beginning farmers on exactly that. After returning to his parents' farm in the early '80s to help them as they retired, he began selling produce at the farmers market and realized he was making enough money to quit his subcontracting work building houses. But he noticed that as sales grew and the farm got larger, so did the headache of managing labor and costs, which caused his profit margins to shrink. The solution he turned to worked so well that he is now teaching that model to farmers throughout the state, with the support of the American Friends Service Committee of New Mexico.

"I started to switch what I was doing completely. I went down to small scale. My profit margins went up, my headaches went away. It's possible for just one to two people to manage three to five acres, and you can enjoy life. That myth of being a slave to the farm is just not true. I tell people if that's what you think you have to do, you've got the wrong formula, man. We've been able to prove that if you set up a small farm like this, if it's managed

correctly and you do your marketing correctly, it can be economically viable.

"The training method we use is simple. When we have our first conversation with farmers, we ask them how much they need. You know you're not gonna be driving a brand new Mercedes-Benz every year, but how much do you need to have food on the table, to pay your bills? And if that's possible, then we'll help you develop a plan to meet those needs. That's what this farm does, and it does it using solar energy 12 months a year. With the greenhouse, we can use 12 months a year so we're not trying to grow everything in 120 days, but 365. So if one thing doesn't quite work, we got two or three other things we can start to develop, and we're able to market those. So, when people ask me if this is economically viable I say yes, depending on your lifestyle, your ability and your commitment to doing the work. It goes against big ag and the paradigm they push. This is about small business, and we train people to be business people and sustainable ag producers.

"We have a farmer-to-farmer training manual which goes through the 19 points of becoming a successful farmer over one year's training. We do a popular education model where farmers are learning hands on from other farmers, and we ask the trainees to participate a minimum of 18 hours a week. During the 12-month training, they have begun to replicate what they're learning on their own sites and start to supplement the income from the trainee stipends we give. We go from business

planning to farm planning to crop planning to management and marketing. It's a natural evolution. We tell farmers, 'If you're gonna go to farmers markets, you want to learn how to grow ten crops pretty well. Learn how to grow two to three crops really well and you'll be good, but if you go to market and you want to make $1,000 a week, you grow ten crops, and you only need $100 from each crop.' That's maybe 50 bunches of radishes, 50 bunches of carrots, 50 bunches of beets, 20 pounds of lettuce, 20 pounds of spinach. So you're not trying to feed the world. People get all daunted, but if you just need 50 bunches of radishes, take a 3 x 10 foot area and plant that area every week, do that with ten crops, dude you got your $1,000 a week right there, easy!

"The last four months of the training, we have the conversation about finances and we help people get the resources they need. We go with them to the NRCS office to apply for funding; we introduce them to the various programs out there that help with getting funding or building things like cold frames. We help people navigate all the loopholes, since some programs are about reimbursement instead of giving money up front. So we talk about microloans and whatnot. Or, if they need help getting land, we help them negotiate leases. If they need help getting into markets — whatever we can help with. Part of our training program is to teach them how the system works and what their rights are in the system and how to create that change. Because I know it can be difficult to get into the system and shake things up. I went through it.

"When I started selling at the farmers market, I had to push my way in. The Santa Fe market was a good farmers market, but it was a little difficult to get into. Even though it was meant for farmers in northern New Mexico, I think it was mostly a certain demographic they were looking for, a certain ambience people wanted for the city, and I didn't quite fit that. So I remember going there and parking at two o'clock in the morning, so I'd be the first one in line and they couldn't get anybody in until they gave me a spot. That was my strategy!"

Don laughs a full belly laugh and strokes his black and gray beard as he smiles, "I did that for a couple years, and then I started to go to the board meetings and started saying how this wasn't right and asking why I was always on the waiting list, never getting to the top. Where was this supposed waiting list, you know? I began asking the tough questions about who the decision makers were. I began really getting involved, and things got a little better. Then we had an opportunity to start a year-round market on a blighted piece of land from the city. First, we had to raise a lot of funding, and a few of us worked hard to do that for three years. But then, after we came up with the money, we were pushed out by the higher-ups. Now the market is thriving, and we're not a part of it. That was a good lesson on power dynamics. And that dynamic is still alive. Even for getting support for small farmer training, the Farm

Bill makes our communities go out there and try to match funding dollars that rich communities have just flowing in.

"The system is so entrenched. I see the way it's set up, and it really disempowers young men and women to participate in a meaningful way because people are so locked into their power roles and their authority. I sit on an advisory council with some professors that grant money to farmers and ranchers, and they want to deny the applications if the right academic language isn't used or words are misspelled. It's bullshit. But I'm just one lone voice against all these Ph.D. professors. The institutional system still has a lot of discrimination. I think there's been a lot of progress made, but there's still a long way to go.

"One thing I think people ignore, and it's a big mistake, is the new immigrant population. A lot of immigrants coming in are agriculturally based, not all, but a significant majority depending on where they're coming from. If we can really work toward engaging the immigrant population in the ag sector in a positive way that empowers them to be owners, I think that'll be a significant step in shoring up our systems across the U.S. We're working with the National Immigrant Farming Initiative and folks down in Chaparral and Las Cruces to transition immigrant farmworkers and train them to run their own farms.

"Everybody wants to start from the top. You know, they say we're gonna put in infrastructure and change policy, but the way I've seen it is we go out there and train the community. Our model is about community members working together to meet larger institutional demands to make healthier communities by creating jobs, healthy foods and healthy people. I see that happening all over. We're working to change community food systems from the bottom up, and we're starting to see the results already in the form of community cooperation.

"We're developing a farming cooperative here in northern New Mexico. It's gonna be great, led by women. So far it's called *Sabor del Norte,* the Taste of the North. We already started another cooperative down in Albuquerque, *Agricultura Network.* It was the first New Mexican cooperative to be certified organic. They are working together to access markets across the state. These models don't depend on any one person. It's about cooperation."

As I sit with Don under the shade tree on his farm watching the acequia run through the land as our conversation comes to a close, I think about how acequia culture created such a strong sense of community cooperation and democracy. It was actually one of the earliest forms of democracy in the United States, with a system based on the number of water users in an area who elect and appoint community commissioners to oversee water usage. The acequia system is rooted in sharing water amongst the community to the very last drop. The tradition is called *equidad* (equality), and tradition dictates that people must never deny water to another living being and that it should never be separated from the land. This tradition also led to community cooperation and shared labor, as well as democratic food systems like the *convite* (invitation) tradition of sharing food during shortages.

The ancient acequia system has managed to survive despite many corporate, political, government and legal forces working to undermine and dismantle it today. I can't help but think about how farmers like Don Bustos are ensuring the survival of that cooperative culture by watering seeds of healthy growth throughout his community, just like the acequias of his ancestors.

Portrait 4:
Gullah
Seedlings

*Marshview Community
Organic Farm,
St. Helena Island,
South Carolina.*

The history of the Gullah islands is based on communal survival.

— Sará Reynolds-Green

BACK IN THE SOUTH, in a corner of the world famous for its preservation of culture, I meet with a couple who are dedicated to continuing that preservation, particularly around food and community. I steer Lucille through the Low Country of South Carolina to what are known as the Gullah Islands to interview a pair of farmers who are focusing on what they consider the seeds of our future: food and children.

Sará Reynolds-Green.

I pull onto the dirt road of Marshview Community Organic Farm on St. Helena Island, which leads me past rows of onions and toward a majestic oak tree with its moss reaching low for the ground. The oak marks the entrance to the house with its large porch, and the backdrop of the soggy marsh sends a breeze to play the wind chimes hanging near the door. I stand under the tree looking at the rest of the farm stretching out from the front of the house. Hens peck at the grass; rows of beans, tomatoes and okra grow in the distance, and I feel an overwhelming sense of peace. This land is special. I can feel it.

"This land has been in our family since 1892," says Sará Reynolds-Green after she and her husband Bill Green come out to greet me and we sit in rocking chairs on the porch watching the sun sink slowly behind the marsh grass. "I saw a deed where my great-grandfather purchased 20 acres of land. And you know, they freed the slaves here on the island in 1861, so 30 years later he was able to purchase 20 acres of land, which I thought was very commendable. I was born in my grandfather's house by a midwife right here on this land. This is my home."

Now Sará and Bill share their historic land with the larger community. They run a ten-acre organic Community Supported Agriculture (CSA) farm, which means they grow a variety of vegetables and sell them to members from the community who sign up to buy shares. They also include their eggs and honey in the shares, and shareholders pick up their shares on the porch of South Carolina Coastal Community Development Corporation, a former produce packing shed on the island. Others in the community buy foods from there also. They are the only community-supported farm in the area. Community and food are at the center of everything they do; they build on what they would both call the historic culture of the island.

The Gullah/Geechee Nation, led by Queen Quet, is a nation of Gullah Geechee people whose roots in West and Central Africa have been tightly preserved since their ancestors arrived here as slaves. The Sea Islands and what's known as the Low Country along the coast from Wilmington, North Carolina, to Jacksonville, Florida, is home to the Gullah/Geechee Nation. The lowlands and marsh of these areas served as the primary grounds for rice production in the 17th and 18th century, and Africans from the traditional rice-growing regions of West Africa were brought to perform the arduous work. Isolated on the Gullah Islands, Gullah Geechee people developed a strong sense of community and were able to preserve more of their African cultural heritage than other groups of African Americans. Gullah people developed a separate creole language similar to the Krio of Sierra Leone, and they continue distinct

Mr. Bill.

cultural patterns in their language, arts, crafts, religious beliefs, folklore, rituals and foodways, in which rice, fishing and hunting play a big role.

"The history of this island is based on communal survival," says Sará. "We were cut off out here on a rural island. Before they built the bridge, you had to take a boat across, into town. So people learned to be self-sufficient and make with their hands the things they needed to survive. This was the epicenter, with Penn School teaching everybody on the island how to farm and create an environment where you didn't need to go to Beaufort for a lot, only those things we couldn't make ourselves. Most of what we had right here in this community was enough to survive.

"We made it like that, by growing and sharing and selling our own food. I grew up in a family of two brothers and four sisters. We all grew up farming and helping my mother on the farm. As we were coming up, every person just about had a little garden and grew something. My mother was known for growing her peanuts, sweet potatoes and tomatoes. Everyone knew when it was peanut harvest time and okra time, and they would be calling her to buy a bushel of peanuts, okra or both. I would deliver the orders, and I didn't mind 'cause I'd get to drive the car. I was about 13 or 14 and the rule for us was if you sat up tall behind the wheel, nobody would bother you. I would deliver all over the island driving on the dirt roads. Moma was also known for her yeast rolls, and every time she baked a few pans of them I'd be delivering them to neighbors who were sick or who called her up wanting her rolls. Food was at the center of our community.

"The main crops that helped sustain us were the cash crops we grew which helped us go to college. My mother grew tomatoes and cucumbers. Those were the two crops that helped really build the island, back when we had packing houses where distributors and large farmers came and bought what local farmers would bring in to sell from their farms. Everyone in the neighborhood knew that during the summer months between June, July and a little of August, all you'd be doing is picking cucumbers and tomatoes and taking them to the packing house. That's what helped my mother to support our college tuition. The farm yielded a lot of tomatoes and Moma had big, beautiful tomatoes, and that was

her income; we were the farmhands and we helped her. We'd be out there picking and hoeing all summer long.

"My other great-grandfather was a county extension agent who helped the farmers and everyone in the area to farm and utilize their land to be profitable and self-sufficient. He also helped the farms on the proper way to raise farm animals. And everyone helped each other in that way. If one person was a farmer and they farmed a lot of sweet potatoes, then they would share that. If someone else grew cucumbers or squash or greens, they shared. If this person was raising cattle, whenever he killed a cow or hog then he'd share a piece of that. It was communal. And everyone knew when someone was killing a hog, it was a celebration, and they would go to that person's house early in the morning to help, and they all had their favorite pieces of meat to take home, so everyone's family was fed. That's how my mother and father's house was built. Everyone came every Saturday, and piece by piece they put the house together. That made life worth living for everyone without much hardship on one person. I love that concept, and I try to live it and try to pass that on."

"The culture of the Gullah man is based on loving kindness," Bill adds in his gentle voice and patois accent, rich with hints of the Gullah language. "The average Gullah person will do for you quicker than any other, and they don't mind helping. It's a very spiritual thing. Going out in the creek catching fish, bringing it back in, sharing it with everybody. Loving kindness. We work with our whole community, our environment too. We love the natural, and we know how to work with the natural things of life. We work with the 'poppers' [porpoise or dolphins], we get out on the boat, 'poppers' run the fish up the creek and we follow them. We bang on the boat so the 'poppers' come back out and chase the fish up to the boat. Gullah people learn how to work with animals and nature; we learn how to respect our whole community.

"We farmed together, we always looked out for one another. I grew up on James Island across the water from here and by the time I was a teenager I already had farming in my blood. I grew up close to the farm, and we all worked on the farm for a living, coming out after school and going out to pick beans for the farmers. I made $13.50 a week, and that was enough to get by. We could go to the store and buy a bag of rice for 50 cents and harvest food in the garden and cook for the whole family."

Cooking is something else Bill has been doing his whole life. He's a chef and owner of the restaurant Gullah Grub, which serves up Gullah dishes on the island, drawing hungry patrons from all over the country, including chef personalities like Anthony Bourdain and Martha Stewart. Much of the food they cook with is grown on Marshview or fished locally.

"I cook Gullah dishes like catfish chowder and shrimp gumbo with okra," Bill continues, "red rice and beans, fish and greens. I use the Green Glaze greens. They are the best green out there. They come straight from Africa, and they have more body, more flavor to them. Back then, meat was expensive so I learned how to cook without using a bunch of meat. It was more about fish. We lived basically off the creek, and that's what we'd eat. We lived off a lot of seafood and whatever we grew. I learned how to cook from my grandparents and some of the ladies that worked around the farms as I was coming up. And with my mom when I was a young fella, working with her when she worked in the kitchen in a private home. I started with cooking a lot of soups back in the '70s, and I would use the community center kitchen here to cook mass amounts and sell at market and to the military base over the bridge. I cook freehand style, no measuring. You just gotta use your common sense and all your senses, smell and sight. It's the old-fashioned way, it's the way I was raised up.

"But this generation doesn't know cooking like that. That culture is getting lost. Even on the farm our culture is gone. A lot of farmers talk about working together, but then they don't make it that way. They have to learn how to work together, when it's supposed to be in their blood. That love and kindness is in all our blood, but it doesn't come out until a mass destruction or something happens like a bad storm. Then people come together, but once it calms down then it goes right back the same way. It's too bad that's the way it is."

"It's all about 'me, me, me' in today's world," Sará adds, "and now we rely on other people for the things that we need, instead of trying to create them within our own means. Starting with the food. Once we stopped growing our own food, we relied on the grocery stores for everything, instead of the garden, the farms and the dirt that we walk on every day. Once we separated ourselves from nature and from the Creator, that's when we started going into man-made products, processed and microwavable. It started to change then, with convenience. Culture goes with the generational changes. When a generation changes, they grab hold to the modern culture and no longer feel tied to their own. I was that way too. I wanted to get away from here as fast as possible, because we thought that this was the end of the world when we were young. One way in and one way out.

"But when I left, I started losing my identity, my connections, even with the food. The way it's prepared, the smell. I had a yearning to come back. Something was pulling me back. The water, the smells, the food, being around family. That's where we get our strength from, that community; it's that energy that pulls you and keeps you together."

"We have to keep ties to our culture and keep trying to love and help each other as a community," Bill agrees. "That's why we're trying so hard here to work with the kids and train them every chance we get."

Sará and Bill, or Mr. Bill as the kids call him, run a youth program on their farm and in the Gullah Grub restaurant. With Sará's passion for working with children as St. Helena Elementary's guidance counselor and Mr. Bill's passion for cooking and passing on Gullah culture, they found a perfect opportunity to teach farming, cooking and food culture to the island's youth. They work with children from 4–18 years old and pay them stipends for working and learning skills on the farm, taking cooking classes with Mr. Bill, and learning the entire process of farm to table. Some of the teenagers end up working in Mr. Bill's restaurant, learning the job skills of cooking and serving, while others work at the farmers market, learning the process of harvesting and selling their crops. Sará started a garden at the school and incorporates food and agriculture and community into her guidance curriculum. She brings many of her students to the farm after school, and more keep signing up as they hear about it from classmates. The youth have called themselves Young Farmers of the Low Country, and I had the pleasure of farming alongside them during my stay on Marshview Farm.

We hoe the rows, and the kids teach me how to pull out the root of the nutgrass, a weed grass that grows all over the area, with a small seed or nut at the end of its root. Sará tells me she sometimes pays them $.02 a nut they collect to encourage them to pull the whole root, otherwise the nut will just reseed. The girls kick their muck boots in the water springing out of a leak in the irrigation tape, a new addition to the farm since the summers have been getting warmer. We are three generations of women talking and working side by side on the farm, all from different families but working together as one.

"I talk with the kids about how one seed can feed a family," Sará says as she hoes expertly across from me. "They couldn't understand that, and I tell them just wait and see. It's a way to show them that if you have one seed, it will produce a plant and that will produce many fruits, and then we save those seeds and the next year we grow many plants with many more fruits, and so on. Then they begin to see how that one seed can feed a family.

"We also talk about the history of those seeds. When we do our cooking classes, we include the history of Gullah culture tied to that food. Mr. Bill starts with the basics, which is how to cook a pot of rice — very important to our culture. We tell the story of rice called the *Rice of Passage,* and it's the first thing we teach them. We talk about how rice came over from Africa braided in the hair of African women. And how rice growers were targeted to be brought here as slaves from the West African coast because of their technical skills of growing rice in their country. The two coasts are very similar. In fact, Sierra Leone's prime minister came here to visit the Penn Center, and he talked about Carolina Gold Rice making its way back to Sierra Leone, and when it got there, they knew it as if it was their own. Our classes tie these stories together as well as environmental conservation. We say 'if you like shrimp gumbo, we have to sustain our rivers and creeks.' Food is life, it's not just digging in the dirt."

After we finish in the fields, the kids harvest food to take home to their families, and I drive to the Gullah Grub to bite into Mr. Bill's red rice and shrimp gumbo. There are two women sitting on the front porch of the restaurant weaving baskets. As I sit in the rocking chair next to them and savor the delicious Gullah grub, I think about the youth, the community and the rich stories tied to each bite. I can literally taste the love of this Gullah island that Sará and Bill hold and work so hard to pass on.

Menkir Tamrat,
Timeless Harvest,
Fremont, California.

> **"**
> I grew up farm to table in the countryside of Ethiopia,
> where there were no grocery stores, so everything was from
> the farm. So it took me a while to make the connection
> that the industrialized food system here was impacting
> the taste of the food.
>
> — Menkir Tamrat **"**

PRESERVING CULTURE even in the place where it is rooted can be challenging, but preserving culture thousands of miles away requires a special passion, dedication, and pure love of home. I head to California to meet with an Ethiopian farmer/chef who is bringing the cuisine and crops of his homeland to the East Bay and working to perfect the taste of home.

⚜

Menkir Tamrat stands in the shade of his acacia tree, a native Ethiopian tree famously dotting the African landscape and known for the thorns that protect its branches from overeating giraffes. Here giraffes are not part of its worry; this tree, grown from seed that Menkir carried from Ethiopia, now lives happily in a suburban front yard in Fremont, California. The acacia feels at home in the similarly warm and arid climate, and instead of a grassy lawn as its companion, it grows next to rows of *gesho, koseret* and *tej* grass. This is Menkir's home garden, a little taste of Ethiopia.

Menkir, a 62-year-old former tech manager now running a farm-to-table

business for Ethiopian cuisine, came to the United States for college in the 1970s. Living in upstate New York, far enough away from the large Ethiopian communities of Washington, D.C. and Toronto, Menkir began to miss his mother's cooking and started searching for the flavors of home. He quickly found, however, that there were some unique Ethiopian ingredients that could not be found in any stores. Even when trying to recreate the flavors in his own kitchen, he knew there was something missing.

"I started to understand one of the reasons I wasn't getting that flavor," Menkir recalls, "is because there were no fresh ingredients. I did not make the connection because I grew up farm to table in the countryside, where there were no grocery stores, so everything was from the farm. So it took me a while to make the connection that the industrialized food system here was impacting the taste of the food. Food here is abundant and cheap, but it is missing the taste.

"At home in Ethiopia, things were made from scratch. In fact, my father would not even buy a fridge until I was in the 12th grade because he didn't want old food to be served. I was insecure about this because other people of our income level had a fridge at the time. But he did not want to eat food that was one or two days old. However, it fit with our eating style. We used to slaughter a small lamb for the family on Saturdays when it wasn't Lent; Wednesdays and Fridays were Lent, so we couldn't eat meat or butter those days. We would feast Saturday and Sunday and then the leftover meat would kind of cure, hanging up the rest of the week."

"With the meat we would have *wat,*" explains Menkir, "which is a red stew that is a basic staple of Ethiopian food. During Lent, it's made with lentils or split peas and shallots, and the base is made with *berbere,* a spicy seasoning comprised of a unique Ethiopian chile plus 11 other ingredients of spices, herbs and aromatics. It's flavors like this and *koseret,* an Ethiopian herb related to oregano, and *gōmen,* a fragrant Ethiopian collard green, that make a dish uniquely Ethiopian." However, it was finding the perfect *berbere* and its complex mix of ingredients that first inspired Menkir's business idea.

"My mother used to always send me a bag of *berbere,*" Menkir continues. "It's how you get the true taste from home here. But when she died, I no longer had those ingredients, and they aren't found consistently in specialty stores here. I started to realize also that many Ethiopian restaurants didn't have a reliable supply chain for key ingredients like *berbere.* Someone's aunt might send over a bag or some stores had it sometimes, but it either tasted a little different each time, or they could never buy it consistently. I started seeing the flavor in the restaurant food was missing because they didn't have the support system to get them high-quality, fresh ingredients that bring back the taste. It's hard to keep a cuisine in a foreign land."

Menkir with an acacia tree.

"So I began trying to make the *berbere* myself with the chilies available to me, and it just wasn't the same. I was forced to grow my own. I got seeds from Ethiopia and began growing them so that I could be sure of the authentic taste and have my own consistent supply. Once I had it perfected, it made me think about how I could help the restaurants bring back the taste."

Menkir has always dreamed of working closely with food, ever since he was a young boy. Growing up in northern Ethiopia in Wollo province where altitudes reach over 8,000 feet and ancient grain agriculture is common, Menkir enjoyed watching peasant farmers plow their land with oxen and later joined a horticulture club at his boarding school. Throughout his career in the high tech industry, Menkir would take workshops and classes on master gardening and viticulture and practice his culinary skills until he was good enough to teach cooking classes. He finally took the opportunity to begin putting his dream together when he was laid off in 2009. He got right to work building a greenhouse in his backyard and finding land to grow over 5,000 Ethiopian pepper seedlings for the *berbere*.

Menkir now grows his peppers from seed he ordered from Ethiopia, plus *gómen, koseret* and other Ethiopian crops on six acres at the Sunol Ag Park in the East Bay, in addition to what he grows in his much more diverse backyard farm. He also works with farmers in northern Nevada to grow *teff,* an ancient Ethiopian grain used to make *teff injera,* the spongy flat bread used as a foundation in Ethiopian cuisine. With the production of his large variety of Ethiopian ingredients, Menkir is producing what he calls "intermediate products," such as the *berbere* base, which can be bought and used by restaurants and individuals looking for fresh and reliable Ethiopian cuisine staples. He calls his business Timeless Harvest and experiments with his products at an Ethiopian restaurant in Berkeley called Finfiné.

Menkir also makes his own honey wine called *'tej* and sells it to several local Ethiopian restaurants. *'Tej* is made from fermented honey, similar to mead, but what makes it distinctly Ethiopian is the bittering agent called *gesho.* Like hops, *gesho* leaves are used to make Ethiopian beer called *tella,* but for *'tej,* its woody stems are used. Menkir's longing for his mother's honey wine started his hobby of making *'tej.*

"My mother used to make excellent *'tej,"* Menkir recalls with a smile as we sit in his living room enjoying a beer together after touring his backyard farm and his farm plot at the Sunol Ag Park. "She would use rich, wild amber honey. One of my favorite memories is when she would make it for the holidays and people would come to visit and drink a glass of *'tej* with my father, but they would always try to find a way to stay longer for a second glass," Menkir laughs softly. "Honey wine is ancient, even before grape wine. It was being made in Europe, Asia and Ethiopia, but the fundamental difference was that the Vikings in Europe were making it without *gesho.* So growing my own *gesho* and making fresh *'tej* has become part of my business and complements the Ethiopian cuisine very well.

"I'm sort of creating an ecosystem of Ethiopian food in America," Menkir explains, "in a consistent, higher quality and sustainable way. But it's not always easy to find a market, the *'tej* has a wider distribution, but the food is harder. The Ethiopian restaurant community is by and large a lower-income immigrant community, and they are used to getting ingredients from home cheaply or doing what they can to keep costs low. So most of them use regular collard greens instead of *gómen* or use *injera* made from barley and wheat flour instead of *teff*.

"*Teff injera* has to be fermented for two to three days, similar to sourdough. Plus *teff* is not so easy to get. Ethiopian restaurants started here in 1975 in Washington, D.C., and at that time farmers here were not growing *teff*. So, many chefs are using this substitute *injera*, but it doesn't have the nutritional and gluten-free benefits that *teff* has. I, however, have been experimenting and have figured out how to make *teff injera* without too much hassle.

"The key," Menkir concludes, "is convincing these restaurant owners that having the authentic and fresh ingredients is worth the higher cost. Charlie, the Ethiopian owner of Finfiné restaurant in Berkeley, is one of the few who have stepped up to the plate. He told me, 'If you make it, I'll sell it.' So that has been my start. My work now is two-fold. I'm not a farmer or a chef, I'm somewhere in between. I like the combination. I can't separate the kitchen from the farm, just like I can never separate myself from Ethiopia."

❧

I was lucky enough, after my visit with Menkir at his home, to be invited to eat with him and his fellow Ethiopian foodies the next night at Finfiné in Berkeley. A group of four of us sat together for hours, eating, laughing and drinking *'tej* and *tella*. After following the customs, including thoroughly washing our hands before joining the communal meal typically eaten without utensils, Menkir excitedly ordered up many of the dishes comprised of his freshly grown ingredients. I was able to taste the flavors we had talked about the day before while standing on his farm.

We folded our spongy *teff injera* and scooped up the delicious red stew made with his *berbere*. We filled up on tasty *shiro,* made with yellow peas, garbanzo beans and lentils. And we ate Menkir's favorite Ethiopian delicacy, *kitfo,* a spicy raw beef dish, sort of like steak tartare, spiced with a distinctly Ethiopian seasoning called *mitmita* which Menkir also made from his chilies. I drank my share of the sweet *'tej* honey wine and tasted the rich, dark *tella* beer. But the best gift was simply sitting with Menkir and this circle of friends sharing food, sharing stories, and literally laughing until I cried.

"The way we eat is by sharing," says Menkir. "It is a sign of humility. It means you're open, you're not hiding anything, and you are offering a part of yourself during the meal. It's like saying you're my brother and we're eating together."

It is that feeling, along with the delicious and distinct tastes of home, that I'd like to think Menkir is preserving — the simple joy and community that comes with food culture.

Part 5: Fierce Farming Women

> Her hands are cracked, reeling from the whipping wind. Split, torn and dotted with splinters, numb to the impact of the wooden shovel. Cuts fade and reappear, garnishing her knuckles. Her palms tell the story of the day's work, etching out the lines with black soil to the edge of her fingers, retracing every inch of land ploughed, every seed planted.
>
> Her forearms are brushed with dried mud, some splattered onto her face. The rest is caked in every crevice of her fingernails and painted onto her faded, tattered clothes. It's too early to see the callouses on her palms, but if you were to hold her hand, you'd feel them.
>
> — Natasha Bowens

I HAVE NEVER FELT MORE LIKE A WOMAN than the day I dug my hands into the soil for the first time. I'll never forget the feeling of my hands after my first season farming. The above poem describes them, and I like to think it describes the hands of every female farmer out there. It is a description that challenges society's definition of feminine beauty. However, with women making up over 70 percent of the world's farmers, I'd say we need to change the picture of feminine beauty to the image of a farmer's hands.[35]

Women feed the world, we always have. We've been the gatherers, the cooks, the ones to provide milk to our babies, the nutritionists, the healers, and even the farmers.

According to the International Center for Research on Women, rural women produce 80 percent of the world's food.[36] That's an astounding contribution to the survival of humanity. To have ownership over such a vital contribution is something to praise.

Yet in some regions, that contribution is not praised at all. Not with rights for women or even ownership over the land from which we feed the world. In many developing countries — responsible for much of the world's agriculture — women only own two percent of the land.[37] Due to the lack of rights for women in many of these countries, and even here, where women are often left out of farmer credits, subsidies and training targeted at men,

Danny Woo Garden, Seattle, Washington.

women cannot gain the ownership they deserve in our agricultural system. We are also discriminated against for loans and fair access to markets, just like farmers of color. Such discrimination from the USDA brought on a lawsuit from female farmers, similar to the discrimination lawsuit filed by Black, Hispanic and Native farmers.

If women farmers had the same access to resources as men, the number of the world's hungry could be reduced by up to 150 million.[38] Imagine that. Hillary Clinton says it best: "Women are the largest untapped reservoir of talent in the world." Yet we are doing our best to tap our reservoirs ourselves and fight for equal access. Here in the U.S., women own or co-own almost half of all farmland.[39] And according to a USDA study, the number of women-operated farms more than doubled between 1982 and 2007, bringing women farmers up to one million strong.[40]

Women are shattering stereotypes here as well, from being depicted as tender backyard gardeners to ranchers herding cattle and managing goat and sheep operations, to reinventing the back-to-the-land movement. Tammy Steele of the National Women in Agriculture Association thinks women are "no longer concerned with breaking through the corporate glass ceiling as they were in the 1960s; now their concern is with tilling the earth and sustaining communities."

And sustaining communities is exactly what female farmers are doing. Community Supported Agriculture (CSA) farms have higher percentages of female farmers.[41] And from what I have seen, so do urban farms and community gardens. Which suggests to me that more women are entering farming to grow community, with growing food and growing a business as an equal priority.

I met with women who returned to or began farming as a sense of duty to their communities — to create access to healthy food, to rebuild neighborhoods or to preserve food culture. Many women I met with started farming as the only option they had to ensure the health of their children. Others wanted to lead by example in proving economic success and independent entrepreneurship is possible for women. And they are doing that with flying colors.

Some women are also using agricultural spaces as education and gathering centers, while others are proudly carrying on a long family tradition of living off the land and feeding community. Many of the popular avenues for feeding community today, such as community kitchens or mobile food markets, have been started and are run by women.

Through food and farming, women are continuing our legacy of providing spaces to gather, food to share and nourishment that goes beyond the belly.

Portrait 1:
Alabama Strong

Sandra Simone, Huckleberry Hill Farm, Talladega County, Alabama.

> You see, to be an independent working woman in the South — where unemployment is so high amongst the men — causes a lot of resentment. There's a lot of resentment and isolation as a woman farming here.
>
> — Sandra Simone

T O KICK OFF THIS CHAPTER on female farmers, I start with a strong Black woman from Alabama who embodies the title of this section perfectly. She is not only fiercely independent after losing her husband shortly after moving to the farm, but her background as a jazz singer, actor, artist, mother and Alabama's 2012 Farmer of the Year demonstrates the ultimate power and perseverance of a woman.

We blow into Alabama from Tennessee. From the cool Smoky Mountains, my partner and I descend into sticky sweet Alabama and head toward rural Talladega County, where I know of a woman farming alone, raising goats and getting praise from networks like the Southeastern African American Farmers Organic Network and Alabama's USDA office. After we arrive at her Huckleberry Hill Farm (named for all of the huckleberries growing wild) and set up our tent near her lone log cabin standing tall behind the trees, farmer Sandra Simone puts us right to work. She and my partner, Crosby, begin working on her old tractor while I hold all the tools along with my recorder and start asking questions.

The goats mill in the pasture behind us, as if awaiting the tractor's return to action so their new grass seed can be planted.

"Girl, I was a jazz singer," Sandra begins in her silky smooth voice, as her long braids sway over the engine of the faded red Ford Jubilee tractor, "I never thought I'd be out here doing all this! I was always a city girl. I grew up in Birmingham and then moved to California and lived in Long Beach for 22 years. My late husband and I raised our daughters there. I was Program Director at the YMCA and then finally got the nerve to begin singing. I had always wanted to sing since my earliest consciousness, but I had a lot of fear instilled in me by others. I was never afraid to sing, but people convinced me I was, and as I got older and wanted to be in the spotlight, because of my darker skin and the discrimination we had against ourselves within the Black community, I felt I would never make it. But then I met my husband, Harold Burke, and he changed me — he flipped me from someone lacking self-confidence to someone who believed in possibilities. He brought me out, and my creative self came alive. I began acting in plays and dancing and painting and having art exhibits, and I loved all of it. We then decided to move to Atlanta to get back to our Southern roots and really develop my jazz singing career. I did a lot of singing in Atlanta at jazz festivals in the parks, hotels and clubs. My husband was so supportive. He was the wind beneath my wings.

"Meanwhile, he was busy working on me about Black-owned land. While still living in Long Beach, we would visit my mother who had moved from Birmingham back to her birthplace of Alpine, Alabama. Harold was impressed with the amount of land my great-grandfather had acquired there. I was told by a great-uncle that it was originally about 2,000 acres. My great-grandfather arrived here in America in about 1868. He had worked his passage from Mozambique and landed in Mobile. Why he chose this area, I don't know. I was told that the hills and the red clay soil reminded him of his home in Africa. My daughters Tynesha and Stephanie and I are researching records to find as much information as we can on how he was able to acquire so much in those times. He had quite a sustainable operation. His family was large — 12 children. They produced what they consumed. Sheep, cows, and pigs, and vegetables, and they even had goats! There was a spinning wheel used to make clothing from the sheep's wool. He had a blacksmith shop, a sawmill, and a general store. Most of the land was sold through the years; it's no longer 2,000 acres. What was left was divided into parcels that went to his eight surviving children. Then you know, it started passing down through generations

and became more sub-divided. (Note: See piece about Sandra's heirs' property loss in the earlier chapter "Black Land Loss.") The family's old land surrounds this acreage that I steward, and extends to the lake.

"My husband really began educating me about the importance of keeping the land here, because I hadn't given it a thought. I left here long ago, and I was through with the South, the country. All I could think of were the summers at my grandmother's, the heat, the bugs, *puhlease*, no! But he kept talking about how Black-owned land is getting away, and how important it was what my great-grandfather accomplished, and how we shouldn't just let it be lost. It took a while, because it didn't mean anything to me at that time, but he kept on talking and educating me until I finally heard him. He would say a family business should be developed over there on the lake where people can make an income. So we eventually took on the 40 acres instead of selling, like so many of my relatives did. But I still didn't think it meant we'd go back and do something with it. It was just nice having the land, coming to get away from it all, connect with nature and honor my great-grandfather's legacy.

"When my mom got sick, I came and stayed for a while, and I would take walks in the woods. I got in touch with the rhythm of nature, the weather, and realizing the things that you can feel as a steward of the land. There's a thing that happens in the air when it's changing from summer to fall; there's a thing that you can feel in the spring — and I had never noticed this before. I started planting a flower garden, I called it my heirloom garden because I was planting all kinds of old-fashioned flowers that I collected from my aunts and other neighbors in the area. Then that turned into a little vegetable garden. I really began to love it out here. That's when I first got hooked. It seemed the Creator had a different plan for me.

"Next thing you know, Harold and I were planning how we could put up a little cabin that would allow us a place to rest after a day of work on the land, before the drive back to Atlanta. Somehow, that evolved to we would live here and see what we could accomplish on the land. We put

Sandra & Natasha give medicine to a goat.

things into motion and after a year or so of planning, we started building this beautiful little cabin. But, before the cabin was completed, Harold was diagnosed with terminal cancer. Within a few short months, he made his transition and passed on."

Sandra, heartbroken in the home she dreamed into fruition with the man who made her unafraid to dream, now had a choice to make. She could stay on the land alone and preserve her family's legacy of Black land ownership and live off the land, or she could go back to Atlanta to be near her daughters and heal from her loss. Pulling from an inner strength deep within herself, she decided to continue living out her and her husband's vision on the land. Now a single Black female farmer, Sandra has not only overcome heartbreaking loss, but she has mounted the hurdles that exist for Black farmers and female farmers — and she continues to meet those challenges.

"Sometimes, I think about everything Harold did for me when he was alive," says Sandra. "I let him take care of everything for me. I got to do what I wanted and focus on singing while he took care of everything else. And now here I am running a farm, working on tractors, doing everything myself and learning what I'm capable of."

"So I kept growing food and tried talking to my relatives to get them involved. With my daughters' help, the Community Supported Agriculture (CSA) shares started back in 2005. The CSA did great. I was a little intimidated by the thought of growing food for people, and taking their money like that up front. So I only did six people the first year, but it went OK, and the next year it was 12 people, then the next year was 24 people. I was doing it by myself. My daughter would come every two weeks to help, but other than that it was just me. And it kept growing up to 48 members. Then the recession hit, and it just jumped all the way back. I was like 'whoa what happened?' I was on a roll and then it was over. And the weather too, right about then it started getting really, really hot, and the drought came. So I had to cut it the last couple years. I wasn't gonna do all that work and just break even on expenses. I wasn't making anything. And, see, my customers were in Atlanta, two hours away. So we had the transportation cost. My daughter would come and deliver the produce to them in Atlanta or I would meet her at the state line.

"I had a hard time recruiting members out here. All my members were in Atlanta and a few in Birmingham. We recruited members through my daughter and our connections in Atlanta at first by word of mouth, then we got on Local Harvest and recruited there. But rural members are hard to find. I think for a few reasons. It's harder to get rural folks or Black folks as excited about organic food. That word sells in the White community and in the cities, but not here. Also even though not as many people have their own gardens as they used to, some still do, and so people are accustomed to getting vegetables for free from their neighbors who grow so they don't want to pay you for them.

"Not only that, but I think it's gender too. In these rural areas, what I've found is that I can't get anybody interested in what I am doing because I'm female. Like with the goats. I started talking about the goats to men in the community here because my friend, who is from Tanzania, was telling me about the difficulty they had getting meat goats in this country. It was around 1999 when goat meat production was just kinda starting here in the States. So my idea was, in addition to raising goats, let's go out and procure goats from people who are ready to sell their herds, and we can put them here, fatten them up and just sell them. Nobody bit. We had meetings. I had representatives from Tuskegee come to talk, the Heifer Project International said they would supply a herd to each of us. I wrote the bylaws for an organization and everything. Nothing. Nobody. Nada. That opportunity is not here like that now, and there's nobody selling goats as cheap as they were then. That's over. So that was a real opportunity, dead. I still ended up getting my goats through Tuskegee, and that's how I started this herd. I'm told that a lot of men just don't feel that it is a woman's place to provide the direction, and that they wouldn't, or couldn't, take me seriously.

"You see, to be an independent working woman in the South — where unemployment is so high amongst the men — causes a lot of resentment. Just about everything in this area that provided jobs has closed down. They used to have textile mills; they used to have Tyson chicken factories — all of that's gone. There's a sawmill still open, so whoever has a job there is very fortunate because there is nothing else that I know of that provides jobs around here. There are some big corn and soybean farms here, wheat, too, recently. But they're all White farmers now, that I know of. They used to be Black farmers growing corn, sugar cane, cotton and watermelon. But they're mostly gone. They either died or lost their farms to foreclosure or family land disputes like so many other Black farmers. And young people aren't encouraged to work the land. They either work at fast food places or leave the area.

"And how many of the farmers left out there are single Black females? Ha. Talk about isolation. Resentment and isolation as a woman farming here. I feel like I am surrounded by people who don't want me to succeed. Even within my community. Especially the men around here who aren't doing *anything* with the land they have available to them. They tell me I try to do too much. I think that it causes them to look at what they are not doing. Maybe they feel that it is a reflection on them, especially if I succeed."

Sandra has not let isolation, resentment, or other obstacles (mentioned in the "Black Land Loss" chapter) stop her. She owns and operates over 100 acres of pasture, where she raises a herd of 50 Boer goats, a South African breed of meat goat that she sells through direct marketing. She also grows and sells produce and was one of the first four farmers in the entire state to become certified organic in 2006 with the support of the Southeastern African American Farmers Organic Network (which she now sits on the board of). She mentors youth in entrepreneur gardening programs in the summer, works with local churches to find volunteers for the farm, and gives demonstrations of her solar energy well pump that she had installed by SURREF (Sustainable Rural Regenerative Enterprises for Families) because there was no electricity on her pastured land. Sandra works closely with Tuskegee University and the Alabama Natural Resources Conservation Services (NRCS) in her efforts, and is leading the way for farmers to operate as sustainably as possible. And she does all that while still going to sing in jazz clubs once in a while. She is Alabama-strong, to her roots.

❧

Shortly after my interview with Sandra in 2012, Alabama NRCS named Sandra Farmer of the Year. When I received the phone call, I could hear the pride in her voice. I smiled thinking about how proud her Harold would be of her, but more so, I smiled with the thought of all the little brown girls all over the South seeing her picture as Farmer of the Year and thinking that could be them one day.

Portrait 2:

American Indian Mothers

*Beverly Collins-Hall,
American Indian Mothers
and Three Sisters Farm,
Shannon, North Carolina.*

I look after my family and my community because I am
a mother. We've got to empower ourselves. Women,
we have the power to do it. We are the healers of
this earth.

— Beverly Collins-Hall

LEAVING ALABAMA THINKING about
what women are capable of alone, led
me to think about what we're capable of
when we come together. I turned Lucille
to a corner of the South where women —
mothers — have come together to change
the future for their children and their
community using the traditional growing
and eating practices of their ancestors.

"American Indian Mothers has survived as an organization for 12 years. I'm
proud of our organization. The survival
came from people believing in us and
us believing in ourselves," says Beverly
Collins-Hall, "Wind in Her Hair," a fiery,
fighter of a woman who sits before me
in her living room in Robeson County,
North Carolina. She is combing her
granddaughter's hair while offering me
breakfast and answering my questions. I
have just arrived, pulling up to her modest
home that has a sign out front advertis-
ing a home hairdresser. Before she started
American Indian Mothers and Three
Sisters Farm, she dreamed of being a wife,
mother and cosmetologist. She became all
of those, and now she runs the non-profit

organization that focuses on health, community and food founded by Native
American mothers.

A small sculpture of the Iroquois *Three
Sisters* in full native dress sits on her coffee
table, and a feathered bow hangs above
her fireplace. "We are Iroquois, but also
Algonquin, Cherokee, Tuscarora and
Siouan," Beverly says. "We're a mixture.
But those are just names, we're all the
same people." Beverly is one of eight in her
family who live close by, spread around the
land where she was raised. We head out
to attend a fundraising event for her sister,
who is raising money to put a children's
amphitheater and community park in the
neighborhood.

"We're focused on helping our youth
here," Beverly begins as we drive along the
country roads. "Here in Robeson County,
we were number one in the nation in
the year 2000 for syphilis. So unsafe sex
was prevalent, but also drug use amongst
our youth. There are a lot of drugs in the
county, still are. The government started a
task force, but we decided as the mothers in
this community we had to do something.
We went out there learning and getting
together with other Native American

groups, and we held conferences. We pulled the kids together, we started talking about safe sex and date rape and drugs and everything. We listened to those youth, it was really important to understand what they were going through. Those were some of the beginnings of the American Indian Mothers, and the focus on health in our community spread from there.

"Robeson County is the poorest county in the state and third in the nation," Beverly explains. "Diabetes and cardiovascular heart disease are prevalent among our Native American community, obesity and cancer as well. I worked in home health with elders after doing cosmetology, and I saw how the illnesses are impacting us, but more so I saw how the program was basically taking advantage of our elders. They have to decide whether to buy food or medicine. And that's just not right, that's not our way. In our community when I was growing up, the elders didn't lack for anything, the children didn't lack for anything. But here I was, watching Native American elders choosing to buy medicine, so they were dying without food. And the food they do give them in the food banks is killing 'em. Feed 'em healthy food! A lot of the health problems we have are actually initiated by these government programs. A lot of the folks that are out there sick, is because they're on prescribed medicine. We got more hospitals, more doctors, and more sickness, so something's not working. Our people are dealing with so much. We're off our balance, and it's alarming."

Robeson County is home to the largest group of Native Americans east of the Mississippi River — around 60,000, comprising about 40 percent of the county's population. The Lumbee Tribe, as well as Iroquois, Algonquin, Cherokee, Tuscarora and Sioux, constitute the Native American population there, and even though they have lived in the area since the early 1700s, the Lumbee are still not federally recognized as a tribe. They have been petitioning the government for tribal recognition since 1888. Without federal recognition, they have no rights to tribal sovereignty, federal services, protections or benefits.

"In order for there to be a change," Beverly continues, "we have to change it. It's up to us. We have to look out for ourselves. What the government is giving out in commodities is not what our people are used to eating. It's not healthy. So we started a food bank for the elders and for the community. And we started a community garden growing peas and butter beans and corn and the stuff we like to eat. You know we can't be dependent on what they are giving out and selling. We gotta be responsible for our food supply and where our water comes from and what our land is like. The soil has to be healthy in order for the food to be healthy. We have to be healthy as a community in every way. It starts with you, you got an elder community, you're responsible, you got children in the community, you're responsible, you got land you want to feed you, you're responsible. So that's how American Indian Mothers started. We got into teaching how

to get back to the preservation of the community, the preservation of the family. We came together and grew into a network of over 200 Native American women across the nation.

"We have to preserve our Native communities because we've been colonized and westernized so much that we've left who we are. In order for us to be healthier people, it's important to know who we are and where we come from and what's unique about our culture and how we lived. That uniqueness is here, but we gotta revitalize it — especially African Americans and Native Americans and Hispanics who have walked away from their world into someone else's world and forgot where they came from. Then the children don't know where they've come from. There's no storytelling. There's no pride in good things like food. Food is a good thing to have pride in.

"That can come from the family. We used to work on the farm together, play together, prepare food together and sit at the table together. With the food, comes a long conversation, knowing what the family's doing and how they're doing — all of that has an impact on children having responsibility, parents, elders, community, everybody having a responsibility. If you don't communicate, then there's a lack of it. Food can be the center of that communication."

A strong family woman, Beverly grew up farming with her parents, grandparents and siblings. She's lived here all her life and is proud of the land her family still owns, as it's been kept in ownership by Native American families over decades. Her grandparents bought the land in the 1940s from another Native American family and grew mostly tobacco and cucumbers as well as corn and other vegetables. She remembers picking cucumbers as a child with her brothers and sisters in the time before her father planted the land in pine trees. Her father came from a family of 14 children, and her grandfather from an even larger family, so when she speaks of preserving family and community, she speaks from deep-rooted experience. However, her family lost some of their land and are working to reclaim it. "It seems ridiculous to have to buy back the land I was born on," Beverly says, "but right now I have to rent the land I farm on. The land I own, however, I will never sell. We cherish our land. It is our voice to our children."

Beverly farms to pass on the tradition of food and farming to the children of the community as well. "We started Three Sisters Farm to bring back our traditions and make food the center of that conversation" Beverly says. "*Three Sisters* is an Iroquois tradition of growing corn, beans and squash together. These three crops are sacred to the Iroquois — as the circle of life relying on one another for survival. They hold a spiritual, ceremonial and celebratory place in the garden. Not only are they rich in cultural and botanical history, but they belong together nutritionally. Corn for grain and carbohydrates, bean for protein, and squash for vitamin A. They work together agriculturally too. They

teach us about companion planting and other sustainable growing practices that Indigenous people have been using for so long. We have always practiced farming, and we've always done it sustainably. We allow the land to rest. We call it the 'Year of the Jubilee,' where we allow the land to rest for seven years so it can build itself back up. That's not what these big farms are doing. They're overworking the land and putting too many chemicals in it, so the land can't yield and give you what you're supposed to with the nutrients and vitamins we need because they're trying to change the land, and now the seeds.

"Why do they have to come in here and change the seeds? To us, the bean is already perfect. It's always someone trying to change us — God's creation. People don't realize the side effects to that [genetically modified seeds]. There's side effects to everything we do. Everything that man puts his hands on to alter because he thinks he knows more than God and he can fix it, is putting us in trouble. We've got to stop and look at what we're doing. The farmers have got to stop and look at what they're doing to the land. If they're on that show-boat of getting money, more money, like those larger farms, then they'll continue to be part of the problem. We have a huge manufacturing plant for poultry two miles down the road. They have spray fields and packed chicken houses, and it's just awful. If you go around it and look at the land, it's awful. It's got fish floatin' in the river, dead, and everything's brown. We've got hog operations, turkey, chicken industries all around here. It's overwhelming mass production.

"They're making the forest sick, the land sick, the people and plant life sick. We have to take care of the earth to let her do what she does best — take care of us. She always takes care of us. We're the ones abusing her. Native Americans can lead the way in taking care of her. We know how to live off the land, and it doesn't have to be large land. You can take a small portion of land and it will surprise you the yield it gives. We have to look back at how our elders did it. We would always grow enough food. It's like that squirrel. He was working all summer to put up because he knew what he had to go through in the winter. Things got hard enough and there weren't a whole lot of grocery stores, but you had to be responsible for your own food supply. Because all these grocery stores and their revenue-based ideals of

sustainability, where you have to buy from somebody else, that's not sustainable, that's dependent.

"So we're growing our own, and we hold workshops and programs with the children and the community to teach not only growing food but also the storytelling and culture and nutrition that comes with the food. We do everything from canning classes, to health education and teaching parenting skills, to having talking circles and a women's gathering each spring. We even support our local small farmers.

"What we can do to support farmers is a service, but at the same time it's effective education because we can teach in our own language to our people who are gonna understand what we're talking about. It's a lot of work to follow the organic practices of the USDA or apply for support from the NRCS. You have to be very knowledgeable, and a lot of our farmers don't have more than a 12th-grade education; some of them might not have that. You read some of these applications, and it's like a foreign language. It's not an application process. It's a process of elimination. They tried to do it with me. They tried to make me look like the village idiot, asking me the Latin name of the peas I'm planting. Why do I need to know that to apply for this grant? They're Dixie Lee peas, that's all I know and that's all that should matter. These people coming up with these applications haven't worked on a farm a day in their lives, and they are just complicating things for people who actually work on farms. Because at the end of the day,

Three Sisters vase in Beverly's home.

when we're sitting here eating the food, nobody's talking about *Triticum aestivum,* you know what I'm saying. We're talking about wheat. It's ridiculous.

"My thing is, simplify things for the folks who you say you're serving. Let farmers serve farmers. It shouldn't matter what our color is, what our race is, what our culture is. As farmers we can communicate with each other. It's these institutions that are the gap in communication. Even these food movement conferences. They're talking about food deserts — how many farmers you think know what that is? I don't know what that is. I've heard the definition, but it's not something I carry around every day. Or what about all this talk about the Farm Bill giving money to socially disadvantaged farmers? They say they have all this money to support us, but that's just a title. By the time the money gets to the state and then to the counties, there's no money, there's nothing that's really gonna make an impact and a change. It goes through too many agencies. The

same organizations supposedly helping these disadvantaged farmers have been getting that money for 40–50 years, and what has it changed? It should be direct. We've got to get these farmers capital and real support. We've got to educate them on all the jargon and empower them to understand how to work the system. I educated myself and intend to help others.

"I've been helping people all my life and don't plan to quit yet. My mother always worked in compassionate service, and now I do too. I look after my family and my community, because I am a mother. We've got to empower ourselves. It's the only way we're gonna heal everything that's hurting. Women, we have the power to do it. We are the healers of this earth."

❦

Beverly is now running for office in her county and opening up a cannery/restaurant to continue working toward her goals for a strong, healthy community.

Portrait 3:
Sisters

Carol Jackson and Joyce Bowman, My Sister's Farm, Burgaw, North Carolina.

Preserve your family tree by staying connected to the soil it grows from.

— Anonymous

I HEAD FURTHER TOWARD THE COAST of North Carolina to meet with two women who are trying to revitalize their family land by growing food organically. They are two sisters in their sixties, now retired from teaching. This area where they grow has changed over the decades and now faces the challenges of land degradation, climate change, and heir property laws. This pair of women teach us that ferocity knows no limitations; sometimes all you need is a sister by your side.

❧

Deep in the lowlands of the North Carolina coast, a small family farm survives. After generations of growing food — through development and floods — the family's land persists. I am standing on that land listening to the tiller's engine run. Behind it walks Carol Jackson; her sister, Joyce Bowman, walks behind her, planting sweet potato slips. These two sisters grew up together in Burgaw, North Carolina; both became teachers for special needs children and after retirement both returned to the land where they were raised to grow organic vegetables together.

They call their farm My Sister's Farm because both are too modest to take credit for the idea and each jokingly blames the

other for getting them into it in the first place. They started over ten years ago, slowly, first to keep busy and active in retirement and then to sell their excess harvest as production grew. They sold shares to consumers in a CSA for a few years and now sell to Feast Down East Cooperative, a community distributor supporting local small farmers by buying their produce and selling to restaurants, markets, schools and large CSAs. They are certified organic and are members of the Southeastern African American Farmers Organic Network, who sent them to Italy as delegates for Slow Food International's largest food and agriculture conference. They also travel the Southeast attending meetings and conferences for farmers hosted by North Carolina A&T State University and *Minority Landowner* magazine.

"Those conferences help us learn," says Carol, or "Sensei," as she's called by those who know her well enough to know she holds a black belt in jiu-jitsu, "I didn't know anything about farming when I started. Even though my dad farmed, I only knew how to chop [weeds], but I didn't know when to plant or how far apart to plant or nothing like that." Carol and I sit on her floor petting her pitbull Sasha. I've just arrived at her house and after just a few minutes we end up sitting on her floor together, talking for hours. "My dad used to give us a little spot to garden," Carol continues, "and I would plant something following his guidelines. We learned by watching him. But we didn't take over the farm.

"I left here and moved to New York City and taught there for 33 years. I only moved back here after 9/11. At that point, I worked as dean of the school, and I was sitting in my office and someone called me and said a plane had just fallen into the World Trade Center. I looked out the window and I said, 'it didn't fall into it, it flew into it.' Then I looked at the Hudson River and saw another plane and I said, 'oh my God, we're under attack.' That was the second time the World Trade Center had been under attack. So I told them that day I was going to leave the city. I moved back here in 2003.

"I didn't want to just sit in my retirement here. Joyce and I began gardening together, and one day I went to the market with my friend and I saw some goats, and those goats fascinated me. I bought four goats. Didn't even have no place to put them. So my friend put them at his cousin's house, 30 miles from here, and he built me a fence for the goats there. Well, goats have babies very quickly. At one time, I had more than 50 goats. I would sell them for a little bit of money. Then I bought two cows and they had a baby calf. I knew nothing about gestation for cows. I ended up with nine cows at one time. I learned how to take care of them through the Internet and by going to those meetings. Not a cow died, not one. I learned how to trim the goats' feet; I learned what medications to give them for worms; some that got a broken leg, I'd put in the bathtub to heal. I did it all. I kept the cows down on the creek on our family land, but now I-40 runs right through it, and it's not so safe for the cows. So I sold them all, and we started using that land to grow on."

Carol and Joyce have seen the area of their childhood change drastically. They have lived through segregation, the civil rights movement, growing development and climate change, all of which have impacted them and affected their family land. Carol and I wrap up our discussion on her living room floor, and she takes me over to the farm on her family land. As we drive, she reflects on childhood memories of the area.

"We grew up down on Burgaw Creek, where the farm is. There were eight of us, five brothers and three of us sisters. There's been so much that's changed since then, I know that much. This road really used to be a dirt road. Now they have a lot of homes that have been built here. There is still farming that goes on here, but I would say mostly on a large scale now. Sweet potatoes, peanuts, corn, soybeans, blueberries and grapes are grown in this area on a big level. Many people grow grapes for the winery, and you'll find that people have large poultry and pig farms around here. But we used to have little people that grew a lot of stuff. During the '50s, they used to grow a lot of cucumber and squash, zucchini squash and yellow squash, and we used to come down here and pick squash. There were also a lot of dairy farms — see, that was a dairy farm there. But now the little people don't grow. It's the big people that have taken over. The little farmer used to be able to take his five crates of strawberries down to the market and sell them to the trucks that would come in, but that's closed down. Instead, what we have are McDonald's and Kentucky Fried Chicken. They just came here in the last 10–12 years."

We stop off at her sister Joyce's home and pick her up for the ride down to the farm. She is out front in her garden when we pull up. She puts her tools down and gets in, smiling. We continue driving and turn onto the main road lined by brown corn fields. It's April, before planting time, and these fields have been cut and sprayed. We begin talking about the effects of the conventional farms that have taken over the area.

"Look at how that's dead out there," Carol says as she points to the fields, "and they're gonna be planting our food out in that mess. I'd like to see all chemicals done away with, the herbicides and pesticides, and turn to a natural way. Because there's so many people that are dying from diseases and sometimes doctors are not able to determine the causes — I think it's from all these chemicals."

"And people try to say it's not possible to grow without them," Joyce adds, "I just don't believe it. We even have people say that about us. They don't believe

we're growing everything without pesticides. It *is* possible, and I don't think it matters if you're growing one row or 20 rows. You don't have to use pesticides and herbicides."

We pull onto the road that leads us down to the three-acre farm. A freeway, I-40, runs over us on the overpass. "This is the road that we used to have to travel," Carol points out. "We used to walk from our home to high school until they gave us a bus. I guess I might have been in the 6th grade. For the most part, the people that lived down in this area were Black. All these people down here had some form of a garden, but now it's very difficult. When it rains, this whole area is flooded out. And at one time, it wasn't that way."

Carol points to the highway, "That is the famous I-40 that destroyed the whole area," she remarks snidely. "It was built around 1982. They moved our old house and put it on the other side of the road to build I-40. I think they did that with a lot of homes. The highway closed off Burgaw Creek that ran here, and our water runoff went into the creek. My dad had ditches set up into the creek. But now I-40 closed off our drainage, so when it rains, the water just comes back down here and floods. We can't grow as much as we used to because of that. We would produce a lot more and could have a beautiful farm, but when it starts raining there's nothing we can do.

"One year, Joyce and I managed to get everything in the ground, and we had okra early, cucumber early, everything was early and looking good for the season and then, of course, it rained, and it all washed away. We would apply for drainage programs through NRCS or EQUIP but we can't do anything permanent to the land because it's heir property."

Heir property (as briefly discussed in the chapter "Black Land Loss") is basically land that has multiple owners, with each owner unable to make land-use decisions without consent from all the owners.

The land has been passed down to heirs as undivided, fractional ownership interests, and they don't have separate deeds to their ownership nor can they claim specific areas of the land until after it has been sub-divided.

Heir property ownership is often the precursor to land loss and is identified by the Federation of Southern Cooperatives Land Assistance Fund as one of the top reasons for land loss among African

Americans. With each passing generation of heir property owners who die without a will or other estate plan, a new generation of heirs inherits ownership of the land. Typically, each successive generation is larger than the previous one. As a result, the land ownership interests grow smaller, yet the number of interest holders, or co-owners, increases. This results in way too many cooks in the kitchen. With so many co-owners over generations, several typical situations arise: heirs no longer live on or even near the land; heirs don't live near one another; heirs don't even know each other; heirs don't know how to find each other to communicate about the land; heirs don't have a connection to or interest in the land.

This makes it very difficult to get unanimous consent for land use or the construction of permanent structures or alterations to the land (like digging new drainage systems).

"We have been writing letters to our nephews," says Joyce, as we get out of the car at the farm and start getting to work. "We've been asking and asking for their consent on doing what we need to with this land. The land was passed down to the seven of us children, but my sister then passed, and her share went on to her sons. We have been asking them to sign the papers so that we can build our hoop house or divert the water, but they won't sign. We're ready to fly to New York and find them with the papers filled out. It's crazy. This land is rightfully ours, passed down from our mother, and here we are having to ask consent from these boys who have no interest in the land."

"I wish we could encourage young people to farm," Joyce continues with a sigh as she starts planting seeds, "I know my son isn't coming in the field to help us, the youth are not doing that. We tried to get Carol's grandson in the field but he said he didn't want to mess up his shoes. He loves to eat the food, but he sure doesn't like to work for it."

"We like the work," Carol adds as she tinkers over the tiller, "and we don't have anybody helping us. Her son calls us independent Black women, and that's what we are. We're out here enjoying ourselves, and that's what we'll continue to do."

Portrait 4:
A Farm of
Her Own

Nelida Martinez,
Pure Nelida Farms,
Viva Farms,
Skagit Valley,
Washington.

We [Latino farmworkers] are the majority, and we come here and it's a lot of humiliation for us, and many of us never think about having our own farm because we feel degraded by the work. But I didn't want to put up with it anymore.

— Nelida Martinez

ABOUT 3,000 MILES diagonally opposite of Burgaw, North Carolina, in the far northwest corner of Washington state, another fierce and determined woman refuses to let limitations stop her. I drove the miles to Skagit Valley, where migrant farmworkers travel the long miles up from Mexico and the Southwest to find work on the abundant farms spread across this fertile valley. One such worker decided she wanted more for herself, but especially for her children. She left the fields she'd worked since childhood and started a farm of her own.

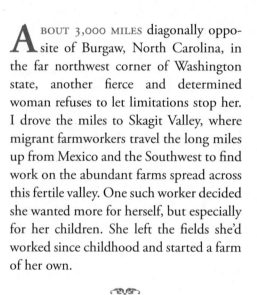

As I drive up through the northwestern region of Washington state, it is raining and gray in late August, bringing the lushness of the Skagit Valley to life. Skagit Valley is named after the Skagit River, which derives its own name from the Native Skagit tribe who called the valley home for thousands of years. Skagit Valley is the richest agricultural area in the Western Hemisphere, with some of the best soil in the world. This is why a diversity of crops are grown, and the economy is hugely impacted by agricultural production. Known for large-scale berry, apple, tulip and dairy farms, the agricultural industry in the valley brings in tens of thousands of migrant workers, primarily from Mexico. Like in many agricultural regions in the U.S., migrant workers face a lot injustice in the fields and have started to protest for better pay and improved working conditions. In fact, while I was in Washington, berry pickers from the Sakuma Brothers Farm, one of the largest berry farms in the state, were on strike, and I listened to the political discussion unfold on NPR as I drove up to the region where Sakuma Brothers operates. Little did I know that the farm I was on my way to visit sat right next to some of their fields and that some of the farmers I was about to meet used to pick for the Sakuma Brothers and now operate their own farms.

As I pull up to the Viva Farms, a farm incubator where small farmers independently operate their own farm businesses on shared land, a large farm stand sits at the corner, drawing in customers from the busy road leading to the highway. Beautiful berries, fruits and vegetables sit on display in this open air market, and the backdrop of the farm boasts rows and rows of the very plants most of the crops came from. The price tags for each product have different farm names scrawled across them, yet the big sign out front reads VIVA FARMS. A handful of people busily work in different sections of the fields while a large truck and a couple guys tinker at the irrigation pumps at the back of the farm. Another team of people are sitting in a trailer at the far end of the farm, sorting through invoices and clacking away on computer keyboards. It's clearly an efficient and busy operation.

A truck pulls in and parks near long rows of raspberries and blackberries. Out hops a little woman with a curly ponytail and a spunky smile you could spot from acres away. Nelida, or La Estrella (the star) as she is nicknamed by many here at the farm, begins working in the rows of berry plants she started by seed. Her delicious berries sell for $3/pint in the farm stand and at market. Across from her berries, tomatillos, jalapeños, lettuce, cabbage and other vegetables grow happily. Everything is dripping and vibrant. I later ask Nelida what her secret is, and she answers, "lots of love and a little compost." She has two acres that she cultivates here, and another two acres of land a few miles away where she grows more. Nelida rents both parcels of land to support her business selling produce and added-value products at local farmers markets. She is a wife and mother of six and says her favorite thing about farming — other than her love for

the plants and fresh air — is working for herself and no one else.

Nelida, a Mixteca native of Oaxaca, Mexico, worked as a berry picker and farm worker from the age of 16. Arriving in the States alone with her three younger brothers after being abandoned by their

alcoholic father and left at an orphanage in Mexico, she found migrant work with large berry and grape farms throughout California, and then Washington. But when her son fell sick, she vowed never to return to where she was forced to work with cancer-causing chemicals. She started her own farm, and now her berry field sits directly across from some of the Sakuma Brothers fields, and she fully understands the cause the berry pickers are fighting for. For her, the problem was not only the wage she was expected to live on while trying to pay for her son's healthcare costs, but more so the environment she was expected to work in and expose her children to.

After Nelida and I are introduced, we sit under the shelter of the washing area on the farm while it drizzles around us. Sarita, the program director at Viva Farms, sits with us to help translate our bilingual conversation. For Nelida, Spanish is a second language, with Mixteca as her first. We sit next to boxes of cucumbers and there are a few flies buzzing around us. But what I feel buzzing in the air is the strength and power radiating off of these two women I sit in a circle with.

"A lot of the farms I worked on," Nelida begins, "would tell us that when we wash our clothes, we shouldn't mix our work clothes with our regular clothes because the chemicals will penetrate our clothes and our children's clothes and will be contaminated. So I really started seeing that the environment where I was working was really bad for us, and it causes us to contract diseases and sickness. They are conscious of what they are putting on those plants and that they're putting us in danger.

"When my son got sick with leukemia, I really started thinking about the chemicals I worked with and how I wanted to have a healthier life for my family. I wanted to grow my own food organically and know where it was coming from and work in a healthy environment. I didn't want to put up with it anymore. Sometimes you just get a knock that makes you realize you need to change your life, and when my son got sick that was my knock, and it caused me to start my own farm."

Of course, starting a farm is not easy. Accessing land and resources is difficult for most beginning farmers, but again, for immigrant farmers or transitioning farm workers the task is far more daunting. Nelida, however, not only had the strength and skills to make her vision a reality, but she also had the opportunity to take advantage of a unique model that gives beginning farmers the head start they need.

Nelida rents two acres at Viva Farms, a farm business incubator on 33 acres of certified organic land. Incubator farms have been cropping up all over the country and can be great ways to provide hands-on learning for new farmers or minimize prohibitive costs for start-up farm businesses. Many incubators provide land, infrastructure and machinery at low rental rates that eliminates some of the most expensive start-up costs for farmers. Viva leases organic land at half the market rate, provides irrigation infrastructure and maintenance, machinery, cold storage, washing facilities and a business center for invoicing and labeling. In an industry that caters to large farm businesses with industrial cold storage warehouses or expensive equipment rental, something as simple as accessible cold storage for the few crates of produce a small farmer needs to chill before delivery, or tractors available on site to rent by the hour, can make that vital difference for survival and success.

Viva also combines their start-up incubator with beginning farmer education. While most of their farmers don't lack in agricultural skill, some need the farm business education. A common trend taking place throughout Skagit Valley and eastern Washington is one where Latino foremen working on farms are taking over family farms they have worked on for decades. Retiring farm owners are handing over the business to farmworkers — who often know the farms better than the owner's children who don't work on the farm, nor have interest in taking over. And while these transitioning farm owners have the agricultural skill and vast production knowledge, they may not have had the opportunity to be in managerial positions and make the business and planning decisions, so the classes help with that.

Viva offers language support in English-dominated markets. They also provide marketing and distribution outlets, such as an on-site market, a CSA, and distribution and delivery to Seattle restaurants and markets, creating a sort of cooperative among the farmers that grow there. Farmers interested in joining the incubator first take the courses taught bilingually by the Viva team at Washington State University (WSU), which cover the nuts and bolts of sustainable farming and farm business planning. They then submit a business plan and get started, with all upfront costs for land, infrastructure and coursework coming to about $5,000.

"We are trying to take the capital needed to start a farm and first reduce it as much as possible and then divide it out into a lease rate so folks can bite it off," says Sarita, the founder of Viva Farms and coordinator of WSU's Latino Farming Program. "It doesn't make farming free, but it makes it low enough that the risk of starting up is manageable. Basically, they can get into farming, and if it doesn't work out, it's not too much skin off their back. And instead of paying off loan debts, they can be saving their income from the farm and setting themselves up to eventually move off site onto their own established farm. Our ultimate goal would be for them to become established enough that they can buy us out if they so choose, taking over this land and developing their own cooperative farm business if that's the direction they want to move. It's about facilitating the goals they've set for their businesses."

When Viva Farms started in 2009, there were six Latino farmers that joined; all of them are still farming here today, in addition to seven more farmers. One couple has now bought their own 13-acre farm after starting at Viva with just an acre. Santiago, another farmer, started with two acres and had a five-year goal of growing to ten acres, which is exactly what he has done. Another couple, who suffered a deportation in their family last year, still have their operation running here and another five acres leased elsewhere. And Nelida, who started out with just a small plot at a community garden in her farmworker

Tomatillos on Nelida's farm.

housing community, found out about Viva and was one of the first farmers to start there.

"I've been farming here at Viva for four or five years," says Nelida with a warm smile, "I was living in the San Jose apartments [a subsidized farmworker housing community] when I met Leah, the childcare coordinator there, and she knew my situation with my son Danny, and she knew that I wanted to create income for my household because my husband was the only one working at the time while I took care of Danny. I told her I needed to do something but wanted it to be something good and healthy this time. She told me about a community garden I could use to grow food and maybe sell at market. I got a plot there and started growing, but after a short time, I already wanted to grow more!

"She connected me with someone who let me use a quarter acre of his land, and I started planting tomatoes, jalapeños, cucumbers and a little of everything. I was growing for my family but also selling a little. I started meeting a lot of people this way at the markets, and I began making enough money to then lease an acre of land to grow more. I started planting strawberries and blueberries and have kept growing little by little. Then I met Sarita and learned about Viva Farms. I started going to the classes and then started growing here. Now I sell my produce and berries here at the Viva farm stand and at farmers markets on Saturdays where I also sell ready-made foods."

Nelida is known as La Estrella because, as Sarita notes, "she is awesome at farmers markets." She makes fresh tortillas, pressing the tortillas and grilling them right there at the market. Customers can buy a stack to go or buy her fresh quesadillas that she makes with squash blossoms, herbs and peppers that she grew. Nelida says, "No soy *tortillera,* I'm not a tortilla maker, I'm a farmer," but she saw the opportunity to harness her culinary skills and the food culture she brings from Oaxaca to create added-value products to sustain her business. She saw that just selling the tomatillos, jalapeños or other crops wouldn't go as far. In a society where many have lost their food culture, this is an added value that farmers like Nelida bring to agriculture.

Nelida's example has prompted Viva Farms to consider adding another aspect to their business incubator: a Seattle-based restaurant where startups can have access to a commercial kitchen while also bringing their culinary skills and farm fresh food to the broader market of Seattle.

"Viva Farms has been so helpful in getting my business started," Nelida says.

"The hardest thing for me is talking with the customers. I can increase my production, but I also need to keep increasing my sales. Viva helps me with that by finding markets and communicating in English. But the best thing is that I have been able to get my business started and now I am self-employed, I don't work for anyone else! Now I want to help others who have been in my same situation get to this point.

"We [Latino farmworkers] are the majority, and we come here and it's a lot of humiliation for us, and many of us never think about having our own farm because we feel degraded by the work. And we don't have the money for land. But it is possible. First there has to be communication about what is possible and what you want to do as a family, talk about your goals. But sometimes you just get that knock, and when you get called to do something, the important thing to remember is that you *can* do it."

In my country we could just walk outside and get whatever food we needed. We wanted to have that again. So we decided to use the land here and grow our own food.

— Sulina

I SET OUT on the road from Washington to Oregon to talk with another fierce farming woman who is proving anything can be done. Over the Washington border near Portland, Oregon, I visit a small Laotian/Hmong family farm led by a strong and humble woman who is defying expectations about what can be grown in Oregon soils and breaking down assumptions about America's family farmers.

☙❧

Sulina of Sulina & Bay's Farm, known for its delicious strawberries and beautiful cut flowers grown organically and sold at Portland markets every weekend, insists that their small family farm is just a hobby. But as I pull up to the ten-acre farm in the agricultural region outside of southeast Portland and see it teeming with vibrant fruits, vegetables and flowers, I see she's just being modest.

Sulina's property is neatly organized with fruit trees, such as Asian pear, fig, persimmon, apple and plum, growing around the house, while the rest of the land is planted in long rows of strawberry and raspberry plants, many varieties of flowers, and just about every vegetable you

can think of, including some you'd never guess could grow here. Her family's garage has been converted into a washing and packing station with stacks of blue-green harvest pints sitting on the shelves. Their tractor sits parked along the side of the house.

"My husband and I never walk out of the house without wearing work boots," Sulina says smiling, as we begin walking around the farm, her clippers in hand and at the ready for the plant or vine in need of a trim as we pass through the rows. "There is always something to be done. You can't just walk outside and not end up working."

Sulina and her husband run the farm with her husband's brother and his family, the Vangs. Both couples and their kids share the work and the income. Running the small farm is a full-time job, with plenty of harvesting and flower arranging to be done each week for market. Yet both families already work full-time jobs.

"I work in production for Leatherman tools," Sulina says as we kneel together in the endless rows of strawberries while she harvests for the day. "We all work at our jobs on swing shift, except for my brother-in-law, who works daytime. So in the morning, we manage the farm until it's time to go to work, then we go to work. This is all we do."

Sulina is also the mother of four, with three of her kids still at home. She and her family continue to work full-time jobs because they don't feel the income from the farm is reliable. "Farmers market income is not dependable," Sulina explains, "sometimes people come to shop, sometimes they come to look. So it is not a dependable income for us." But Sulina and her family continue to grow for the extra income and for the health of their family.

"In Laos, we were farmers," Sulina continues. "We had no income, so basically we grew everything. Everything we ate, we grew. So when we got here, we bought this property and wanted to keep farming a little bit to keep all of us in shape and keep food on the table."

Sulina came to the United States with her parents in 1984. They settled in Fresno, where there is a large Laotian and Hmong community and where agriculture is a big industry. Sulina then met her husband who had been living in the United States since 1980, and together they decided to move to the Portland area and buy some land. They bought this land in 2001.

"In my country," Sulina recalls, "we could just walk outside and get whatever food we needed. We wanted to have that again. So we decided to use the land here and grow our own food. We try to grow things that we use daily, so we can use it

whenever we want, without having to go buy it. It's more fresh. It's also more convenient. We don't have to run to the store for one little green onion."

Sulina also wanted to be able to have food that reminded her of home without having to look for it in the stores. Though many of the plants are best adapted to growing in Laos' tropical climate, Sulina decided anything was possible, and she began planting what she missed most.

When I had first arrived at Sulina's farm, she was a little hesitant to talk to me and kept insisting she didn't have much to share. But now, when I ask her if she's growing anything that reminds her of home, her face brightens and she waves me on to follow her, "Oh I'll show you!" she exclaims excitedly, as she turns to walk toward the back of the property. "I'll show you what I grow that reminds me of home!"

We walk past the raspberry rows and under the soft shade of tall sunflowers on the right. On the left sits an arbor of *chayote,* a Mexican squash known by many names in different parts of the world, including "Buddha's hands" in China because its shape resembles two hands pressed together in prayer. Finally, we pass the unruly vines of large Asian cucumbers to find a thick wall of bamboo, standing tall.

"You know, at home we harvest young bamboo during bamboo season," Sulina points out. "We just go pick bamboo and eat it fresh. So I try to grow a lot here, and in the season when the baby bamboo is growing, we actually come out and harvest it just like at home."

There are more than 1,400 different species of bamboo, and they grow in a variety of climates. Many grow in warmer and tropical climates, and while these tropical bamboo will die at or near freezing temperatures, some of the hardier species can survive temperatures as low as -20 degrees Fahrenheit.

"We also grow these Asian cucumbers," Sulina says pointing back toward the oversized, soft green cucumbers hiding under giant leaves, "we call them *dib hmoob* in my language. They grow even bigger back at home. When we first moved here and the soil was still rich, they would grow that big," she says spreading her hands to the size of a watermelon, "but now we used the soil here for many years, so they don't grow as big.

"We like to make a drink with these cucumbers. We scrape off the seed and use a spoon to scrape the meat and put it in water with ice and sugar. It's called *kua dib* or *dib kaus* and it's *really* refreshing. It reminds us of being back in our country where we work on the farm the whole day, and it's very hot, and we would drink that to cool down, so it always reminds us of home.

"We save our own seeds too. If we lose the seed for this, then we lose our memories of home. So we make sure we keep saving the seed so we can keep having the food we had in Laos. It's important to save seed, to save culture." Sulina continues walking and pointing out other crops from home like Asian squash, pumpkin, and cabbages such as *pakchoi,* as well as Chinese long beans, or yard beans. She takes me through thick rows of corn and peels back their husks to reveal a rich purple-and-white row of corn kernels, an Asian corn called *pob kws quav npua* in Hmong.

"But now," Sulina says with a smile and a twinkle in her eye, "I will show you what I am growing that is totally, totally home." She walks me toward the greenhouse and inside, among rows of lemongrass and a plant similar to the tropical taro, stands a vibrantly healthy cassava tree.

Cassava trees grow primarily in tropical and subtropical regions, and its tuberous, starchy roots, dried to make tapioca, are a great source of carbohydrates. In fact, cassava is the third largest source of food carbohydrates in the tropics, after rice and maize, making it a major staple food in the developing world.[42] But Sulina and her family know the cassava tree, which they call *qos ntoo,* not for its roots, but for its leaves.

"We eat the cassava leaves like a vegetable. Back home we were poor, so this is what we ate. In Laos, meat is for rich people, so if you're poor this is what you end up eating. We steam the leaves or boil them and dip it into a hot sauce made with tomatoes, green onion, peppers, cilantro and fish sauce. This is the thing that *really* reminds us of home. Everybody said I wouldn't be able to grow it here. But here it is," she lovingly strokes the leaves and grins proudly. "Nobody else grows this in this area, as far as I know. It won't make it outside. This variety doesn't have the roots like the cassava at home though. It isn't warm enough to grow that one, so we grow it for the leaves."

Sulina doesn't add anything to her tropical plants to get them to grow, nor does she add much to the soil. She simply keeps them protected and warm in the greenhouse, and maybe gives them extra love. She's all about "keeping it natural," and even has a laid-back attitude toward pest control.

"It is important to us to know that our own produce is safe to eat," Sulina says, as we continue out of the greenhouse and down the first of many rows of her famous strawberries. "We would see what's in the markets and wonder why the products are never perishable. Our products are very perishable because they are natural and not sprayed. That's the main point is trying to avoid all the chemicals. We don't spray for pests, and we only use fertilizer when we have to. We use organic fish fertilizer.

"We actually don't get a lot of pests, and when we do, we let the bugs eat. We just pick the good ones and let the bugs have the others. I've always said, 'you either eat with the bugs, or you die with the bugs.' Whatever you spray to kill them may eventually kill you too. So we choose to eat with the bugs."

Many organic and sustainable farmers grow with this philosophy of "no spray" and use Integrated Pest Management (IPM) techniques instead. This is basically a fancy way of describing common sense, natural approaches to deterring bugs. These techniques range from focusing on growing a healthier plant which will use its own biology to resist pests, to planting unique crops nearby that deter or divert certain pests, such as marigold for the tomato horn worm, horseradish for potato bugs, or nasturtium for squash beetles. There are also many non-toxic or even homemade chemicals used in IPM, such as pepper spray, garlic spray or Neem oil, which comes from the Neem tree in India.

Sulina & Bay's Farm is not certified organic, but they let their customers know that they don't spray and everything is naturally grown. For their regular customers, which I saw they have many of when I visited them at the Lents International Farmers Market in southeast Portland that weekend, that knowledge and the healthy produce they find each week is enough. For other customers, there is a sense of disbelief, beyond awe and inching toward insulting.

Sulina with cassava tree.

"People always ask what I use for spray," Sulina recounts as we stand now among her rows of beautiful golden raspberries, "and I tell them I've been growing berries for many years and I don't know about any spray, I just don't use anything. And they don't believe me. They think it's impossible to have such big, healthy berries, especially the strawberries this time of the season [the end of August]. One woman kept saying the strawberries must be from California, so I told her to come to the farm and see them for herself. She came, and she was embarrassed and apologized. But some customers can't believe it, and they don't even talk to me, so they don't want to buy it."

Such assumptions about what small farmers are capable of producing can be detrimental to their business; while the initial disbelief can be taken as a compliment, a conclusive disbelief about their growing practices can be taken as an insult. Particularly because it lends itself to a sense of distrust. This is what small farmers are up against. There's a general assumption and lack of consumer knowledge about what is possible in sustainable agriculture — a distrust of anything that competes and even exceeds the perfection of the conventionally and commercially grown, because it is the same, if not better, quality without any of the same inputs.

And for small farmers of color, the distrust may be even greater. While Sulina was telling a story of overhearing customers at market — customers who wouldn't even stop and simply ask her whether she grew the food or whether she sprays and take her word for it — I couldn't help but think about the parallel issue Cynthia raised in the "Transforming the South" chapter, where Black farmers trying to sell their organic produce at market were getting a lot of distrust without the certified organic sticker.

Maybe with an immigrant family behind the table at market, there are assumptions about what their role is on the farm, and those assumptions lead to decisions about whether or not to communicate with them. Racial stereotypes dominate, instead of clearly seeing: this is simply another family farm in America defying the odds and growing delicious and healthy food for their community.

Part 6:
Generation Rising

 Radical simply means grasping things at the root.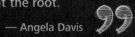

— Angela Davis

THIS GENERATION — my generation — labeled as "millennials," labeled as "entitled and lazy," are the huge group of young people born anywhere between the early 1980s and the 2000s. With an equally huge number of articles out there describing us, we are apparently not only entitled and lazy, but self-centered and slow to cut the cord from our parents.

Yet, we're also being touted as the change-makers, the more open-minded, tolerant and tech savvy generation, stirring up political revolutions and starting million-dollar social media companies. We're a rainbow of colors and ethnicities, orientations and identities — finally fusing together, as if to heal the mistakes of our ancestors' past.

We may be slow to figure out our paths, but I'd like to think it's because we want that path to be legendary. We want to do something different than the generation before us — something meaningful, something that speaks to our diversity of identities and builds on our values. And our values are often based on being true to ourselves and correcting the wrongs of the generations before us. We carry the responsibility of fixing the broken planet our parents and grandparents have left us, and we must spread awareness about the toxic foods the system has been feeding us. We carry the task of transforming the unjust perspectives and governing philosophies society has held for so long. We carry the revolution.

So, how is picking up a plow and stepping into one of the oldest trades known to man revolutionary? Because, this generation recognizes the power of how something as old as subsistence can be a tool for resistance. Unlike generations before us, this generation is trying to learn and heal from the past with a dedication to pass our knowledge on to the next generation in a new way. We are serving as bridges for real change.

Looking back at the degradation of our environment and how industry and corporate greed has led us to a broken system, many young people today are looking to not make the same mistakes. We're looking for a healthy alternative, and we're looking at the dirt right underneath our feet. I've met hundreds of young farmers whose reasons for picking up the pitchfork are strictly out of environmental concerns or maybe because they want a healthy *spiritual* environment, one with an office among the plants and in the sunshine instead of in a dark cubicle.

But particularly for young people of color farming, our motivations go beyond fixing a broken food system and an ailing planet. We are finding our cultural identities through food. And we're using food and agriculture to preserve that identity. We're liberating our communities from oppressive and unjust systems. We're healing from that oppression and healing from the toxic foods and environment by bringing back our ancestors' foods and stewardship practices — honoring the legacies they left us.

Young farmers of color are unearthing holistic ways of life in our heritage, sustainable farming practices, and cultural food traditions that, when applied today, are the very solutions to the broken system we're all looking to fix. We are rebuilding our grandfathers' farmer cooperatives, keeping our elders' foodways alive, and re-thinking land ownership based on models that existed pre-colonization. We are finding our voices in this movement and carrying on the voices of those who came before us who were historically unheard.

Young urban farmers and food activists of color are also speaking up for the unheard by addressing food insecurity in our neighborhoods and injustice in our community food systems. Like the women mentioned earlier, young farmers are leading the way in using food and agriculture as tools to build and feed community, but these young farmers are also using food as a tool for justice. This generation is not just inventing social media apps, we're creating innovative food businesses and bringing back revolutionary agricultural movements to ensure food access and fight for control over our food. Some of us recognize that these practices never left, and we're sitting at the knees of our elders to relearn these valuable skills. Others are also learning from what hasn't worked in the past and adding in their own brilliant, radical philosophies and concepts for change.

With such a beautiful picture of vibrant young people flocking to farms, holding up old traditions and feeding and empowering community, it's hard to be anything but optimistic about the future.

But this would be a narrow, deceptive view of the possibilities within our flawed system. While in some states there has been a rise in young farmers over the past decade, it remains that over a third of the national farming population is 65 or older, with half retiring in this next decade.[43] And according to the USDA Census, only five percent of principal farm operators are under the age of 35.

There are many huge obstacles in the way for young people who want to run their own farms. Finding and purchasing land, as well as coming up with the hefty capital to get started, is the first hurdle. In the heart of agriculture in the Midwest, farmland prices have soared to almost $15,000 an acre for top-quality land that sold at just $1,900 an acre ten years ago.[44] Keeping urban land for farming and spaces for community building is also at risk due to the gentrification and development that prices people out of their neighborhoods, particularly people of color. Facing this and the other soaring costs in today's economy, plus the weight of student loans for young people, the lack of job security or income in agriculture and community empowerment work, as well as a system still rife with discrimination and inequities, this generation has seemingly impossibly steep hurdles to overcome.

But that's where our ingenuity, radicalism and determination are proving to be helpful. This generation is bridging old models of cooperative ownership with new models of cooperative investment along with social media like crowd-source funding to get farms going and expand outreach. We're bringing old mobile farm distribution into new foodie trends to boost market reach for small farmers through such means as mobile food markets and farm-to-food trucks. We're giving a whole new meaning to *farm to table* by fusing our culinary and agricultural heritage together for food businesses that are both authentic and new. We are taking farmer training courses or getting started on incubator farms — unique programs for beginning farmers that young farmers themselves are creating in some cases. Young farmers are also starting associations to band together and pool resources, knowledge and skills. We're coming up with ways to connect landless beginning farmers to retiring farmers with land. And we're leading policy advocacy programs to change the system for beginning farmers.

This generation is also involving the next generation of our communities in the movement and on the farm. Youth educational farms are sprouting up nationwide and have been some of my favorite farms to visit. But young farmers of color are using farm education as a way to pass on the tools to fight for justice; we are cultivating empowerment and education based on values. This generation is adamant about educating the next generation in alternative and transformative ways and looking to our ancestors and elders as our best teachers.

We refuse to settle for anything less than transformation and what we think is just.

My hope is that this willpower, along with serving as the bridge between our past and our future, will truly revolutionize not only the food system, but the way we live on this planet.

Tahz Walker, 37 (at time of photo) and Cristina Rivera-Chapman, 32 (at time of photo) Tierra Negra Farms, Durham, North Carolina.

> Vivette, my friend and elder, has really pushed me to understand that the earth beneath our feet is the dust of the bones of our ancestors. It's really important to us to understand that there are people that have their people beneath our feet. It's not light work.
>
> — Cristina Rivera-Chapman

MY FIRST STOP VISITING with young farmers is with a couple who is bridging the gap between themselves and their ancestors by building connections with their elders and passing on their knowledge to the youth of their community.

~※~

I had heard a lot about Cristina and Tahz of Tierra Negra Farms in North Carolina. All the way up in New York City they were well known among young food-movement activists and urban gardeners there. So as I pull up the long driveway to the land they are renting outside of Durham, I am excited to finally meet them. A white and tan Catahoula, a beautiful dog bred for wild boar hunting in Louisiana, trots up to greet me as Lucille rolls to a stop in front of a shimmering pond next to their gardens.

Tahz looks up from his work tinkering under the hood of a car, and Cristina emerges from the cabin with a warm smile on her face. I hadn't realized until that moment how much comfort it gives me to be with farmers of my generation. I have immensely enjoyed my time with elders so far on this trip, but there is a different energy of solidarity that I feel as soon as I am in the company of Tahz and Cristina.

They welcome me into their home, and we talk like old friends into the night over a dinner of lentils and kale. I get to know them and how they came into farming as well as their experiences as people of color in agriculture. Cristina shared her memories of growing up racially ambiguous in the eyes of the White, liberal community she lived in outside of Boston where her mother's Chilean culture stood apart, and she always felt being "other" was part of her identity. Tahz reflected on his days growing up exploring the woods north of Atlanta and often being the only person of color in the nature camps and farms he worked on.

"I spent a lot of time in nature and lived in a lot of rural areas in north Georgia," Tahz reflects in his steady, gentle voice. "There were definitely some aspects of racism that weren't subtle. Where it was like, 'you're not supposed to be out here.' And you know, there is a lot of that fear that's been put out there that mountains and rural areas aren't for us. But I'm like, 'this is mine as much as it is yours, I'm still gonna come out here. My people have been here just as long as your people have.' So it's helpful for me to know my place in this and that I'm connected to this land."

Tahz's family is from the Black Belt of Kentucky; his grandparents had a farm there, and his great grandparents were sharecroppers. His genealogy research about the agricultural legacy in his family, as well as his affinity for nature and desire to save money by growing his own food, is what led him to farming.

Cristina, however, would say she completely stumbled into farming at the age of 22. While waiting tables at night to pay off college loans, she was looking for daytime work when she answered an ad looking for help at a family farm. As a self-described "apathetic young person who hated any food that wasn't candy," farming was the last thing Cristina saw herself doing.

"It was just so transformative on so many levels," Cristina recalls pensively, "but the most basic level was that I was eating vegetables — that had not happened before. I also really fell in love with the feelings that I had from farming: I physically felt good, I emotionally felt good, I felt like I was making a difference — and it was real and not theoretical. It helped me understand systems in a way that felt empowering. Growing up, all of our systems seemed oppressive and as if there was nothing I could do about it. But there was something about being part of a natural system and seeing that my little part mattered that I hadn't experienced before I started farming, so I just chased that feeling."

Cristina wanted to share that feeling, particularly with younger people. She and Tahz are now both educators as well as farmers. Together, their experience in teaching workshops has ranged from therapeutic drumming to sustainable farming to revolutionizing the food system. The next morning I accompany Cristina to her off-farm job educating youth at SWARM (Students Working for an Agricultural Revolutionary Movement), a non-profit based in Goldsboro, North Carolina. After spending the day with her and the youth there, Cristina strikes me as a brilliant educator who cares deeply about cultivating thought and independence and making space for understanding perspectives.

"I wanted to work in the garden with people who grew up like me," Cristina explains, "and didn't necessarily have a connection to land or growing food, and thought of dirt as something that you wash off of you and not something you put your hands in. The little ones, they would get magical revelations about growing food. Just digging in the dirt and eating new things would blow their minds, it was so powerful. To question where our food comes from, to question where anything comes from, like our history books or authority, I wished I'd had that in my pocket as a seven year old. It's about food, but it's also about deep change."

Cristina first started working in the garden as an educator in Brooklyn and then began developing curriculum for an urban farm non-profit in Red Hook where she worked with youth for five years.

Youth cooking class at SWARM.

(I happened to have volunteered at the same farm and wrote a controversial piece about their food justice principles for *Grist* magazine in 2010. We found out while standing in Cristina's kitchen that the letter of thanks I'd received for raising the issues had been from her — after she'd left there due to the same concerns.)

"There's a real problematic dynamic in a lot of urban farm non-profits," says Cristina as we start the long drive back to Durham at the end of the day with SWARM. "One of them concerns the support of youth in the ways they really need it. It was a readily vocalized concern at the farm in Red Hook. The youth age out of the program and are left in the dirt without enough in their toolbox to support all the transformation that needs to happen. I hear from youth and they say, 'we need jobs.' They are really passionate about wanting to transform the food system, but they also need to bring resources into their own homes. A huge factor in whether or not they are able to commit the time that they do is if they are paid. There are a lot of youth of color involved in farming here, but it's through non-profit organizations who are giving the staff positions and paid jobs to mainly White constituency. So a lot of these youth are being targeted for the grants but not targeted later for the positions."

"I get organizations' need to fill a position based on job qualifications," Cristina continues, "but I think it's important, especially in this work, to prioritize someone's lived experience as a job qualification or quality you're looking for. Computer skills or the skill to articulate in a grant format are the easy skills you can learn, but the lived identity stuff is priceless. We need to be supporting young people, especially young people of color and working-class young people coming into their own identity of feeling like 'I'm knowledgeable; I'm supposed to be here'; or, 'I'm vocalizing something that's important.'"

Cristina and Tahz are interested in ways of working with youth to figure out a partnership that creates a job cooperative of sorts, where they can have their finger on the pulse of what the paying gigs are for youth. They also plan to continue their educational workshops along with their farm business. However, their own obstacles as young, landless farmers of color have put them into a perpetual cycle of transition and struggle.

After Cristina and I return to the farm from Goldsboro, we meet Tahz and all jump back in the car together to drive to an event in Mebane, North Carolina. Tahz and Cristina both have an off-farm job there. Together they generate their main income off-farm while they work toward securing permanent land for Tierra Negra Farms. Until then, they feel like they can't expand their farm and so have to diversify their streams of income.

"We started Tierra Negra Farms in Mebane in 2009," Tahz explains as we drive toward Mebane. "We wanted really to try on our own, not as a non-profit organization, to form a model of community food sovereignty, just by testing things out on a small scale. We're trying to figure out what makes the most sense for our survival while still getting food to folks who need it. We started with a food share that we called *Grains and Greens.* We had weekly shares of our vegetables and baked goods from our friend's home bakery. We structured the food share after we polled people to see what they would want and how much they paid for groceries. But by the end of the season, due to underpricing our produce in order to have prices our customers could afford and being too far from the city to have a viable work trade, we didn't break even, not even close. We even had to hustle and clear out sheds and sell equipment just to buy seed.

"The next year we got a grant to purchase a greenhouse, and we decided to grow seedlings and teach about gardening and food systems and sustainable farming practices. We wanted to promote backyard gardening, and we saw a niche for organic seedlings. Also, just to put the sovereignty into food sovereignty, we wanted to sell seedlings to folks to grow their own food, and those sales helped offset the cost of the food share a little bit. We sold to schools and individuals and some organizations. Things were going great. But then we had to move off of the land we were renting. While we're now in this awesome place closer to Durham, it's still not our own. So it's hard to think about the sustainability of our farm without land security."

Land security is a big issue for young farmers. With more than half of all U.S. farmland owned by farmers 55 and over, and farmland disappearing with development or prices increasing beyond affordability for new farmers, many are forced to rent.[45] Young and beginning farmers have the highest rates of leasing farmland, with the majority of acres in operation by farmers under 35 consisting of rented acres.[46] This provides no security for a business invested in literally putting down roots. Lack of land security for such a business results in job insecurity. According to a report by the National Young Farmers Coalition, 73 percent of young farmers surveyed rely on off-farm income to make ends meet.[47]

"We keep running into this wall," Cristina adds. "It's hard to ignore the fact that we need our own land. We need land to invest in for the next generations. We need to be able to put up structures and not have to walk away from them and start over each time. I think for both of us, but

maybe more so for Tahz, who has been farming a little longer, there's a certain amount of heartbreak to keep investing time and energy into the soil and have to start over again somewhere else the next year. We don't even know if we'll still be on the land we're on now this time next year. That doesn't feel very powerful.

"Also, it takes time to build up soil. We're reclaiming and renewing land; we add value to the land we work. Landowners should be paying us, if anything! At this point, for me, it's been eight different pieces of land I've worked, and Tahz, his family is coming from lines of sharecroppers, and he can't repeat that. It's all about who owns the land. All these new initiatives we are trying in this movement don't shift power unless we shift who owns the land."

"I think it's critical," Tahz adds, "especially in the South, with what's going on with Black land loss, for folks to figure out how to stay on their land. There's this weird cycle where folks are on land and it's a working farm, but once the farmer ages out, the rest of the family cashes out. There's gotta be a way to think of stewardship beyond just one or two generations. I think the ancestors who were securing land at the time of the turn of the century were trying to avoid that. I think they were thinking really broad. They were thinking about their kids and their grandkids and those kids' kids."

"I think that's what families need to be doing," Cristina says, "figuring out some ways that we can take care of ourselves as families and think long term and not be pushed apart because we gotta go chase the buck. Sometimes we have no other choice. I think about how as a society we're forcing our next generations to choose between saving the land or being able to retire when they get older or feed their children. That's what we're seeing families here having to decide between. They just can't afford to continue living and keep their land. It's messed up.

"I think working within the framework of money and capitalism — which we know is all about explicitly trying to screw one group over another — when we talk about land ownership is always going to give us that result. One family's loss over another. It's how the system pits us against each other. So why am I trying to think about land in those terms? So that the system can gain and we lose? There's part of me that's like, why should we even be *buying* land? I'm entitled to it. If it's owned by the U.S., that's me, it's ours; this land should be all of ours. It can be a collective ownership. I'm not saying I'm ready to squat or overtake land, but I want to think beyond the current framework because it seems like that's where the solution will be. But here we are, fighting the system and at the same time trying to work within it."

Tahz and Cristina are looking into how to own land communally with a group of fellow young people of color also interested in land stewardship or simply obtaining land security for their families. Tahz found a lack of organizations in Durham that focus on connecting young Black farmers

to available land. (Although there are powerful organizations in Durham helping farmers of color *keep* their land, such as the Land Loss Prevention Project, which was founded in 1982 by the North Carolina Association of Black Lawyers to curtail epidemic losses of Black-owned land throughout the state. They now provide legal support and assistance to *all* financially distressed and limited-resource farmers and landowners in North Carolina.) So he started his own elaborate letter-writing campaign to absentee landowners found through county tax records. He is meeting with lawyers to map out the legal logistics of how to own land communally. And their group (who also meet for what they call "Just Us" dinners, which provide a safe space for people of color in their community to share their ideas and grow their work) is being advised by local Indigenous elders who Tahz and Cristina have formed friendships with over the years.

"Our friend Vivette, who is a member of the Occaneechi Band of the Saponi Nation," Tahz says, "lives here and can trace her family back to the 1600s, and she's going to help us frame some of the conversation as far as remembering what communal models have already existed. I think because of what Cristina was talking about with the current models of land ownership, we need to reach out to models that existed pre-colonization. I think that's where solutions are. In some ways it's intimidating because there's really no systemic support for that now, but we know that there are systems that existed before this system. And Vivette is teaching us to tap into that ancestor database and realize that we have support in the room, and we don't have to disregard our ancestors when having these conversations about communal land and stewardship."

"Another elder mentor, Elwood, who is Black and Occaneechi, has passed on many different skills to me," Tahz continues, "and when I ask him about his identity with the land he always talks about the elders. It's like he forgot the question and just mentions the elders. But it's just a different type of relationship to land; there's no disconnection between thinking about land and elders. Our ancestors are synonymous with the soil. So I think we have to start connecting with what they would have wanted and what they would have done and our relationship as humans to the Earth. It's a tough concept though, and this culture doesn't value that at all; for my generation it's like, 'when's the next iPhone coming out?' But the value of land goes beyond this individual generation. It's about honoring people even if they're not here."

"And it's also about honoring those we still have here with us," Cristina adds, "our elders and our family members who have gifts and talents that could be supportive, not just in getting on or staying on land, but for the whole picture of survival. If we all utilized each other's gifts and talents as a family, it might make it easier to survive and stay on your land and do what you need to do to be in the world. I think it's important to find ways to have conversations as family about that kind of

collective, long-term survival. That could then spread to build strong communities.

"If we used our collective skills and talents as forms of trade within communities, think about how vibrant and dynamic the community could be. Like the one we work in now, where we are working toward structures to share resources like our toolshare program, or where we are creating child care for others to be able to do their thing, or trading food for gardening. Systems like that feel more compelling to me. I'm not interested in everyone becoming farmers. It's more about how to make a cooperative economy that's dynamic enough to support what everyone needs to do. That may not eliminate the need for money, but it would try and offset it as much as possible. Again, for me, it feels like money is the trap."

"And those communal trade systems are already there," says Tahz, "we don't have to invent anything. These systems have been laid out by our ancestors, and they might still exist in some communities, but it wasn't that long ago when they existed widely. I remember talking with an elder farmer who told me about his experiences of always farming in different places, and I was confused because I knew he had his own farm. But then I started to understand that this was what farming looked like then — it was just communal. It was like building community was just what you did 'cause there was no way that you alone could do what needed to be done on the farm. So there was constantly a sharing of resources. This farmer told me about how when they would process corn, they would start on one farm and then for a whole day they would move from farm to farm to farm, and whoever's house they landed at by the end of the day would feed everyone. That was all encapsulated as farming. It's just what it meant to be a farmer. It meant you worked with your neighbors and you could call on them."

As we arrive in Mebane, Tahz and Cristina tell me the land here is Occaneechi land. The Occaneechi Band is a lineal descendant of the Saponi Nation and related Indigenous peoples who occupied the Piedmont of North Carolina and Virginia in pre-contact times. Tribes from the region formed a confederation after settlers arrived, and the confederation included the Saponi proper, the Occaneechi, the Eno, the Tutelo, and elements of other related communities such as the Cheraw. All of these communities are descendants of the much larger Siouan communities that lived in North Carolina and Virginia in prehistoric times. The Occaneechi Band consists of those that remained in the area after most tribal members fled north during 18th-century warfare. Today the Occaneechi live primarily in Orange, Alamance, and Caswell Counties, North Carolina, and in 1984 they petitioned the State of North Carolina to be accepted as a recognized tribe. In 2004, the Occaneechi Band of the Saponi Nation became North Carolina's eighth recognized Native American tribe. The Occaneechi operate a tribal office in Mebane and own sacred land in the Pleasant Grove Township of North Carolina, where many of the 950 tribal members live.

We walk across the lawn of the house and enter the event. After we eat and folks gather to catch up with each other, I head outside to walk the property alone, thinking about those who walked this same land before it was lost to them. I find myself drawn to a beautiful pecan tree with a wooden swing hanging from its strong, bowing limb. I swing under the tree as the sun dips down and think hard about my own ancestors and wonder how my generation — our generation — can bridge the gap that lies between our ancestors, our elders, ourselves and our youth. How can we move forward collectively to transform systems as such a large intergenerational group? It's hard enough moving forward on small projects with small groups. I know my experience in communal farming, progressive organizing, and attempts at communal living has jaded me against collectivity on some levels. But in my heart I know that strong communities are the answer, not only to transforming our food system, but to changing all of our systems.

Communal work, however, is not easy. Consensus is hard to reach, particularly when dealing with a diverse group who carry a variety of perspectives and lived experiences. On the way home, I ask Tahz and Cristina more about their group working toward owning land together and their experiences as young food activists working to build community intergenerationally.

"Well, the intergenerational piece is significant," answers Tahz. "The eldership

I have here, particularly with elder farmers of color, is what has kept me here, because I've never had that before. But outside of those relationships, it feels really disconnected between generations doing this work here in North Carolina. There's a lot of older kind of activists and farmers and landowners, but I don't know how much they're connected with the younger urban areas. I even felt that at the Black Farmers Conference I went to in New York, it was missing that connection to what folks are doing in urban areas or what's hot for young people to get them involved and keep them excited. And the rural elder farmers that came up mentioned the same disconnect from the urban youth. So I think that's something that feels like a big gap."

"Also taking the time to build relationships across the group," adds Cristina. "Working toward consensus is a slow process, what we have to remember is that this shit takes time. Transforming systems, building community, it doesn't happen overnight. Taking the time to first build trust really makes the difference. I think that's one of the reasons why I love our Just Us dinners, because it isn't about getting together to work on some crazy big project. The crazy big project is getting to know each other, relationship-building and building trust. For me that is huge, and I think it's undervalued. If you don't trust, then pursuing consensus gets overshadowed by the distrust.

"I feel like that's where also a lot of the healing work is really important too.

Especially for people of color around land and farming, which has historically been incredibly oppressive, and there's deep family history in that. Joining a community of farmers or a community garden project with a diverse group of people and not acknowledging the internalized oppression and racism that folks are carrying is absurd. Sometimes we don't even realize we're carrying it and that it got passed down. Even when we're fighting against it, we still pass it down if we're not doing the processing. It's not something you can check off a list. There aren't road maps; it's different for different people. My experience farming is not the same as someone who is sitting on a trust fund doing it or someone who is African American and two generations removed from farming, or someone who has migrated here to farm so they can keep the land in their country. It's just not the same, and it's not always about us in this lifetime; we're carrying things passed down to us. So we have to be explicitly processing that and recognizing that we're all carrying generational distrust and exploitation and hurt, which is why there might be distrust today in the group."

"I think another thing we try to do in our group," Tahz says, "is support multi-visions instead of just one homogenous vision. I think that's where things have broken down in the past. Groups get stuck on pushing one vision, and it breaks down because some people don't want to do all that. They just want to grow food or have space to organize their own programs, or they just want to take care of their family.

When you're working toward consensus for one homogenous vision, I think that's where it gets scary because you have to trust this person to hold your vision in mind."

"It's also important that it's the right solutions," Cristina adds, "and if it's right, then it will work out, but it has to come from the larger community — we have to be careful about getting too insular and too exclusive. Neither of us is interested in communes. Because your world gets too small. We've shied away from being at group meetings about all different things every day of the week, and it's always the same people. It's like, I go to your fundraiser to give you money that you just gave me at my fundraiser. We need to make sure we're not getting sleepy."

I feel charged with inspiration by how awake and conscious Cristina and Tahz are to the issues facing their generation in this movement. How cautiously they step and critically they think about their own actions and processes on this journey toward building food sovereignty as a community.

Their profound insights and beautiful energy stay with me as I say my good-byes and leave the next morning. I carry their charge with me on my way to interview two elder women farming on North Carolina's coast. I keep a feeling of hopeful and determined responsibility as a member of this generation tasked with the duty to honor and gather answers from the wise who came before us, while guiding and supporting those to come after us.

Portrait 2:

Breaking

Down

Borders

Borders are the oppressive scars of history, greed and power.

— Anonymous

L ATER IN THE TRIP, I end up in the Southwest, near the Mexican border, where I meet with several young farmers and activists who are also serving as bridges between generations and doing it while bridging two nations. Their stories stand separately as students, educators, non-profit directors or beginning farmers in their own unique identities, yet they also run parallel in many ways, including a tie to the Southwest and Mexico, so they are woven together in this chapter.

❦

I'm sitting at a community center in Austin talking with Kandace Vallejo, a 2012 Food and Community Fellow with Kellogg's Institute for Agriculture and Trade Policy (IATP). She is 28 years old and works as the youth educational program coordinator at Proyecto Defensa Laboral (Workers Defense Project), a labor rights non-profit and community center in Austin's Latino immigrant community. Kandace identifies as half-Mexican, or Chicana, and she tells me the Mexican population makes up about 80 percent of Austin's immigrant community. Kandace comes from a worker justice organizing background, which led her to working with the well-known Coalition of Immokalee Workers (CIW), a powerful coalition of immigrant farmworkers putting pressure on the food industry for worker justice. However, her experience with them led her to food justice work, as she saw the impact of growing food, building relationships with farmers, and addressing racial injustice.

"I started to learn a little bit more about how our economic system is affected by

Kandace Vallejo, 28, Austin, TX.

capitalism," Kandace explains as she reflects on her time with CIW, "and how it is basically built on the exploitation of predominantly people of color and people from the Global South. I started to see how that started with the slave trade and imperialism and still continues today with the imperialistic trade policies we have in place which cause the migration of people here to power our capitalistic food system."

Kandace teaches justice to the youth of the labor organization's members by using food as a tool. "Working with CIW was kind of a process of self-discovery for me," Kandace continues, "and I learned a lot more about who I was in the world and where my family comes from and those cultural and food-based traditions that I had lost over the years through my mother's migration and assimilation. Because food touches so many parts of culture and so many different parts of our economic system in so many ways, it's a way to use something really concrete and expand and be able to talk about all kinds of other things. I often say that food for me is not the issue, that justice is the issue and food is a tool to be able to teach about that.

"There are a lot of projects out there that are working with youth around different kinds of food issues," Kandace continues, "a lot of stuff around nutrition and teaching kids agriculture. But I think a lot of times, those programs tend to run in a political vacuum where there's not really a justice-oriented lens placed on the program itself, and there's not really an arc toward talking about some of those issues

and contextualizing them. So I think that is really where the crux of the issues lies for me. Here, we do talk about food and health and nutrition and we do gardening, but we focus on what is really at the root of all the issues — justice. We talk about what justice looks like, and we do that in a variety of ways through food."

Kandace tells me about some of the curriculum she's implemented with youth from ages five through college age. Being that most of the youth are the children of the community of Latino laborers utilizing the center, they talk about things like why there is a prevalence of nutrition-related diseases and illnesses in the Latino community and other communities of color. Kandace even has the students locate where those communities are and go into the neighborhood, looking at where there are different food access points, looking at convenience stores versus healthy food stores, and also looking at the housing and the cars and what all the material property values in those different areas look like. They take pictures and bring them back and analyze them, always looking with an eye toward what is shaping the reality that the kids live in. All of that makes it possible for them to start talking about issues of economic justice as well. They look at the ways in which corporations decide where to put grocery stores, how they advertise, who they target when they advertise. Kandace mentioned a class where they looked at the prevalence of "Hip Hop-themed" McDonald's ads and how the kids figured out who was being targeted.

"This youth education and empowerment program has three different goals," Kandace explains. "First, to develop the skills and abilities of young people to be leaders in their communities. Second, to make it possible for these kids to self-actualize later on in life, so name and self-determine what their options in life really are. And third, is academic support to make those other two things possible, and we do that in a variety of ways through mentoring and helping them out with their homework, all kinds of activities that help facilitate that knowledge. So really for us it's more about giving a values-based education that cultivates certain kinds of values as opposed to didactically teaching about all kinds of issues."

Kandace seems deeply dedicated to education. Her focus is not traditional education, but transformational education. She just finished her Master's at the University of Texas-Austin in Education and Cultural Studies, where her thesis focused on theories of education and how education can be used to develop leaders and propel transformative change. She looked at injustice, the history of social movements and how education can be used as a tool for liberation.

Kandace's vision for the future is to build a school that is a movement-based, educational leadership development institution that is serious about developing the next generation of civil rights leaders for the immigrant community, and using food and agriculture as tools to teach about justice. Her vision was inspired by

her time studying with the Movimento dos Trabalhadores Rurais Sem Terra/MST (Rural Landless Workers Movement) in Brazil who have their own movement-based schools. And because the organization is now almost 30 years old, she saw how a lot of children who were brought up through their movement schools have come back to be the teachers for the movement.

It was there that Kandace began to understand how change is made and activism is sustained. She's carrying that torch forward, learning from leaders before her and cultivating our next generation of leaders. (Note: Kandace now does multicultural consulting work for labor organizations fighting for justice in New York.)

❧

I have just trekked across the state of Texas with Lucille chugging along in the blistering, dry heat of June to find myself in El Paso, the highly militarized border town where tensions are high, migrant workers cross in daily to find work, and many long-time residents have grown up feeling a part of both countries. Residents like 27-year-old Ivon Diaz, who was raised in El Paso, Texas, frequently visited her family's hometown of Ciudad Juárez, Mexico, just over the border. She talks about working toward food sovereignty and wanting to dedicate her work to her community, while dealing with the serious pressures of living on the border.

"I've always been interested in farming," Ivon says as we sit in the shade outside of El Centro de Trabajadores Agrícolas

Fronterizos (The Border Agricultural Workers Center, discussed in "Forced Migration" in Section Two), "Ever since I was a little girl I have loved the idea of it. My dad has an acre in Nombre de Dios Durango in Mexico, and we would go there in the summers, and I remember it has a little acequia running through the back.[48] And I just got a kick out of having to water and wait 'till an area was filled up before going to open up another little path. I think that is what really did it for me." Ivon laughs a sweet laugh reflecting on the simple start of her affinity with farming.

Ivon and I sit outside of El Centro where she volunteers and is part of *El Instituto,* a leadership program at the Center started by the younger volunteers to bridge the generational divide between the *campesinos* (ag workers), the elders, and the young volunteers. Ivon is studying for her Master's at New Mexico State University where she is focused on ag education. She is also a farm student with the AFSC (American Friends Service Committee) Farmer Training Program in New Mexico where she hopes to learn skills that she can bring back to her community and share in the urban gardening work with the *campesinos* at the Center.

"We are trying to get land here for El Centro," Ivon explains, "through the collaboration we have with La Mujer Obrera, a community-based organization in the Chamizal area of El Paso, and another group called AYUDA, located in San Elizario, Texas, we are raising funds and

looking for land. We want something concrete; we don't want to work something for a year and have it taken away from us. For now, we have the raised beds garden here, which we've been doing with the *campesinos* for a few months. And whatever I learn in the farm training, I bring it back here. But the *campesinos* don't always come out — they work a lot of hours and they are tired. I'm stretching myself

Ivon Diaz, 27 (at time of photo), El Paso, TX.

thin too. I keep taking on more and more projects, maybe to escape the pressures of living here on the border. But the more I do this work, where there is not much money, if at all, the harder it is to ignore those pressures."

At this point, Ivon becomes overwhelmed with emotion as she explains the dichotomy of agricultural work and personal survival, "My family came out of poverty," she begins, her eyes wet. "My mom was the first one to get an education, and if I finish my Master's, I think I'll be the first one to get a graduate degree. So that's all important, but what I learned here I would have never learned in college. Poverty is the label that farming carries, so it's hard for my family to understand my choice. They want me to have a job with benefits and be secure, you know. We take stability very seriously around here.

"I'm supposed to be a teacher with my degree, and I could teach science and math; I was even offered a job, but I said no. Because I know if I go into traditional education, I can't be as involved in this work toward food sovereignty as I am right now. I don't know what I'm going to do in the future. There's not a lot of work or money in this — I'm not looking to get rich, I just need to pay the bills. But I feel a connection to doing this work because of my small experiences as a child in Durango, and because of my culture and my community here."

At one point, Ivon left El Paso to conduct undergraduate research in Colorado, where she fell in love with the landscape and the liberal mindset. She decided to move back there after she graduated, but after returning and living there another year she began to miss home. "I missed speaking Spanish," Ivon recalls, "I missed my grandmother, I missed the food. I came back and really felt like things needed to happen here. This is my home, I love this community. I feel safe here, as awkward as that sounds considering we're across from Juárez. People don't get that, but I do. The pressure here is high, but I feel like this is what I need to be doing."

Ivon, like many of this generation, had a calling to return home and fight for her community. She has since completed her year of farmer training with AFSC and went on to become a Farm Trainer for the new training class of 2013, leaving only to give birth to her baby boy. She is now the marketing coordinator for the AFSC program, and she and her partner, who owns a food truck, farm a plot of land in Anthony, New Mexico.

❧

Another young Mexican American activist just a few miles away in Anthony, New Mexico, (who actually connected me to Ivon) also answered the call to return home to her community and carry the torch forward for her generation, as well as the younger generations after her. Cristina Dominguez-Eshelman, co-founder and farm director at La Semilla Food Center, came home after college and a stint in AmeriCorps to dedicate her time to building alternative food systems in her

community. Her dedication to community food systems began at a crossroads where her cultural identity and her relationship with food met, sparking her journey back home and into food and agriculture work.

"I did all kinds of volunteering in college," Cristina says as we drive around Anthony in her car, getting a tour of the land La Semilla is developing and one of the school gardens they started, "I worked at the service learning center which was very much based in service and social justice. But I couldn't pick just one thing to focus on. So I served as an AmeriCorps VISTA at a Latino community center in Columbia, Missouri, after college. And I had never been so far away from my family before. I had never been so homesick. In

college, I hadn't been as homesick because there were lots of Mexican Americans and people from border communities, but here I was the minority. Growing up on the border is different than being some place where you're one of the only people of color. So I just kind of had all these identity questions. It was just a big transition year. I had this crash, and I went through a depression, and I began getting sick, and I couldn't eat much. I started thinking about my family at home and realized how much time I really spent with them, and how much of that time was always around food. I grew up with certain food staples — like my grandpa would always make chili and batches of beans and bring them over — and I realized I really missed

Cristina Dominquez-Eshelman, 32 (at time of photo), Anthony, NM.

that and I missed my family, the food, the culture. I decided I wanted to move back. It was a difficult decision because I had also fallen in love with someone there, but I got him to fall in love with the border, so he moved here and now we're married!

"I got better when I returned home and I started looking for a job and got hired with Heifer International, a non-profit organization whose work all ties back to food. So I'd just gone through this whole year of not being able to eat and not feeling healthy and now I was working on the social justice issues around eating and health, so it all started coming together."

Cristina worked with Heifer for over four years, learning about food and food systems and having opportunities to work with youth; it was there that she discovered her passion for youth agricultural education. She soon left and began working at the Anthony Community Garden where she wanted to learn to grow more seriously. She was accepted into the UC Santa Cruz Agro-Ecology Apprenticeship in 2010 where she improved her agricultural skills and, after completion of the program, decided to return to Anthony and start La Semilla with two of her friends.

La Semilla's mission is to build healthy, self-reliant and sustainable food systems in the Paso del Norte region of southern New Mexico and El Paso, Texas. They work with children, youth and families to build awareness around food issues, provide informed analysis on transforming the food system and creating alternatives for healthier environments and communities. La Semilla

has worked to strengthen several farmers markets in the area, including recruiting and providing support to local farmers (like Luis Castañeda in "Transitioning to Sovereignty" in Section Three). La Semilla uses their 14-acre farm for agricultural education, and they participate in Farm to School programs by influencing policy and starting school gardens. (Note: As of 2014, La Semilla supports seven school gardens through their Edible Education program.)

"Loma Linda Elementary school is one of the school gardens we started," Cristina says as we pull up to the school. "We really thought the gardens would be the entry point in having those conversations about farm to school and food systems within the public education system. This work is step-by-step; you have to meet people where they're at, and I feel like where a lot of people are at right now, is starting with community gardens, farmers markets and school gardens. And that's great, it's a start. There are so many more things that need to be in place to support that and the food system development that includes growing growers and encouraging community members to see that they can play a role in that. But we're going one step at a time.

"Growing new growers is definitely a focus, which is why we partnered with Don Bustos [see his story in "Acequia Culture" in Section Four] and AFSC's Farmer Training Program. AFSC also provides us with guidance and will be providing us with a hoophouse. We partner with multiple other groups and organizations doing this work in the region too. If we're gonna supply farmers markets, we need farmers, and right now that's a challenge. The aging farming population is highest in Texas, Arizona and New Mexico. The farmer training program at Santa Cruz was great for growing growers, but you learned to grow in the California soil, not here in the Chihuahuan desert. So I really envision La Semilla's farm space as a training center, except we'll be teaching local new growers how to grow in this soil and climate. It also allows for residents from the community to have access to opportunities they would otherwise have to travel to reach. This way it's more affordable and allows people to stay right here in their communities. People like Catherine, our FoodCorps volunteer."[49]

La Semilla was the only organization in southern New Mexico to apply to make a FoodCorps position available; all the other volunteer positions were in northern New Mexico. The position allowed them to bring in someone to start their school garden program at Loma Linda Elementary and it gave their first volunteer, 26-year-old Catherine Marlene Yañez, an opportunity to work in her own community.

Cristina and I walk into the school, and she introduces me to Catherine, who is working in the garden with the summer school students. Catherine begins telling me her story of jumping into agriculture and food work. After experiencing weight gain and health issues of her own and within her family, she decided to learn more about the food she was putting in

Catherine Yañez.

her body. With diabetes and heart disease present in her Mexican American community, Catherine wanted to create change, and she started with her family.

"I thought it would be crazy if the whole family got in a competition to see who could lose the most weight," Catherine says with a triumphant smile, "And so we did. We had about three sessions over two years; it was designed to be a healthy process, not a crash diet. So we all got together and ended up losing 200 pounds between all of us. Different people did different things — some just walked, some of us worked out to videos, some ran by the river. And we started eating differently. We always get together at my grandma's every week and eat, and we started doing a lot more grilling of our food. And I just tried to share what I was learning, even before La Semilla and FoodCorps. We'd find healthy recipes and re-educate each other in terms of food. We started eating stuff that may be common to a lot of people but not to my family — like asparagus," she laughs. "My cousins were putting it on the grill and saying, 'try it, it's good, I know it looks kind of funky, but try it!'

"I became really inspired by that, and when I saw this FoodCorps position, I applied. The most exciting part for me was when my brother, who has different mentalities than me, started asking when I was going to start a garden at home. That made me ecstatic. I'm now expanding what I've learned and teaching it to these kids and the community through La Semilla, but it's really impacted my family, the people I care most about."

La Semilla means "seed" in Spanish, and it's clear that Cristina, along with the team she works with, is planting seeds for change that are growing out through the entire community and touching each generation.

(Note: La Semilla's Community Farm has been thriving since I visited at the early stages of development. They now have a hoophouse, a drip irrigation system, a solar PV system, and have expanded farm production to include cover crops, bees, fruits, herbs and vegetables. They have also expanded their educational programming to include a farm summer camp for children and youth farm apprenticeships. Catherine has since completed her FoodCorps year and now works with La Semilla providing leadership and coordination for their farm educational programming.)

༄༅

Another young farmer in the AFSC Farmer Training Program in New Mexico shyly agreed to talk with me before I left the Chihuahuan desert. Manny García, a 25-year-old Mexican American resident of Anthony, born in El Paso, is passionate and shy; he's also funny, if you listen carefully for his quiet, quirky quips. He has some fresh produce harvested and waiting for me when I arrive at the Anthony Community Garden where he and Ivon have their training farm space. We sit in the shade eating sweet cantaloupe and talking about how Manny became concerned about the origins of his food and started his own detailed research into the ingredients used in the prevalent fast food chains in his community.

"There's an epidemic of sickness among my people, my community," Manny says. "It has a direct correlation with the food, the food that we eat and the food choices that are available to us. It's important for people to know how important their diet is to their life. I began researching the foods in the typical diet around here, which meant going around to all the fast food restaurants. I would get their menus and study them and find out the ingredients and go back and ask them if they knew what was in their food. And most of the time, they didn't know what they were even serving their customer. It's typical — they're a franchise owner; they don't have any control over it you know, it's at the policy level.

"I studied all sorts of food, fast food and non-fast food, preserved food,

Manny García, 25 (at time of photo), Anthony, NM.

different food ingredients. It's surprising actually. For example, the McDonald's chicken nugget has a chemical compound called *dimethylpolysiloxane* in it. And it's found in many foods, I think Pop-Tarts have it; Reese's peanut butter cups have it. And it's the main component of Silly Putty — that's in your chicken nuggets, man! The reason for that is it's an anti-foaming agent, which means they use it for safety purposes so it won't foam over and create a fire, at least that's the justification for it. Why would you use such a thing in food? It's absurd. There's another chemical compound called *tertiary butyl-hydroquione,* abbreviated TBHQ, and it's a petroleum-based chemical that they put in food. It's been shown to cause carcinogens in lab rats, especially of the stomach lining, and it's found in chicken nuggets, fries, many things. There's all sorts of stuff, and the USDA is approving the use of it all. It's all politics, you know, it's people with power putting that stuff in our food. It's mind boggling. I can only try to make people aware."

Manny, who has a degree in criminal justice and turned down a border patrol job to start the farmer training program, began printing out fast food ingredient lists with information on each one and posting them up in the restaurants and shops throughout his community.

"I've been trying to spread the word of what I'm learning," Manny explains. "You know people are gonna eat whatever they want, and that's fine — I used to eat fast food too; you can't control what people do. But I think people are deceived about what they're eating, and that's wrong, man. There's blatant deception every day, and people may choose to ignore it, or they just don't understand it. Like with GMOs, I think people should know about GMOs because we're putting them into our body, so we should know they're there. But these companies will have a significant loss of profit when people stop buying from them 'cause they don't want GMOs, and those CEOs know that, so it's not gonna happen. We're up against the man. I'm just trying to do my part."

Manny's sister, who worked at the Anthony Community Garden, pushed his interest and passion for real food in agriculture, and he applied to the AFSC training program, where he's now learning about land management, crop planning, irrigation systems and integrated pest control. He now also works at a nearby farm and wants to spend his days growing.

"I've decided now that I don't want anything to do with the man," says Manny. "I'm a novice at farming, but I have a great interest in learning. I just want to grow real food and feed people. My ideal work is to be out here. I'm not really a people person I would say, so my line of work is just to be out here by myself with the plants, with nature. I want to work and save up money to buy land and live off the grid one day, just me and my turtle," Manny's face breaks into a goofy grin, "he's one of the fiercest predators in the wild, man."

After a few more laughs and a farm tour, I bid Manny goodbye and drive north out of the Chihuahuan desert that spans Mexico and the U.S., taking with me a feeling that this generation has the ferocity and the heart to rise above any border or barrier put in the way of our future.

(Note: Manny completed the AFSC training program and went on to continue his agricultural training at the UC Santa Cruz Agro-Ecology Apprenticeship Program in California. He volunteers on the La Semilla Community Farm, and in 2014 became a farmer trainer for the AFSC Farmer Training Program.)

Eugene Cooke, 41
(at time of photo),
Grow Where You Are, LLC.
and (formerly) Truly Living
Well, Atlanta, Georgia.

> The only thing we're doing out here as farmers and gardeners is creating the environment for electromagnetism to do its thing. Electric energy is masculine, magnetic energy is feminine, and, from that, all the diversity happens.
>
> — Eugene Cooke

I F THE YOUNG FARMERS and activists near Mexico's border are breaking down borders, Eugene Cooke is working to transcend them. A deep and spiritual brother based in Atlanta, Eugene is all about the elusive energy alive in everything around us — including plants and food. He himself is the definition of live energy. He carries his energy and radiates it outward with everything he does, including cultivating food and art. He welcomed me with a burst of energy to Truly Living Well's urban farm in the MLK Historic district of Atlanta directly next door to the Martin Luther King Jr. memorial site. And, as I spent the next few days with him, he taught me the significance of the various kinds of energy involved in growing an abundant food system wherever you are. This is the premise of his book on urban agriculture, *Grow Where You Are,* and it's the mission of his sustainable food systems company, Grow Where You Are, LLC. His unique experiences learning from his elders, along with his own philosophies and insight, give a fresh perspective for this and the next generation of growers and food movement activists.

With his wild locks bouncing and Nas and Damien Marley bumping softly in the speakers, Eugene sits relaxed with one hand on the steering wheel of his truck while he tells me his life story as we drive around Atlanta on a sunny spring morning.

"My maternal grandparents," Eugene begins, "Frank and Virginia Patterson, had an 80-acre farm in Kansas while I was growing up. We lived in southern California but we stayed there every summer, and I would spend time walking the farm with my grandfather, who was a mix of Native American and African. My memories of him are not so much of talking, it was just being with him and doing what he did. I would just follow him around, wake up early and do the work. That was my first instruction to farming, and I had no idea how much that would influence me later.

"It just altered my whole perception of living because there was just nothing out there. It was just us, my sister, parents, cousins and them. There were only three channels on the TV, which would go off at ten at night. They had a well you had to hand pump; they had pigs, chickens, geese and cows in the front yard; there was a pond my grandfather dug out in the back. It was so different. Back in Cali, my sister and I were raised as latchkey kids, while my parents worked late — my mom as a schoolteacher and my dad for the city water department, so we were given a garden to take care of to keep us out of the streets. I still ran the neighborhood with my friends, skateboarding and getting into trouble. But I carried those times with my grandfather with me."

Eugene grew up interested in art and drawing and went to school for drafting with a hope to become an architect. He was drawing houses at a young age, and by the time he turned 19 he worked for a large gas company called Union76 designing their gas stations all over the state of California. While he would now say he was working for the "enemy" then, he carried that eye for design and structuring spaces into his first urban gardens.

Eugene later left the gas company and settled down in a college town with his wife and their first baby on the way while he began focusing on his art, letting his creative energy flow. Part of that creativity came out in the cultivation of food. Soon, his entire backyard was overflowing with food, growing on every surface, crawling up wall murals and attracting their young neighbors. His backyard garden became the hangout spot for the community of young folks, offering a creative space for inspiration and connection.

"So our house became a mecca for that," Eugene says with a reminiscent smile, "people would see the backyard and were like, 'whoa, I never thought about planting this or doing that.' Then my uncle Jimmy came from Kansas to visit when our son was born, and when he saw the backyard he was like, 'oh, so you were paying attention to your grandfather.' Soon, people started pulling me out into the community and pushing me to go into L.A. to teach urban gardening."

Eugene began sharing his energy and gifts of creativity and cultivation with the youth community of L.A., teaching art, poetry and gardening in a program called *From the Ground Up*. Soon after, he was introduced to his next elder mentor, one who would pick up where his grandfather left off and have a long lasting, powerful impact on him. Adonijah Miyamora El, who lived out of his van in the middle of Watts in south L.A., was the epitome of a guerilla gardener. He jumped fences and planted all day long all over the city. He grew everything from peaches, cherimoyas, zapotes, avocados, loquats, lemons and bananas to raised beds full of food. He asked Eugene to work with him — no pay — just growing food for the community. Eugene accepted and soon moved into a tent with Adonijah and created gardens in L.A. for the next three to four years.

"I first found Adonijah gardening at Crenshaw High School," Eugene recalls, "where he had jumped the fence to revitalize their abandoned greenhouse and garden plot. He was from L.A., and he chose Crenshaw because he'd graduated from there in the '70s. He'd gone all over the world to learn about gardening: Hawai'i, the Philippines, then he came back and asked to use the garden at Crenshaw. They took too long navigating the politics of it, so he just hopped the fence at night and planted.

"So that's how we grew; we'd plant at night mainly, and he taught me the value of night gardening. There's a different energy at night. Think about what happens as a society at night, busy consciousness is at rest, sexual energy is heightened, the moon is up, there are powerful energies at night. He also taught me the value of gardening on holidays for the same reasons because there's a mass amount of animal sacrifices happening on holidays, the whole country is feeling an ebb of love and energy, that's when you need to be gardening.

"Adonijah's energy and mine worked well together too. He's a Sagittarius, so he would move through like a brushfire, just burning the space out, and I would come in behind him as a Pisces and, like a river, I would just wash it clean and shape the design of the space. He would turn around and be shocked. There'd be pathways and structures and the art was crazy."

Eugene and Adonijah's work created a buzz, as bountiful gardens sprouted up across the city, people wanted to know who created them. Soon they were designing landscapes and gardens for Hollywood celebrities and simultaneously working with troubled youth in the state parks. His time with Adonijah would soon end as he began to work with yet another elder mentor, who, upon returning from a trip to Ghana, would invite him to move to Atlanta and start Truly Living Well.

Rashid Nuri, former appointee to the USDA, asked Eugene to bring his growing skills and design gifts to Atlanta to help start the Truly Living Well Center for Natural Urban Agriculture. Eugene would say Rashid carries different gifts than Adonijah. Eugene watched him in his strength of pooling resources together and quickly making things happen. They started building structures and producing food immediately. Truly Living Well now has five farm sites throughout the metro area and grows produce for the community, sold through two year-round farmers markets and a CSA, as well as to restaurants and Black-owned markets like the Boxcar Grocer. As of 2010, they were selling about 10,000 pounds of produce annually; today, it has grown to much more than that. Truly Living Well also runs a youth summer camp, a new farmer training program, garden classes, garden consultations, and farm tours, and they are highly involved in the community.

Eugene and I arrive at the Wheat Street Garden, one of Truly Living Well's farm sites in the MLK Historic District. Eugene and the operations coordinator at Truly Living Well, Nicole Bluh (who is now operations coordinator for Grow Where You Are, LLC.), walk me through, giving me the tour of this beautiful and abundant urban farm. It is only May, and already their squash plants are flowering and fruiting, their young plum trees are offering up juicy plums, and they gift me with endless amounts of food to try as we walk and pick our way around the farm. There are herbal gardens, greenhouses, an on-site market stand, and even bees; mushroom logs are tucked away in the surrounding trees. They make their own compost for everything to grow in, and their straw bale and drainage pipe compost operation is on point, with food scraps collected from various community restaurants and markets and dried leaves collected from residents' landscape bags left on the side of neighborhood roads like unwanted treasures. They also have a relationship with the local saw mill and brewery for sawdust and spent grains to help heat the compost more quickly.

The trainees for the day show up in high spirits and full of energy, seemingly feeding off of the energy that I can feel pulsing through the garden. I ask Eugene and Nicole why their farm feels (and looks) so different, so much more vibrant, healthy and alive, than any other I've visited. They both smile at each other and excitedly began to tell me about their energetic philosophies and how they impact the plants. "It's all about the masculine, feminine energy," says Nicole, "the electromagnetic energy and also the spiritual effects in the environment for these plants."

"That's the long-winded answer," Eugene says, "really it's about facilitating beauty. Just understanding that the only thing we're doing out here is creating the environment for electromagnetism to do its thing. Electric energy is masculine, magnetic energy is feminine, and, from

that, all the diversity happens. So making sure there's water and minerals and making sure we submit to the order, that's all we gotta do. There's this order that a lot of us growers don't wanna submit to; we want to control it. If we're gonna have control, then we have to be responsible for whatever results, so I try to eliminate having control and just be a partner in the dance.

"So we say OK, we know when the energy is high and we know when it's low and when there is a certain kind of environmental factor, like you know when we have a wet spring or a dry spring, that impacts the energy. We have to understand how to channel that energy and have this kind of communication with the plants and know that all that energy has been pushed up into higher energy centers in the body that make us more receptive to a whole 'nother frequency. We let that guide our work. And when we're in there working, it's about our energy too. We carry all kinds of energies, including our own sexual energies. So there's this real interesting sexuality that is infused into the garden.

"We also carry and bounce off different energies with each other," Eugene continues. "A lot of other gardens here are monocultural. I'm not talking about what they're growing, but who is doing the growing. If it's Black folks growing, then it's all Black folks, if it's White people, then it's all White people. And most of the gardens don't take interns or volunteers, they don't like a lot of volunteers because they are for profit. They're trying to make money, so they don't do tours and education programs. We do school tours, we have elders come out, we have children, we have our trainees, volunteers — it's really diverse. And we all bounce off each other. Our trainees, Chris and Jeremiah, have a really interesting way of cracking jokes on each other, making Rochelle, another trainee, laugh. So what does the plant do if it gets to hear a beautiful woman laughing all day, you know? The plant responds to that. So this powerful exchange of energy happens all day. And you know night-growing is where it's at, so we come in at night and we're keying all that energy up and focusing it and driving it into the greenhouse and the fields.

"And this is happening right in the middle of the hood, it's supposed to be the hardest place for things to go down. But people come out to the farm and they're blown away by these plants. It's beautiful."

I look around and can't help but agree. Eugene and Nicole leave me alone to try and capture the beauty with my camera, while they gather the trainees for the morning's agenda talk. The plan is to continue working at one of their newest sites. So we all jump in the trainee van and head over. It is a site they are developing as a mound agriculture site, also known as *Hugelkultur,* derived from an indigenous practice in Eastern Europe and Germany where woody debris and soil is used to build mounds — sometimes up to three feet off the ground — in which the plants grow.

Eugene and Nicole designed the site which, upon arriving and walking the curving mounds laid out in an ancient symbol shaped similar to pinwheels, I could see was a display of Eugene's gift in artistic design. Hugelkultur was also a good solution for them because the farm site is low-lying and prone to flooding, and two large trees on the site were dying when they began development. So they decided to look at the available resources in an innovative way.

We all get to work building up the mounds with branches laid over the foundational oak stumps which serve as the bones of the mound structure. As we work, I ask Eugene about the trainee program. "We got a three-year grant from the USDA that brings in 20 people at a time to go through 12-week intervals of training," he explains. "The first interval is working out here. They work two days a week and have class study one day. The next phase will be entrepreneurial — like how to make their living from it. The third part is them getting on land. Ages range from 25–50, and they all get paid. It's unlike any program that we've seen where somebody's learning urban ag and getting paid."

At that point, Rashid and Carol, the chief administration officer of Truly Living Well, arrive at the farm. I begin talking to them as Eugene and Nicole continue to work with the trainee crew.

"Truly Living Well is a three-legged stool," Rashid begins, as he gives the big picture of what I've seen so far as a well-operated agricultural center. "One leg is to grow quality food and sell it directly into the hands of the community. The second leg is agricultural education where the community can attain horticultural literacy and propel the local food movement. The third leg is community building and community development, which includes economic development and job creation. This has an immense impact in urban areas, where unemployment rates are high and healthy food access is low. All of our farm locations are in what the USDA has termed "food deserts," and we placed them there before there was a term. We placed them there because we wanted to be where people need food."

This trend of targeting "food deserts," which are predominantly communities of color and low-income, with new food movement initiatives like farmers markets or urban farms is on the rise. But often the initiatives are led exclusively by middle-class, White organizations or groups. This has caused another rising trend of hitting community engagement obstacles and sometimes failure.

"In some communities there needs to be a trust factor," Carol comments, "there needs to be cultural sensitivity. So if you don't have those things, that could create some problems. It's important to look at the power dynamic when asking members of the community to come out and volunteer or work on the farm for you. Here, we are out there working with them. We've even had people comment on that, that we're one of the only gardens that work right alongside our volunteers. There's nothing Rashid, Eugene or Nicole ask the volunteers or trainees to do that they haven't done themselves."

That's especially important when working across races and cultures, particularly with the oppressive power dynamic in agriculture that's so closely tied to race throughout this country's history. Later,

Mound agriculture site, also known as Hugelkultur.

Eugene and I talk about this dynamic and his experience with addressing it when various youth groups and students come to the farm for tours or summer training.

"There is definitely an oppressive stigma tied to people of color and farming," Eugene says, "and here we are farming on land owned by Wheat Street Baptist Church [pastored by civil rights leader William Holmes Borders during the civil rights era]. That's a beautiful thing. But when young Black students come out here, I don't even address that stigma with our history in farming. I just turn them out and we get to work. Because they're not even thinking about that stigma, so once I introduce it to them and go, 'we were slaves and we used to have to do this for nothing' — What? They just came to see a farm. It's unnecessary. But when White students come out here, I address it very clearly, because it's important *they* understand the history so not to get it twisted. Black folks shouldn't have to carry that stigma and feel like they have to just because they were born Black. That stigma only turns into a problem today when White folks are ignorant of that history and when their words and actions show that.

"One time we had a group of junior high students come and they were working on a social justice project and their teachers — who were White women that I've met before at the farm — asked how we felt about growing on land that we don't own. I addressed her question by explaining how throughout history we've hardly ever grown on land we own, because of slavery or sharecropping and denied land rights. But also we as indigenous people never talked about land as something to own. So that is the piece that I talk about with White folks: the concept of owning land. And how their ancestors invented the concept, and on that concept leveraged ultimate economic gain — that's all land ownership is about. I've never owned a piece of land and I've grown all over the planet. That's all we've ever done. I want to ask most landowners: How do *you* feel about owning land but not growing on it?

"We get ourselves into all these interesting paradigms," Eugene continues passionately, "these invented, unsustainable concepts like owning land and chasing money. It's interesting that right now people who are trying to change the system are being led by the system's money, when we know it's not real and it's not sustainable. How is the sustainability movement being led by the U.S. dollar? It's completely unsustainable. We've taken that dollar and we've turned it into commodities, possessions, precious metals to be sold and traded. Why not take that dollar and buy fruit trees, build farms? We are being blinded by something completely unreal. It makes it clear what we're motivated by.

"It goes back to the issue of White organizations coming into communities of color to start farms and markets," Eugene emphasizes. "The only reason they are coming into the hood is because of funding. Otherwise they'd do it in their own neighborhood. The funding dictates that you do the work in underserved communities. So my answer to them is to at least partner with someone in the community who's already been doing that work for, you know, 20 years, because they *are* out there. There's an organization here in the 4th ward called Operation Peace — they've been doing this work for 14 years, not agriculture particularly, but community building, youth empowerment, and they live in and operate in the community, and we are partnering with them.

"It's a real issue otherwise," Eugene concludes, "because not only are these organizations coming in and sucking up the funding, but they are also misrepresenting the movement in the media. Leaving the folks who have been doing this work in the shadows. Now I'll admit it was partly a hurt ego when I saw Truly Living Well left out of a popular local magazine article about Atlanta's upcoming young urban farmers, but that hurt became more profound when I saw all of our trainees and how slighted they felt. This article, like so many you see, featured mainly White male farmers in the city, and that's just a misrepresentation of what's really going on. Now, that has a rippling impact. Our trainees pick up the article, they show it to their families and say, 'look an article on urban farming,' and their families are like, 'damn, they didn't even talk about the farm where you're working. Didn't even mention it.' OK, that sucks. But this is where it gets crucial. Now, a regular resident of the state of Georgia opens it up and sees a misrepresentation of the population, particularly the percent of the

population that's looking for work. So if my son opens it up — or any young Black man looking for work — and sees this, he feels like he can't even think about a career in this, not even this lifestyle, because he's not represented there. But all of the young White males can look at it and say, 'oh I never thought I could do that, I see myself represented four out of five times here, I can do this, this is for me.'"

This paradigm is happening all over the country in urban areas like Detroit, Oakland, Chicago, Brooklyn and New Orleans. But I've seen in all of these cities, and rural areas alike, activists and growers from communities of color coming together to form coalitions that help elevate the work they are doing and reverse the misrepresentation and exclusivity of funding. Once such coalition in Atlanta Eugene informed me of is called URFAM, Urban Food Abundance Movement. He tells me how the work they are doing here is crucial because they are basically a trade organization of people who are working in the food movement on every scale, including food retailers like the Boxcar Grocer, a healthy food retailer run by sister and brother Alison and Alphonzo Cross, whose mission is to strengthen urban communities by providing access to healthy food. Representation in every facet of the food system is a key component for addressing food access in communities of color because when people walk into a food store or a farmers market and not only the owners, but the patrons too, are of a diverse population, it allows people to feel like that space and that food is for them, that they belong there eating healthy food too.

"It's gotta be consistent," Eugene remarks, "because the barriers in place are consistent. The systems we're trying to change are consistent. If we can be half as consistent as the enemy, we'd be so successful. It seems that anytime people are working toward positive change, we're way less consistent than the negative — they work 24/7. They work while we sleep, through the night. By the time we wake up in the morning, the negative power has been on their job for hours — like the train that honks in the middle of the night, they don't care whether it's three in the morning, whether it's Christmas or New Year's, they are shipping their products, and they don't care what you say. So if we can be half as consistent as that, then we're on the right track."

Eugene is dedicating his consistent, positive energy into the soil all over the world. Surely making his grandfather and his mentors proud, he is building abundant food systems through garden and urban farm development from Atlanta to California and many states in between, and from Jamaica to Haiti and Africa. His "Grow Where You Are" workshops based on his introductory book on urban agriculture are well received around the world. While he teaches this and future generations the importance of growing food, he emphasizes the fact that growing our own food locally is an ancient practice, reminding this generation once again to rise up as the bridge to our ancestors' wisdom.

Portrait 4:

Kitchen Kwento

Aileen Suzara, 29 (at time of photo), Berkeley, California.

THERE IS ANOTHER POWERFUL ENERGY involved with food, one that takes place after the planting, the growing and the harvest. It takes place in the kitchen, where food and the rich storytelling that accompanies food traditions come to life. I drove to California to meet with a few young farmers/chefs who are not only renewing connections to the cultural food traditions of their ancestors, but are exploring their own sense of farm to table through fresh and heirloom culinary skills.

悗悗

Decolonization work is usually about resistance. But we also have to relearn, reconnect and heal. I spent my college years healing in the kitchen and providing that therapy for others. I would cook to say, 'I am here' but also as a sort of therapy.

— Aileen Suzara

"I probably grew up eating more Spam, Vienna sausages and corned beef than the foods my ancestors ate," Aileen Suzara begins, as we sit basked in the rays of the setting sun on her back porch in Berkeley, California, where she has just started a graduate program in public health. "I am the daughter of two migrants from the Philippines, and their story parallels with the history of a larger Filipino migration, when thousands of Filipino health care workers were being recruited here, and still are. Both of my parents were health care professionals and during my childhood we moved all over the country to find work at hospitals near military bases. We lived in eastern Washington, in the Mojave desert of California, in Texas, Florida and Hawai'i. And in these American military communities, those were the food choices my parents had available to them. I didn't know it then, but this fact, this disconnect from my ancestral foods, would follow me throughout my life as I became more and more obsessed with food."

Aileen is a trained natural chef, as well as a culinary educator, and has been cooking for people since she was eight years old. I first connected with Aileen through her blog called *Kitchen Kwento,* where she shares recipes and writes about the relationships of food, stories (*kwentos*) and land with a Filipina American lens. She sees the kitchen as the place where everything begins — the heart of a home and of a community. Those that know her well know Aileen has always been at home in the kitchen.

"I was a weird kid growing up," Aileen explains as we enjoy fresh slices of cantaloupe she put out for my visit, "and living in the Mojave desert of southern California, we were very isolated. So I tried to keep busy by spending a lot of time in the kitchen. My family was not very big on cooking, so they gave me free range over anything in there. It was really great that my parents trusted me and gave me that freedom. I remember loving to read and digging through all these cookbooks we had stored up and covered in dust. I was just immediately drawn to them right away. I wanted to teach myself to cook. Then, when I was eight years old I found this one book buried under everything else. It was this little softcover book that was starting to fall apart. It was a Filipino cookbook, the only one in the pile. I remember looking at it and reading these simple little recipes and thinking, 'What *are* these ingredients?! I have no idea what these foods are!' I was so curious, and I began to ask my mom about all the ingredients that seemed foreign to me, and ask her why we didn't eat these things.

"So we began talking about all the recipes in this little book, and she and my father would remember the flavors that they grew up with, and they had the memories, but this cookbook was my portal to another dimension of food. We actually started to try to hunt down some of the ingredients, and I would try to recreate some of the recipes, even though I didn't know what the original flavors tasted like. I mean some Filipino foods had filtered through for me while growing up. Like sometimes my dad, who was busy, busy working all the time, every once in a while a recipe would just bubble out of him. This didn't happen a lot, it was just an act of nature. But I can remember some days coming home from school and something was cooking on the stove, and I was blown away by the amazing smells coming out of the kitchen. It would just be something he remembered. But otherwise, we ate a fair share of the processed American diet, and I kept pouring over this book and experimenting with the foods of my homeland.

"In that same year, my parents decided to make their first return trip to the

homeland in almost 30 years. This was a very big turning point for me. I was eight years old, had just become exposed to and interested in Filipino foods, and it would be my first time in the Philippines. Just being there, tasting all these flavors, seeing family. It was amazing. I wasn't hit by the culture shock that my sister was, who was nine years older and an angsty teen trying to process privilege and all these things. No, I was just like, 'Give me a mango, I'm having a great time!' I got to taste the classic Filipino heritage dish that my dad made once in a while called *adobo,* which comes

Aileen Suzara.

from where my dad was raised in Bicol. The region is known for its chili peppers, its coconut milk and its general spiciness. In my opinion *Bicolano* cooking is some of the best from the archipelago. *Adobo* is a noun and verb at the same time. There are a lot of *adobos* from around the world, but the Philippine one has these basic elements: *adobo* has to have something sour, like a vinegar or a sour fruit or an acid; you can use different meats — I've always used chicken; you can even *adobo* [that's when it becomes a verb] vegetables, like mushrooms. You just need to have that tangy sour flavor and you add coconut milk, lots of garlic, lots of onions, chilies and pepper. Anyway, it was a life-changing trip. And needless to say, it propelled my passion for cooking even further."

Aileen continued to cook for her family, and when they moved to a small rural town in Hawai'i where farmers and fresh foods were abundant, her relationship with food transcended to another level. "The food culture in Hawai'i is so rich," Aileen reminisces fondly, "there's just so much. You can eat a mixed plate with all of these foods from different cultures of people, and it's like you're just eating a piece of history right there. The availability of what was grown there was different too. You could actually eat the papaya that was grown on your neighbor's tree. Food was just very beautiful and vibrant and connected to land and ag. Where I lived I was very lucky to see people who were still subsistence farming or who would spear fish or hunt in the woods for pig, and 'eating

local' wasn't fetishized, it was just what people did.

"But there was another side of it too," Aileen continues, "being that it is an island with the military history and current reality that it has, there is a lot of processed food introduced there too. For example, per capita, Hawai'i is among the highest consumers of Spam in the world. Spam actually issued this collector's edition Spam can that has a hula girl on the front to commemorate that. I spent a big chunk of my undergrad delving into food culture and health. I started out doing a lot of research on Spam. I think because I was being uprooted from the place that felt like home back in Hawai'i and being transplanted in New England for college, whether I wanted to or not I started looking at home with different eyes. I was looking at foods from home and learning and making connections as I was looking at military toxins in my environmental justice classes. There was this whole parallel track of what happened in our food systems and our food cultures. So I started looking at Filipino food culture and the colonization of the Philippines and realizing that when the U.S. came after Spain in the takeover of the Philippines, they not only mandated that English be spoken in schools, but they also sent cooks and nutritionists to teach native people how to cook. That's the big irony. I found some documents from that timeframe, and it was just kind of lamenting the fact that Filipinos were eating rice, fish and vegetables when they should be eating wheat and grains and a processed Western diet. So there was this less visible strand of colonization: the re-shaping of food culture."

The Philippine archipelago was originally inhabited by the Orang Asli, a Malay term for aboriginal people (European settlers named them "Negritos," so they are also known as the Negrito people). Migrant settlers known as Melanesians and Malayo-Polynesians also arrived to inhabit the islands at least 30,000 years ago from Borneo, Sumatra, Malaya, and other areas across what is now known as Southeast Asia and Oceania. Over time, social and political organization developed and evolved among the widely scattered islands, and the Negrito and Malayo-Polynesian cultures took precedence. Today, those cultures are evident among the varied ethnicities, languages, foods and other aspects of Filipino culture. However, the Spanish and American colonization of the islands from the 16th through the 19th century has also impacted Filipino culture. For example, the Filipino *adobo* gets its name from Spain, but the cooking technique remains indigenous to the Philippines. In the 50-year U.S. military occupation of the Philippines after the Spanish-American War, Western foods like canned goods became abundant in Filipino food culture.

"Decolonization work," Aileen explains, "is usually about resistance. But we also have to relearn, reconnect and heal. To me that's part of decolonization work. Looking back, I spent my early 20s healing in the kitchen and providing that therapy for others. It was a comfort for homesickness while away at college, but it was also bigger than that. I was in this old agricultural region of New England and was one of few Filipinos for a 200-mile radius, so I felt alienated but also sometimes like I had to hold it down. I would cook to say, 'I am here' but also as a sort of therapy for myself and other island folks. There was a sense of pressure too, like I had to make the best dish now because whatever I cooked would be defined as Filipino food for this group.

"When I first arrived there, after sobbing uncontrollably, my suitcases stuffed not with practical things like sweaters, but with foods from home like *li hing mui* plums, I convened with a bunch of other island women who were hungry for the flavor of home. We would cook for three days straight and feast and offer people food. I ended up spending a lot of time cooking for and with people. I became the president of the Hawai'i club and would cook for them and all kinds of other clubs too. It was a really big part of being there. People would just gravitate toward kitchen, it was sort of like kitchen therapy for all of us a little bit. It was powerful. And so good to hold onto that food culture. I knew I wanted to continue officially the work of relearning and preserving food culture, so I started training as a natural chef. But something I continue to struggle with, is wanting to learn the craft of cooking and farming from Filipino teachers. I still crave that way of passing on knowledge."

Aileen was able to garner some knowledge from a Filipino family she worked with in their small vegan Filipino restaurant, but she still seeks that mentorship and solidarity in her work not only as a chef but also as a food justice activist and farmer. After years of cooking, Aileen felt something missing. Something nagged at her mind, and she knew it would deepen her relationship with food as well as with her own roots. Aileen decided she wanted to farm. She was accepted into UC Santa Cruz's Agro-Ecology Apprenticeship Program where she was finally able to dig into the soil and connect in a new way with the foods she had been cooking all these years.

"I felt physically very alive at that time," Aileen recalls, "it reminded me of growing up as a kid on the island. After the apprenticeship I moved to work on another farm with livestock and pastured chickens, and I just felt really tied in to the cycle of the animals and what they needed. It made me reflect on the connection to the kitchen. It was the first place I was able to do a chicken slaughter. There I was thinking, 'man I have made so much *adobo* over the years, and this is my first time to actually face the chicken after all this time!' I kinda felt like I just had to get permission to make *adobo* from that moment. It really deepened my appreciation. But there was also something about digging into California soil that suddenly hits you, in the sense of who has farmed here in the past and the history and pain and separation they experienced. When I was farming, it just made me think about the fact that I was the first generation of my family born here on this land, but it also caused me to think about what took us off

of our own land. And what it means to now be on soil where other people have been oppressed. That all felt very physical for the first time."

California soil holds much history for Filipino Americans. Many of the first migrants from the Philippines arrived here and worked as farm workers and joined and led some of the first farm labor resistance movements of our time. The well-known United Farm Workers (UFW) led in part by César Chávez gets credit for some of the biggest farm labor strikes in history, such as the Delano Grape Strike against grape growers in Delano, California, from 1965–1970. However, the strike began with the lesser-known Agricultural Workers Organizing Committee (AWOC), a group of mainly Filipino farm workers in Delano led by leaders such as Larry Itliong, Phillip Vera Cruz and Pete Velasco. They later merged with Chávez's group to form UFW, but, in the words of the late Filipino American labor leader John Delloro, "many Filipino farm workers had over 30 years' experience fighting and striking in the field since they arrived in the late 1920s and 1930s."

"Often when you hear about agricultural struggles, those stories are left out," Aileen says as we talk about some of the history of Filipino American farmers, "and even within our own communities we don't get to hear that history, so there's a huge gap in understanding our role. To actually understand the role and history of our own people and have that historic perspective changes everything. All up and down the coast of California, Filipino farmworkers are here, this is it, there's rich history. Yet in my own experiences apprenticing on organic farms, I often felt like a rarity. When I was farming on the central coast, I had people come into the farmstand and say 'What's a girl like you doing here?' or 'Oh you must be one of those urban youth kids.' Just because I was a person of color selling at the market. Like that's the only reason I'm here growing food.

"Race and history still matter and need to be understood, even with the rise of the 'new' good food movement. It's something our generation of food justice activists needs to address. We're here too, and we have to go deeper. I learned so much from my apprenticeships, but at times would struggle and try to imagine what that experience could be like if it was led by, and grounded by, folks of color. A training center with a curriculum that really embraces what we want to learn and can support the elements important to us is what we need more of out there. There's just something about having that knowledge transferred from folks of color with folks of color.

"Wanting that kind of experience for myself helped me realize that I want to be that teacher for others. Which is why I call myself more of an educator than a chef. It's about passing on that cultural tradition and honoring it. What I've really been dreaming about is starting a school of living tradition with a culinary and agricultural focus. It's a model I've seen in the Philippines, maybe they are elsewhere too, a space where cultural traditions can be renewed. We have to renew who we are and how to live in a good way on this planet, and we need to keep having spaces for that. The kitchen, to me, is the perfect space."

(Note: Aileen has since been involved with the launch of a Filipino foods program and urban garden in Union City with Filipino Advocates for Justice. She is also working on Sariwa (Fresh), a healthy Filipino foods pop-up series and budding food microbusiness.)

❧

> 66
>
> It's interesting how it's turned out, having been adopted away from Korea and now coming back to my roots through food. It's very validating.
>
> — Kristyn Leach
> 99

Another team of young foodies in California is also preserving the cultural food traditions of their ancestors in culinary and agricultural spaces. In San Francisco's Mission District, I met with the chef and farmer behind the popular Korean restaurant, Namu Gaji.

"*Namu* means tree or wood," explains Dennis Lee, the 33-year-old chef and co-owner of the restaurant he started with his two brothers, Daniel and David. "One sort of philosophy that we practice is a natural or *Dāo* approach to things, and my *Dāo* constitution lacks a wood element, so it's kind of a good thing for me to be surrounded by wood. Hence, *namu*. And since this is the second restaurant, this one became a branch of the first one, *gaji* means branch."

Dennis Lee, 33
(at time of photo),
Namu Gaji Chef and
Co-owner.

open up a second restaurant; however they lost their lease on Namu before opening their doors at Namu Gaji in 2011. Walking through the doors of Namu Gaji brings you immediately close to the wood element Dennis referenced. A large candle chandelier sculpted into the shape of a tree branch hangs from the ceiling, running down the center of the restaurant above the long family-style wood table. All the tables are wood, and the space is warm and inviting yet still young and modern.

While looking over the wood counter into the small, open kitchen, you can see jars of labeled ingredients like shiitake mushroom powder and farm fresh pickled chilies. While listening to fresh Hip-Hop beats over the speaker, patrons chow down on Korean tacos, *kimchee* fried rice, and what they call their Korean staple: The Stonepot, filled with *kimchee,* veggies, *koshihikari* fried rice and *gochujang* (a strong fermented Korean condiment made from red chilies and fermented soybeans).

"Our menu isn't very traditional Korean," Dennis says, as we sit by the window in the sunny back corner of the restaurant, "we try to explore many new uses of the traditional ingredients, but we certainly use some traditional techniques as far as pickling, or making chili paste. We draw from a very authentic experience, but the purpose of what we're doing isn't to try to remake or recreate something old. We're kind of honoring those things and putting them into a modern concept and exploring that, just like we would in our own life experiences and identities. My food culture

Dennis and his brothers started cooking what they call New Korean American food in a concessions food stall in Golden Gate Park after they moved to the Bay area 11 years ago. That business evolved quickly into a small cafe and then a full service restaurant in 2006. The brothers were so successful that they began making plans to and culinary heritage is all very rooted in growing up in a very traditional Korean household, albeit an immigrant household. So I'd be pretending I was somebody else if that wasn't showing in my expression of cuisine in some way.

"My mother taught me how to cook. And I grew up cooking with her and fell in love with it. My mom grew up in Jeollado in southwestern Korea. Her older sister emigrated here to Boston where she opened the first Japanese restaurant there in the '60s. The rest of the family ended up emigrating here too, working at the restaurant at various points and moving on to start their own culinary careers. My mom and all three of her sisters have all independently owned and operated restaurants in the Boston area as well as Chicago. And my grandmother made her living cooking as well. So I've been around food my whole life.

"When I moved here from Boston, I saw a lack of real personal cuisine in the restaurant scene. I think that's important and something that's not as present as it should be. For us to be doing something from the background that we have is definitely something that's not on every corner. I think cooking in a way that's not so cookie cutter and sourcing local ingredients is something that's lacking. There is the trend picking up around farm to table and that's great, but we try to make it more about a relationship between farmer and chef that's not so industrial."

Just at this moment, the front door to Namu Gaji opens, and a bright young

woman walks in carrying a crate full of vibrant vegetables and herbs. Multi-colored tomatoes and peppers peek out under leafy greens and bulky melons. Behind her two more young people walk in with their arms also loaded with produce. The young woman is Kristyn Leach, 31-year-old head farmer at Namu Farm, the restaurant's

Kristyn Leach, 31 (at time of photo), Namu Farm Manager.

farm which has been in production for two years.

"So-called organic farms these days are very industrial," Dennis continues, "where it's about yielding product that is consistent or the same size each time because of the pressure of modern retail. But Kristyn and I observe how the weather and land affects the harvest. Our relationship is largely based on talking about that fluctual result. We discuss my feedback about skins being bitter or tough or sweet, and she helps me understand why it might be that way. It's a very visceral approach to cooking and farming."

"Kristyn's approach to farming is very unique," Dennis continues, "it's a much more comprehensive approach to growing things. Her relationship to the land is about creating a sustainable ecosystem, and becoming a part of that system as opposed to manipulating it. And what we're doing here is similar; it's not just about following the farm-to-table trend but more comprehensively exploring how it allows us to tap into my family history, our cultural roots, and also resources my family has like gardening skills and seeds from Korea. The time that's elapsed between my parents' generation growing food out of necessity and my generation growing as a trend is so short, so there's still a lot of resources available to us. My father's family is from an agricultural background; they were all farmers. My father was the first in his family to graduate from high school and pursue other things besides working on the farm. And my mom's mother had a garden next to my aunt's restaurant in Boston because at that time there weren't a lot of Korean ingredients available, so she grew and made a lot of staples from scratch.

"Farming for Namu Gaji kind of facilitates relationships with my parents and my extended family. I love that connection between growing and cooking food and how they both preserve and build relationships with family and community, it's all kind of symbiotic and connected."

Kristyn finishes bringing in the harvest and comes over to talk with me. A young farmer born in Korea and adopted by an Irish Catholic family in New York, Kristyn got into farming by hanging out at community gardens as a teenager and exploring how growing food brought people together. Once out on the West Coast growing more formally on larger farms, Kristyn sought out something she could grow that would help her to explore her own roots.

"I wanted to grow something distinctly Korean," Kristyn explains, "and I sort of stumbled upon the seeds for perilla [known as *deulkkae* or *ggaennip* in Korean]. I didn't really know what it was, but I grew it and really loved it — it's an incredibly beautiful plant. It's a really tall broadleaf plant with purple undersides to the leaves. It's in the mint family and is related to *shiso,* a popular Japanese herb. Perilla is a staple Korean herb and subsequently after growing it, everyone Korean who has seen me growing it is blown away. All the old Korean ladies I would see growing it in Seattle had an immediate visceral response to the plant. As did David when I walked into Namu Gaji with it for the first time.

"David and Dennis's reaction to the plant was magical when I walked in telling them I had a lot of it and didn't know what to do with it. They couldn't believe I was growing it. I decided I would bring it in to them every week, and that's how our relationship started. After a while, they began talking about finding land to start a farm for the restaurant, and I knew of some land available at the Sunol Ag Park where I'd previously farmed for someone. They respected my growing style, and so it went from there. They hired me as their farmer, and now we grow all kinds of Korean herbs and vegetables on about an acre.

"It's interesting how it's turned out, having been adopted away from Korea and now coming back to my roots through food. It's very validating. I work for an older Korean lady who is a mushroom vendor here in San Francisco, and I brought her some perilla and she tried it and said to me, 'you are 100 percent Korean.' She would have me show it off to all her customers, and she was so proud that someone from my generation is growing perilla.

"I love how food can instantly cut to the core of someone like that and how it allows this shared connection. This plant touches us so deeply, all the way back to our shared roots."

Portrait 5:

Foods Are Our Teachers

Valerie Segrest, 31, member of the Muckleshoot Tribe, Community Nutritionist and Native Foods Educator, Auburn, WA.

How can we live like our teachers, the plants and foods around us? How can we learn to grow and thrive in diversity and be big medicine in the world?

— Valerie Segrest

WHILE FOOD AND PLANTS seem to be able to touch us deeply and build connections across generations, I know of a young food activist and Native foods educator who would say that they also serve as our teachers, passed down from generation to generation. I steer Lucille north to Washington state to learn from this young community leader who is sharing what wild foods, along with her elders, are teaching her.

Driving through the Puget Sound area of Washington state, I am struck by the wild beauty of the region. Cedar trees and mountains give way to the coastline of the Sound and its many interconnected lakes, rivers and inlets leading out to the Pacific Ocean. The Puget Sound is a part of the Salish Sea that extends up to British Columbia, Canada, and is named after the Indigenous family of Salish and Coast Salish, or Co Salish, peoples who have inhabited the Puget Sound area for thousands of years. Over 65 different tribes comprise the Salish peoples today. I can't help but think about how the beautiful landscape I am driving through has supported the diverse food system that's sustained them for centuries.

I head toward one such tribe on the Muckleshoot Reservation south of Seattle, home to the federally recognized Muckleshoot Indian Tribe, who are descendants of the Upper Puyallup and Duwamish people, or *Dkh'Duw'Absh* meaning "the people of the inside" in the Salish language of Lushootseed. I am on my way to meet with 31-year-old Valerie Segrest who is a member of the Muckleshoot Tribe, a community nutritionist and a Native foods educator who founded the Muckleshoot Food Sovereignty Project in 2009.

She welcomes me into her home on Muckleshoot land in Auburn for a quick interview while her 12-week old daughter sleeps soundly in the front room. We speak softly about Valerie's upcoming birthday when she plans to take friends and family up the mountain to harvest huckleberries as she does annually.

"Huckleberries are in season now," Valerie starts, "and every year on my birthday I get a group of people together to go up there and pick. I tell them this is your birthday present to me, pick a gallon of berries," she laughs, "and in that way, birthdays are awesome. Huckleberries are incredibly high in antioxidants, so they're incredible anti-agers. We hear stories like that of my auntie who lived to be over 100 years old with a diet of berries and fish; berries are long-life givers. They're high in fiber and vitamin C, and they do not raise the blood sugar; they actually help balance blood sugar. So they're anti-diabetic in a way, and diabetes is such an epidemic in our community."

Though the Muckleshoot don't have a public health department doing research on the impact of diabetes and other illnesses in the community, Valerie has no doubt that the entirety of enrolled members (which is documented as 1,600, but she guesses is closer to 2,500) is affected by diabetes.

"Anybody you meet is impacted either personally or in their family," Valerie explains. "When I go to the school and ask the kids to raise their hand if they have a relative that has diabetes, every one of them raises their hand. Also cancer, it seems like everybody has cancer these days. It's getting to the point of asking, 'when are we going to announce that this is an epidemic?' because it's happening everywhere. In the last year I've lost three of my really great teachers to cancer, and two out of those three also had diabetes for a very long time and had even lost fingers from it. Diabetes is here and it's rampant."

Valerie decided to study nutrition with a focus on the traditional foods and medicine of her ancestors as the answer to tribal health. She has worked as a community nutritionist since graduating with her bachelor's degree in the field, giving workshops and talks within the community and also working for the K-9 tribal school designing the nutrition program and trying to put more traditional foods on the school's menu. Valerie also started a research project to find out what the barriers were to accessing traditional foods in the community. Part of that research involved talking with tribal communities throughout the Puget Sound about all of the barriers and possible solutions to Native food access. This work sparked the creation of the Muckleshoot Food Sovereignty Project, which addresses barriers such as a loss of rights, a loss of land, environmental toxins and a lack of education within the community.

"Some of that cultural knowledge about our traditional foods hasn't been transmitted to all families," Valerie explains. "Certain families still carry it, and people certainly do practice their traditional food culture, but not everybody has equality and access to that education in the community. So we try to create spaces for that to happen, and we identify spaces in the community where food can be grown and harvested. We've planted several community gardens and held workshops and events, like just yesterday where we were honoring cooks in the community to make sure people feel like their work is important. It's important to honor the skills and knowledge we carry; it's a wealth in our community."

Valerie also teaches nutrition at the college level at Northwest Indian College, where she teaches courses like "Honoring Northwest Native Food Traditions" and others that focus on traditional plant use and traditional medicines and foods. She feels the message from the traditional food movement in tribal communities is not that different from the messages we're hearing from the good food movement.

Valerie Segrest

"There are some traditional food principles," Valerie says, "that emerged from the research project I did with my research partner, Elise Krohn, where we were going around and interviewing elders and community members from tribes throughout the Puget Sound. And these common themes kept coming up, which are as applicable today as they were generations ago. Firstly, traditional food is at the center of our culture. Since people traditionally harvested, processed, prepared and shared meals together, this unity is an integral part of our cultural identity. Eating food helps feed the desire for wholeness within us, and it can be amplified when the entire family participates in a meal together. Our ancestors also understood that food is precious, a gift from nature, so we should make sure that we're eating foods that honor the food web or the food chain and work with our food in such a way that we're honoring that web. We should also cook and eat traditional foods with good intention. Finally, traditional foods are whole foods — they are seasonal and they are local.

"Our food culture is so place-based and so season-based, like right now the huckleberries are out, and that's all anybody talks about. And there are 20 different varieties of huckleberry that grow here in the Northwest; they are a food that we would traditionally follow as the different varieties ripened. So it's a huge cultural keystone food for us. Also, our hunting season just opened up, so it's time to go get your elk and store that meat away for the year. My partner, that's his work, so he's now busy getting stuff ready for hunting. It really is a community-based food system. It's just coming from such a humble community that I don't think people see it as anything else but just what they do — maybe I romanticize things, but I think it's very valuable what people do around traditional food.

"My teachers really taught me to look at that, and one teacher who really put into motion the work that I do today is someone who I think started the traditional food movement in the Northwest, though our ancestors really have been doing this for a long time. Bruce Miller or *Subiyay* which is his Native name, passed on in 2005 but is a Skokomish elder who was such a revolutionary man. He's the person who was so bold about sharing his knowledge in a time when people were feeling very disturbed about sharing their knowledge because you don't know what people are going to do with it. But he was so charged with this drive that we don't have time, we don't have time to pick and choose who we're going to share this with, it's out there and it's real. He watched whole populations of food plants that he and his family would harvest disappear. He felt really inspired to act on it and for that I'm really grateful.

"So I was inspired to pick up that work and create cultural continuity. Even that phrase 'cultural continuity' comes from another one of my teachers, Hank Gobin, a Tulalip elder who would say things to me like, 'How are you going to contribute to cultural continuity?' Or 'I know you're a nutritionist and really excited, but nowadays our traditional harvesting grounds are Albertson's and Safeway, so how are you going to help people go through the grocery store with their ancestors by their side?' That to me is a really great teacher. What a wonderful question to ask somebody.

"And then there's Roger Fernandes, who is an artist and a storyteller. He's Lower Elwha, from out on the peninsula, and he grew up in Seattle his whole life. He always presses me to remember the story behind my teachings. He pushes me to look at the lessons that are coming from that story and revisit them over and over again because the power of storytelling, he says, is how we learn. Stories teach us how to behave in the world. All of our traditional foods carry a story. Nettles, salmon, huckleberries. You just sort of get connected in a different way when there's a story being told.

"I don't know where I would be without the advice, strength and even spiritual support from my elders, my teachers. It's medicine for us of this generation, but it's also medicine for them. They are able to share their stories and pass on that knowledge and cultural continuity. They can feel like they are leaving the future of our people, our culture and the rights we have to sustain ourselves in good hands. As our ancestors did before them. Like with our traditional foods, continuing to pass on that knowledge is how we are able to maintain our food culture and our access to these foods in particular. That's the way I interpret food sovereignty.

"Though the food sovereignty movement is getting bigger and is providing a sort of space for people to talk about a different food system and do community gardening and all of that important and wonderful work, there's also an ancient system that has been here a long time and fed people a long time, and we have to remember that system. For tribes at least, food sovereignty carries a different weight. Every time I go and harvest, I'm expressing sovereignty, and to think about it in that way is really important; it's what our ancestors traded land for.

"That was the number one priority of our ancestors when they signed the treaties here in 1859, to ensure we always have access to our foods. And it's a treaty right to access these foods, but it's also our responsibility to take care of them and to make sure that there is enough for generations to come, as they did for us. I think it's a key piece to our community health, because it's a direct message from our ancestors saying, 'we know that these foods have sustained us for a very long time. They've maintained our health and they're going to sustain the health of the future as well.' So when we're looking at the barriers to accessing our foods and sustaining our health; it's a heavy responsibility we carry to remove them.

"Take our salmon issues, for example. We know Coast Salish people have been fishing and eating salmon for 10,000 years, and we're the generation that may watch the last fish come up the river. Salmon is overfished, and there are barriers in natural restoration of the wild salmon population. There are literal barriers blocking the fish from coming back up river to spawn, with work going on up river around dams or development or just European land management styles. Then, some of our fish are just dying; the temperatures of the waters are so high with climate change that they're being cooked on the way home. And the rivers, like the Duwamish River, which is part of Muckleshoot fishing grounds, is so heavily polluted that it's been deemed by the EPA a Superfund site, meaning a top priority for cleanup due to a century of heavy industrial use that's left the waterway contaminated with toxic chemicals.

"There's also issues with our food on land due to environmental toxins and huge development. Food sources such as camas prairies were so abundant here in the Northwest, they could be what we call nowadays a community garden. It was a place where several families would gather and dig camas bulbs [the bulbs of this perennial flower were traditionally roasted or boiled and taste similar to sweet potatoes] every year and camas was, next to salmon, one of the most traded items in the Northwest at one point. The prairies were so abundant that you could walk through the prairies from Canada all the way into northern California, and now we have less than three percent of them intact. So development has been a huge barrier, but also there are barriers in how to manage the remaining prairies and also how to manage our huckleberry meadows. Traditionally, we would use burning methods to manage our berry meadows; now we have Smokey the Bear who tells us that fires are terrible. So our huckleberries and our camas fields haven't been burned in a very long time, and they need to be managed and continually harvested to continue growing.

"But we live in a time where our natural resources department in the state of Washington is looking at our natural resources as cultural resources now, which is great. They've made some compromises on burning issues, not quite what we'd like to see, but it's a start, and we're talking about how to clean up the rivers and be good partners and stewards. So I think we're in a really important time where both sides are listening to each other and saying we need to do something. And we're getting better at hearing each other and working with people where they're at. We also have this spirit of the land and the water and the food telling us that we don't have much time and we have to take better care of them."

Our country's early reaction to this realization that we need to take better care of nature was the conservation movement of the 19th century; national parks were created and the beauty of our wild lands preserved. But, while Valerie is a fan of conservationist literature like that of Walden and Thoreau, she feels it misconstrues the role of man in nature.

"While I'm still in love with and respect literature's take on nature," Valerie comments, "they have this message that whenever man steps into nature we wreck everything around us. But that's the exact opposite of our view here in tribal communities. We are

about finding a balance with nature where you're working together and not having dominion over that space. Even as foragers, we use harvesting techniques that make it look like we've never even been there while also actually benefiting the plant. Most of our foods are perennials, so we use harvesting techniques that increase the growth. For some of the berries, for example, if you don't harvest them, they produce less and less every year. And if you do harvest them, they produce more. It's a relationship we're a part of.

"I understand the need to protect — we have our own conservation we're a part of, protecting our traditional harvesting grounds. We have certain areas where we harvest that we can't bring a non-tribal member to. People are hesitant to share their spaces because one day you go out to visit your medicine patch and it's been dug up with a backhoe. So I get it, but conserving nature from man entirely is not the way."

Humans and nature working symbiotically is an Indigenous philosophy we can all learn from. The Muckleshoot Tribe once based their entire economic, social and food systems on that symbiotic relationship. Systems which were structured around generosity and sustainability instead of greed and power.

"Here in the Northwest," Valerie explains, "our food system was our economic and social system, so certain families would carry certain foods. You may have been a family of saltwater fishermen or a family of huckleberry harvesters, or your family may have maintained a certain part of the camas prairie, and that was really important to our social structure because in our tradition your wealth was judged by your generosity. We had gatherings called the *potlatch* where people would gift their guests with beautiful, lavish gifts. Sometimes you would just give away everything that you owned, that was an indicator of how wealthy you were. Your wealth was also indicated by the way you would set the table. So when it was nettle season, my family would go to the patch and harvest,

and then we would set the table and invite the community in to come sing blessing songs to that food and to enjoy it with us, and it was sort of an announcement to say, 'this food is now in season, we're opening up our space to you and we're feeding you and look at how much we have to offer.' If you took really good care of your patch and you prayed for it and fertilized it well, then you'd be able to set the table pretty well, so it was this sort of idea of generosity and abundance. "

Today's potlucks, where guests bring dishes to a party, got their name from the *potlatch;* however, in many tribes a *potlatch* was not just a party, but an entire type of economic system. The main purpose of the *potlatch* was the regional redistribution and reciprocity of wealth through gift giving. The word itself can be translated as "a gift" or something that is given away to others. Families hosting the *potlatch* would sometimes invest a year in planning the event and put a lot of effort into making or buying gifts for each guest. Many *potlatches* in the Puget Sound, where all the tribes of the Northwest would gather to trade, would be held in preparation for trading. They were events that were key in building allies across tribes and relationships among prominent tribal members. *Potlatches* continued until banned in the late 19th century by the U.S. and Canadian governments. Both governments claimed that the custom was destructive and unnecessary. In 1934 and 1951, the U.S. and Canada respectively repealed the law, and *potlatches* could once again be legally held.

"Nowadays people still have them," Valerie continues. "We obviously are dealing with the effects of a superimposed diet and a total change in culture, but not total because we still carry those things with us. If there's a certain function or funeral happening, certain families will be bringing fish or they'll be bringing the huckleberry pie, so there's still that tie to which family works with which food. And we're seeing more and more people participating in that system as we offer more trainings through the Muckleshoot Food Sovereignty Project. My family now harvests nettle every year and stores it away for anyone who may need it. I am a big advocate of stinging nettle and consider that plant to be my very first plant teacher.

"Nettle is an incredible food source. Just one cup of cooked nettles is all you need for your calcium, magnesium, iron, phosphate — all the things our body uses to build blood and to detoxify the liver. So it's a really incredible food, and it comes out in spring time, when we need our bodies to build strength and detoxify after winter to get prepared for the year to come, so it's got this really cool seasonal rhythm to it. And I can't think of a more useful plant. You can eat the leaves in the springtime; in the summertime you can harvest the leaves for tea; and right around now [start of autumn] the stalks get up to ten feet tall sometimes, and you can harvest those. The stalks were traditionally used as cordage for fishnet. It's one of the strongest fibers in the world. Nettles [like *net*] were used for fishing nets and sometimes armies would use nettle fiber for uniform material. I've seen them bring schools of herring out of the water with it. This food source has many different functions.

"I have certain nettle patches I visit, not just when it's harvesting time, but just to go and be with them. You see, my elders taught me that plants and foods are our greatest teachers. And that they're waiting right outside the door for us. In that way, they are much more than a commodity or food source, they inform us about how to live in the world in a very metaphorical way. When you're looking at how nettle is so strong or how huckleberries feed more than just us, they feed the elk and other animals, or how the salmon people return to the rivers every year, it causes us to look at what that means and how we can live our lives like the salmon people and the plant people do. How do we grow and thrive in diversity and be big medicine in the world?"

Epilogue and Acknowledgements: *Coming Home*

> Everything that we see is a shadow cast by that which we do not see.
>
> — Martin Luther King, Jr.

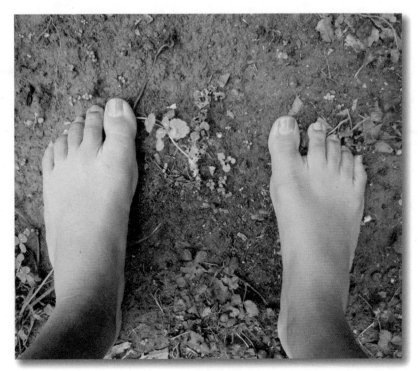

I STARTED THIS PROJECT after standing on a small organic farm, proud with my pitchfork and wondering where all the other brown folks were. Only now, after that thought led me on an incredible journey both physically and spiritually, do I realize how blind I was.

I was blind to the many farmers and food movement leaders of color because I was looking at the food and agriculture movement through a lens that most do: a lens that shows us that healthy food is for people with certain incomes, who live in certain neighborhoods and have certain skin tones; a lens that shows us a monochrome picture of who small, organic farmers are; a lens that promotes books and documentaries on farming and good food from an exclusive community of authors, directors and film subjects; a

From Top Left: *Shirley Sherrod of New Communities, Ben and Darnella Burkett of B & B Farms, Matthew and Althea Raiford of Gilliard Farms, Dr. Ridgley and Sister Ann Muhammad of Muhammad Farms, Ralph Paige of Federation of Southern Cooperatives.*

From top left: *Winona LaDuke of Honor the Earth and White Earth Land Recovery Project, Clayton Brascoupe of the Traditional Native American Farmers Association, Dolores Huerta of The National Farmworkers Association and the Dolores Huerta Foundation, César Chavéz of United Farmworkers, Philip Vera Cruz and Larry Itliong of UFW and Agricultural Workers Organizing Committee and Nely Rodriguez and members of the Coalition of Immokalee Workers.*

lens that only points to farmers of color when highlighting statistics about their rapid land loss and plummeting census numbers; and a lens that only shows black and brown faces when talking about farm labor or food shortages.

Looking through that lens, I failed to see the principal change-makers in food and agriculture whose shoulders this movement stands on — whether the movement acknowledges it or not. They have been steadily paving the way and impacting the lives of our farmers and communities for decades. Prominent agricultural leaders such as Shirley Sherrod, Ben Burkett, Ralph Paige, and Dr. Ridgely and Sister Ann Muhammad who have been blazing a path for the Black Farmer Resistance Movement, leading the way for farmer co-operatives across the South and laying the foundation for Black land trusts. They and many of their colleagues and fellow farmers have been at this work long before today's mainstream agricultural movement was created. Some, like Burkett and his family, or like Matthew and Althea Raiford of Gilliard Farms, have been farming their land for over 120 years.

With agricultural roots on this land that extend further back than that, the food and farm movement also unknow-ingly stands on the shoulders of leaders like Winona LaDuke and Clayton Brascoupe and the strong coalition of Native American farmers and traditional foods activists who have long been working to preserve land and food culture that came under threat with colonization. Also, historic agricultural leaders such as Dolores Huerta, César Chavéz, Philip Vera Cruz or Larry Itliong, who started working for migrant farmer rights as early as the 1930s, paving the way for today's impactful leaders, like those of the Coalition of Immokalee Workers.

Looking through the narrow lens of today's food and farm movement was beneficial for me because it inspired me to look elsewhere. And I quickly saw that many current leaders who I share heritage with were fed up with the narrow lens as well and were making enough noise to be heard in the national dialogue on food and agriculture. Influential Black farmers and food activists like Will Allen, Erika Allen, Malik Yakini, Karen Washington, LaDonna Redmond, Dr. Monica White and Dr. Gail Myers are all making an impact through innovative sustainable agriculture practices, urban farming and food justice work, and research on African American agricultural history. I was personally drawn to these Black change-makers and honored to join them in solidarity.

As a young activist and beginning farmer, I was also drawn to leaders from my generation who echoed the need to claim our community's agricultural legacy and the important stories that come with it. Fierce farmers and activists such as Tanya Fields, Jalal Sabur, Chris Bolden-Newsome, Blaine Snipstal, Leah Penniman, Navina Khanna, Hai Vo, Sarita Daftary, Gerardo Marin and Nina Kahori Fallenbaum among many others — some of which were featured in this book — were all

From Top Left: *Erika and Will Allen of Growing Power, Malik Yakini of Detroit Black Community Food Security Network (DBCFSN), Karen Washington of Black Urban Gardeners, LaDonna Redmond of Campaign for Food Justice Now, Dr. Monica White of DBCFSN, Dr. Gail Myers of Farms to Grow (pictured with Farmer Wil Scott, Jr. of Freedom Farmers Market).*

From Top Left: *Tanya Fields of The BLK Projek, Jalal Sabur of Sweet Freedom Farm, Chris Bolden-Newsome of Bartram's Community Farm, Blaine Snipstal of Five Seeds Farm and Harriet Tubman Liberators Garden, Leah Penniman of Soul Fire Farm, Navina Khanna of Live Real, Hai Vo of Live Real and California Food and Justice Coalition, Sarita Daftary formerly of East New York Farms, Gerardo Marin of Rooted in Community, Nina Kahori Fallenbaum of Hyphen Magazine.*

instrumental in planting seeds of empowerment and inspiration for me.

This community of farmers and activists are just a few of the many who provided the support for this project to get off the ground, help me raise needed funds, and aid me in taking on the ambitious task of reaching out to such a vast community of farmers. Friends and community also stepped up to support this at the very beginning with donations to my crowd-source funding campaign on IndieGoGo. Generous donors included wonderful folks such as Sandra and Wil Blake, Jarad Bowens of Genius Entertainment, Tyler Caudle, Mark Coleman, Michael Coleman, Alison and Alphonzo Cross of The Boxcar Grocer, Belkis Muldoon, Sean Muldoon, Kristin Russell of The Sentient Bean, Jalal Sabur, Naomi Sobel, Dan Sternberg, Henry and Meryl Triplett and Julie Vanderlee. And many thanks have to be given for the generous project grants given by Farm Credit's contributions department.

Priceless support from friends and mentors such as Asantewaa Harris, Kolu Zigbi, Cynthia Hayes and Monica White were invaluable in helping to shape this project through farmer and community outreach, fundraising advice and research and writing guidance. Authors like Mark Winne and the numerous press editors I pitched this book to were also helpful in the shaping of my novice book proposal skills. And, of course, this book wouldn't be in your hands and presented with such keen expertise without the entire team at New Society Publishers.

What is often lost in this and many movements, however, is the structural support lacking for those putting all of their energy into making a difference in an area that their heart and spirit are called to. The sacrifice and hard work of farmers and activists in the food movement is often not valued nor rewarded or financially supported, making the long journey of continuing the work while trying to survive extremely difficult. Therefore the people in their lives that stand behind them with invaluable support and an unwavering belief in their mission make it possible for them to continue their work. While my journey to complete this project over the last five years hardly compares to the plight of the very farmers and activists in this book, I could not have done it without the patient support and love from my husband, my mother and amazing family.

Finally and most important, are the incredible people sharing their stories in this book and the many more who welcomed me with open arms into their homes and onto their lands. Spending time and listening to such inspiring people and their brilliant insight, powerful personal histories and beautiful cultural legacies has truly changed the course of my life. I can only hope that, in sharing their stories, a change in thought befalls the audiences most in need of hearing them. I'd like to include these farmers themselves in that audience because I hope that they see the value of their stories and their knowledge.

When I was out on the road interviewing and photographing farmers, some were hesitant to share with me purely out of a modest disbelief that I wanted to sit at their knee and listen to what they had to say. Other hesitance of course stems from the long history of exploitation in communities of color when foreign folks intrude, prying for information. But most of the time I was just met with a humble denial that they had anything to say or anything noteworthy to share. These farmers firmly explained that they "just do what they do."

I of course would always disagree, and somehow, every time, would end up with them for hours as they slowly and then more openly and jubilantly shared their stories with me. And each time, after the last word was spoken and I clicked off the recorder, we would share a long breath and moment of satisfied recognition that they did indeed have something to say. And just like that, the lens through which we saw this work was shifted.

What I've learned is, when you want answers for how to change the world, sometimes all you have to do is ask. So my hope for this massive movement working toward a sustainable and just future in food and agriculture, is that we can broaden our lens, honor the diversity of stories that exist within this fight, and learn that sometimes you should just sit back and listen.

Collage: *We Are Here Too*

This book, of course, is just the tiniest tip of the iceberg representing all of the wonderful farmers of color across America. And this collage, also small in its representation of the vast diversity of farmers out there, is simply to honor the farmers I interviewed who did not get featured in the chapters, as well as some farmers whom I never got the chance to interview but respect so much. This collage, like this book, is a small way to send a big message to the food and ag movement: *We Are Here Too.*

Appendix

Take Action and Stay Connected:

HERE'S JUST A SHORT LISTING of some farmer and food activist organizations supporting farmers of color, food justice, food sovereignty and cultural food preservation work. Reach out, learn more and support!

African American Farmers of California
Afroculinaria
Agricultura Network
American Farm Labor Organizing
   Committee
American Friends Service Committee
American Indian Mothers
Applied Research Center
Association for the Advancement of
   Hmong Women in Minnesota
Association of African American Vintners
AYUDA
Backyard Gardeners Network
Black Family Land Trust
Black Farmers and Agriculturists
   Association

Black Oaks Center for Sustainable Living
Black Urban Gardeners
BLK Projek
Border Agricultural Workers Center
Boxcar Grocer
Brooklyn Food Coalition
California Food and Justice Coalition
Campaign for Food Justice Now
CANFIT
Center for Cherokee Plants
Center for Diversity and Environment
Center for Global Justice
Coalición Rural
Coalition of Immokalee Workers
Community 2 Community
Community Vision Council
Detroit Black Community Food Security
   Network
Earthworks Urban Farm
East New York Farms!
Farms to Grow
Farmworker Association of Florida
Federation of Southern Cooperatives
Filipino Advocates for Justice

Foodchain Workers Alliance
Food What?!
Friends of the MST
Global Advocates for Justice
Groundswell International
GROW NYC
Growing Food and Justice for All
  Initiative
Growing Power
Grown in Detroit
Habesha
Harlem Seeds
Heurto de la Familia
Hmong Farmers Association
Hopi Foundation
Horagewi
Indigenous Environmental Network
Indigenous Womens Network
International Council of Thirteen
  Indigenous Grandmothers
Just Food
Just Harvest
La Finca del Sur
La Mujer Obrera
La Semilla Food Center
La Via Campesina
Land Loss Prevention Project
Live Real
Marshview Community Farm
Minorities in Agriculture, Natural
  Resources and Related Sciences
Minority Land Owners
Mississippi Association of Cooperatives
Muckleshoot Food Sovereignty Project
Mvskoke Food Sovereignty Initiative
National Black Farmers Association

National Family Farmers Coalition
National Farm Worker Ministry
National Immigrant Farming Association
National Latino Farmers and Ranchers
  Association
National Women in Agriculture
  Association
Native Harvest
Navdanya
NC Field
New Mexico Acequia Association
NOLA Food and Farm Network
North Leupp Family Farm
Nuestras Raices
People's Grocery
People's Kitchen
Presbyterian Hunger Program
RAFI
Real Food Challenge
Rooted in Community
Soul Fire Farm's Black and Latino
  Immersion Program
South Central Farmers
Southeastern African American Farmers
  Organic Network
SURCO
Three Sisters Farm
Timeless Harvest
Traditional Native American Farmers
  Association
Truly Living Well
URFAM
White Earth Land Recovery
Why Hunger
Wisdom of the Elders
Viva Farms

Notes

1. "The *USDA v Pigford* federal discrimination case revealed highly disproportionate levels of support given to white farmers versus farmers of color." — "Disadvantaged Farmers: Addressing Inequalities for Farmers of Color," Institute for Agriculture and Trade Policy, 2012.

2. "Black farmers in the U.S. have been losing their land and going out of business at the rate of 1,000 acres per day; three times faster than the national average." — "Returning African-American Farmers to the Land: Recent Trends and a Policy Rationale," Dr. Spencer Wood and Jess Gilbert, 2000.

3. "Nearly a fifth of all African American children, and nearly a quarter of Mexican American, are obese, compared to a tenth of white children." —"Access to Healthy Food," Policy Link, 2012.

4. "The food justice movement advances self-reliance and social justice by acknowledging that community leadership is the way to authentic solutions." — Growing Food and Justice for All Initiative.

5. A food desert is an area where affordable healthy food is difficult to obtain, particularly for those without access to an automobile.

6. "Approximately 56.2 million acres make up 326 Indian land areas in the U.S." — U.S. Department of the Interior, Bureau of Indian Affairs.

7. "Asian American farmers make up just .5% of all farm operators." — USDA 2007 Census of Agriculture.

8. "The National Resources Inventory," USDA Natural Resources Conservation Service (NRCS) and Iowa State University's Center for Survey Statistics and Methodology, 2007, www.nrcs.usda.gov.

9. NAFTA: The North American Free Trade Agreement passed in 1994 to eliminate tariffs on trade between U.S., Canada and Mexico.

10. "How US Policies Fueled Mexico's Great Migration," David Bacon, The Nation, 2012.

11. "Exposing the Myth of Free Trade," International Forum on Globalization, February 25, 2003; "Tariffs and Tortillas," *The Economist,* January 24, 2008.

12. "Senate Bill 2109, or the 'Navajo-Hopi Little Colorado River Water Rights Settlement Act of 2012,' was introduced by Arizona Senators Kyl and McCain on February 14, 2012 and asks the Navajo and Hopi peoples to waive their priority water rights to the surface waters of the Little Colorado River." — Ed Becenti, Censored News, April 2012.

13. The Long Walk of 1864: forced deportation of the Navajo by the U.S. Army. They were forced to walk by gunpoint 300 miles to Ft. Sumner at Bosque Redondo where they were held for four years.

14. "Senate Bill 2109, or the 'Navajo-Hopi Little Colorado River Water Rights Settlement Act of 2012,' was introduced by Arizona Senators Kyl and McCain on February 14, 2012 and asks the Navajo and Hopi peoples to waive their priority water rights to the surface waters of the Little Colorado River." — Ed Becenti, Censored News, April 2012.

15. "In 2011 $36 million went missing from the Navajo Nation Council Chamber and whistleblowers reported internal corruption." — Marilyn Berlin Snell, High Country News, August, 2011.

16. "Disaster Risk Assessment Case Study: Recent Drought on the Navajo Nation, southwestern U.S.," UN Global Assessment Report, 2011.

17. "Disaster Risk Assessment Case Study: Recent Drought on the Navajo Nation, southwestern U.S.," UN Global Assessment Report, 2011.

18. "Labor Organizing Changed the Hawaiian Islands Forever," APWU, AFL-CIO, 2003.

19. Picture brides were brides selected and sent from their homelands (primarily in Japan and Korea) to Japanese and Korean workers in labor camps in Hawai'i and the West Coast.

20. "After Internment: Seattle's Debate Over Japanese Americans' Right to Return Home," Jennifer Speidel, University of Washington.

21. "Notes on African American Farmers, Agricultural Law Update," Christopher R. Kelley, August 1999.

22. "Soiled Legacy: Black Farmers Hit the Road to Confront a 'Cycle of Racism' — Many Lost Lands, Dignity As USDA Denied Loans Whites Routinely Got," Roger Thurow, *The Wall Street Journal*, May 1, 1998.

23. "Food, Farming, and Sustainability," Susan A. Schneider, 2011.

24. "Notes on African American Farmers, Agricultural Law Update," Christopher R. Kelley, August 1999.

25. "The State of the Climate Report,"

The National Oceanic and Atmospheric Association, 2012.

26. "Climate Change and Agriculture in the United States: Effects and Adaptation," USDA, February, 2013.

27. "State of the Climate Report," National Climatic Data Center, 2012.

28. "Disaster Recovery: Preliminary Estimates of Cumulative Economic Impact from Hurricanes Katrina and Rita to Louisiana Agriculture," LSU Ag Center & Research Extension, October 5, 2005.

29. "Report: Building a Future with Farmers," The National Young Farmers Coalition, November, 2011.

30. Dr. Ridgley Muhammad is a Black farmer in Georgia farming 1600 acres owned by the Nation of Islam. He has his Ph.D. in Agricultural Economics, lectures around the country, serves as the Vice President of the Black Farmers and Agriculturists Association and has written four books.

31. "Virginia has six poultry processing facilities employing 10,000 people with corporations such as Tyson, Cargill and Perdue. There are over 1,200 poultry farmers in Virginia that supply the facilities." — Virginia Poultry Federation, 2006.

32. "The Farming Systems Trial," Rodale Institute, 2011.

33. "About Genetically Engineered Foods," Center for Food Safety.

34. Center for Native Health, 2003.

35. "Women, Agriculture and Food Security," Food and Agriculture Organization of the United Nations.

36. "Women, Food Security and Agriculture in a Global Marketplace," The International Center for Research on Women.

37. "Gender Inequalities in Ownership and Control of Land in Africa," International Food Policy Research Institute, 2013.

38. "The State of Food and Agriculture Report," Food and Agriculture Organization of the United Nations, 2010–2011.

39. USDA 2012 Agricultural Census

40. "Characteristics of Women Farm Operators and Their Farms," USDA Economic Research Service, 2013.

41. "The National CSA Farm Survey," University of Wisconsin-Madison, Center for Integrated Agricultural Systems, 2004.

42. "Cassava," Food and Agriculture Organization of the United Nations, 1995.

43. USDA 2012 Agricultural Census

44. "Returning to the Farm," Randy Mertens, CAFNRNews, 2012.

45. "Aging Farmers and Land: The Numbers," Farm Aid, 2013.

46. "Farmland Ownership and Leasing: Implications for Young and Beginning Farmers," University of Kentucky/USDA, 2014.

47. "Building a Future with Farmers," National Young Farmers Coalition, November 2011.

48. Acequia: a community-operated irrigation canal system. See the chapter "Acequia Culture" in section four of this book.

49. FoodCorps is a national volunteer organization where service members spend one year working with youth in school gardens and food education.

About the Author

NATASHA BOWENS is an author, beginning farmer, and community activist who focuses on building empowerment and community with food and storytelling. As a young biracial woman in today's agricultural movement , she is dedicated to honoring, preserving, and amplifying the stories of Black, Native, Asian and Latino farmers and food activists. Her multimedia project *The Color of Food* evolved from her work exploring the intersection of race and agriculture for *Grist* magazine, and from her blog *Brown.Girl.Farming*, where she writes about issues related to racial inequality, food sovereignty, and resilience. Natasha has interviewed and photographed over 75 North American farmers of color; her work has garnered her national media attention, and she has been featured on Bill Moyers, *The Atlantic*, and *Colorlines*.

If you have enjoyed *The Color of Food,* you might also enjoy other

Books to Build a New Society

Our books provide positive solutions for people who want to make a difference. We specialize in:

Food & Gardening • Resilience • Sustainable Building
Climate Change • Energy • Health & Wellness • Sustainable Living

Environment & Economy • Progressive Leadership • Community
Educational & Parenting Resources

New Society Publishers

ENVIRONMENTAL BENEFITS STATEMENT

New Society Publishers has chosen to produce this book on recycled paper made with **100% post consumer waste,** processed chlorine free, and old growth free.

For every 5,000 books printed, New Society saves the following resources:[1]

33	Trees
3,018	Pounds of Solid Waste
3,321	Gallons of Water
4,331	Kilowatt Hours of Electricity
5,486	Pounds of Greenhouse Gases
24	Pounds of HAPs, VOCs, and AOX Combined
8	Cubic Yards of Landfill Space

[1]Environmental benefits are calculated based on research done by the Environmental Defense Fund and other members of the Paper Task Force who study the environmental impacts of the paper industry.

For a full list of NSP's titles, please call 1-800-567-6772 *or check out our website* at:

www.newsociety.com